EVIL SPIRITS

MANCHESTER
UNIVERSITY PRESS

ANGELAKIHUMANITIES

editors
Charlie Blake
Pelagia Goulimari
Timothy S. Murphy
Robert Smith

general editor
Gerard Greenway

Angelaki Humanities publishes works which address and probe broad and compelling issues in the theoretical humanities. The series favours path-breaking thought, promotes unjustly neglected figures, and grapples with established concerns. It believes in the possibility of blending, without compromising, the rigorous, the well-crafted, and the inventive. The series seeks to host ambitious writing from around the world.

Angelaki Humanities is the associated book series of

ANGELAKI – journal of the theoretical humanities

already published

THE NEW BERGSON John Mullarkey (ed.)

ANGELAKIHUMANITIES

EVIL SPIRITS
nihilism
and the fate of modernity

edited by gary banham and charlie blake

MANCHESTER UNIVERSITY PRESS

MANCHESTER AND NEW YORK

distributed exclusively in the USA by St. Martin's Press

Published by Manchester University Press
Oxford Road, Manchester M13 9NR, UK
and Room 400, 175 Fifth Avenue, New York, NY 10010, USA
http://www.manchesteruniversitypress.co.uk

Distributed exclusively in the USA by
St. Martin's Press, Inc., 175 Fifth Avenue, New York,
NY 10010, USA

Distributed exclusively in Canada by
UBC Press, University of British Columbia, 2029 West Mall,
Vancouver, BC, Canada V6T 1Z2

British Library Cataloguing-in-Publication Data
A catalogue record for this book is available from the British Library

Library of Congress Cataloging-in-Publication Data applied for

ISBN   0 7190 5642 X *hardback*
      0 7190 5643 8 *paperback*

First published 2000

07 06 05 04 03 02 01 00   10 9 8 7 6 5 4 3 2 1

Typeset
by Northern Phototypesetting Co Ltd, Bolton
Printed in Great Britain
by Biddles Ltd, Guildford and King's Lynn

to the members of the haslingden house church
whose inspiration has here met an unexpected fate

and to ella and freya
who reminded us how the demonic and the angelic
are always mutually enfolded

CONTENTS

CONTRIBUTORS

Keith Ansell Pearson is professor of philosophy at the University of Warwick, where he has taught since 1993. His recent books include *Viroid Life* (1997) and *Germinal Life* (1999). His current research is focused on Bergsonian and Marxian approaches to questions of matter, time, the event, evolution, complexity and virtuality. He has recently co-edited the volume *Nihilism Now! Monsters of Energy* (2000) with Diane Morgan.

Gary Banham divides his time between lecturing at Bolton Institute of Higher Education and teaching philosophy in adult education in Manchester. He has held a research fellowship in philosophy at Manchester Metropolitan University (1994–96), and taught at the University of Hertfordshire (1992–94), Manchester Metropolitan University (1992–93), Keele University (1991) and Hertford and Balliol Colleges, Oxford (1989–91). He has published articles on Nietzsche, Derrida, James Joyce and Wyndham Lewis, and most recently a book, *Kant and the Ends of Aesthetics* (2000).

Charlie Blake has taught literature, philosophy and critical and cultural theory at the universities of Oxford, Cambridge, Oxford Brookes, Hertfordshire and Manchester Metropolitan, and is currently lecturer in literary and cultural studies at University College Northampton. His recent publications include *Intellectuals and Global Culture*, co-edited with Linnie Blake for *Angelaki*. He is currently working on a study of drugs, delirium and critical theory, from Thomas De Quincey to Gilles Deleuze, and an introduction to literary and cultural theory.

Howard Caygill is professor in historical and cultural studies at Goldsmith's College, University of London. He is the author of *Art of Judgement* (1989), *A Kant Dictionary* (1995) and *Walter Benjamin, The Colour of Experience* (1998), and co-editor with Keith Ansell Pearson of *The Fate of the New Nietzsche* (1993). He is currently working on a study of Levinas and the political.

Daniel Conway is professor of philosophy and director of graduate studies at Pennsylvania State University. He is the author of *Nietzsche and the Political* (1997) and *Nietzsche's Dangerous Game: Philosophy and the Twilight of the Idols* (1997). He has published widely in the fields of political philosophy, contemporary continental philosophy and the history of philosophy.

Antony Easthope, prior to his death in the winter of 1999, was professor of English and cultural studies at Manchester Metropolitan University. He was the author of numerous volumes and articles on cultural theory, and most recently published *Englishness and National Culture* (1999) and *The Unconscious* (1999).

Joanna Hodge is reader in philosophy and director of research at Manchester Metropolitan University. She is on the editorial board of *Women's Philosophy Review* and *Angelaki*. She wrote her doctoral thesis at Oxford on the concept of truth in *Being and Time* and is author of *Heidegger and Ethics* (1995). She is currently working on the question of time in contemporary thought and on a book entitled *Derridean Temporalities*.

Alphonso Lingis is professor of philosophy at Pennsylvania State University. He has published numerous articles and books, including most recently *The Community of Those who have Nothing in Common* and *Foreign Bodies*.

Jill Marsden lectures in philosophy at Bolton Institute of Higher Education. Her principal interest is in the work of Nietzsche, but she also writes on aesthetics and twentieth-century European philosophy. She is currently writing a book on Nietzsche and the philosophy of ecstasy.

Diane Morgan is senior lecturer in literary and cultural studies at University College Northampton. She is the author of *Kant Trouble: The Obscurities of the Enlightened* (2000) and co-editor with Keith Ansell Pearson of *Nihilism Now! Monsters of Energy* (2000).

Graham Ward is professor of contextual theology and ethics at the University of Manchester. He is the author of *Barth, Derrida and the Language of Theology* (1995), *Theology and Contemporary Critical Theory* (1996), *Balthasar at the end of Modernity* (1999), and *Cities of God* (1999), as well as being editor of *The Postmodern God* (1997), *Radical Orthodoxy* (1998) and *The Certeau Reader* (1999). He is senior editor of the journal *Literature and Theology*.

James Williams teaches philosophy at the University of Dundee. He is the author of *Lyotard: Towards a Postmodern Philosophy* (1998), *Lyotard and the Political* (1999) and a series of articles on Deleuze and Lyotard.

ACKNOWLEDGEMENTS

Special thanks are due here to Gerard Greenway for his constant encouragement and support for this project, which he was instrumental in making possible in the first place, as was Pelagia Goulimari, to whom we are also especially indebted. Thanks are also due to Matthew Frost and Lauren McAllister for their patience and guidance through the travails of editing and publication, and to Jim Urpeth for his exemplary readings and invaluable comments on the chapters which now make up this book. The support we have received from Linnie Blake and Don Milligan throughout the project has, of course, been inestimable.

INTRODUCTION

The suggestion in the subtitle of this book of a relationship between nihilism, fate and modernity under the aegis of the demonic was initially inspired by a conference organized by one of the editors at Manchester Metropolitan University in 1996. It struck the editors that within the discourse of modernity something had been repressed; and, as is invariably the case with that which has been repressed, certain effects have been generated which have been growing more substantial as the history of modernity has unfolded. In order to flesh out this suspicion, as it will be developed in this book, it is necessary to give a preliminary characterization of modernity.

Modernity can be understood as a project of measurement which is based upon two fundamental assumptions: that the world has a scope that permits calculative investigation and that relations between parts of the world are assessable by linear connections. If we simply present the project of modernity through the guise of a pair of theoretical postulates it should soon become clear that these postulates have immense consequences. The first postulate is based upon a transformation of *techne* into an exact and exacting mechanism. The nature of this mechanism is programmatic, intended to pose and replicate a set of assumptions whose formality will in principle if never in practice permit the delimitation of all physical possibilities on the basis of a grid which makes no differentiations between types of matter but reduces all to basic coordinates. The second postulate is a drastic delimitation of the principle of causality. Whereas Aristotle had suggested that there are four types of cause (formal, material, efficient and final), the modern system operates through the restriction of causality to a linear model of efficient causality. This underpins and legitimates the levelling of all types of matter into one underlying substratum of operation.

Together these two postulates have signal effects. The thought of life as containing a specific principle of organization is disallowed and with this comes an assumption of determinism which prevents cognizance of the self-understanding of the very types of being who have formulated the postulates in question. Purposes are, as a consequence, expelled from the world.

The fate of the traditional repositaries of human purpose, the religions of the book, is particularly noteworthy here. The great monotheistic religions arose in battles against the domination of necessity. The pre-monotheistic systems of worship broke upon a wheel of necessity invoked as a consequence of ultimate powers which were not defined as separable even in principle from nature. The Greek *daimon* is a form of 'fate' and Plato suggests at the conclusion of the *Republic* that in the period between incarnations each of us chooses the fate which will bind us in the next cycle. Both within this work and in others Plato suggests that there is a possible cure for the sickness which is the cycle of necessity and suggests, most famously in the *Phaedo*, that this cure resides in learning how to die. This course of learning has the name of philosophy.

Christianity inherited from Plato and even more from the neo-Platonism of Plotinus the lesson that to be controlled by the passions, to be dominated by nature, represented being subordinated to the power of 'demons'. The great lexicons of demonology that Christianity subsequently produced are organized around the power of the flesh, the seduction of the spirit by matter. Within Christianity this assault upon the demonic power of the passions produces assorted movements which successively are recognized to be heresies. Heresies are of many types and can be organized around virtually any detail of the Gospel but the two central and recurring heresies are both reducible to the same name: gnosticism.

There are two major forms of gnosticism: asceticism and libertinism. Usually both forms cohabit within a given sect, with the *illuminati* given to licentiousness (which is possible for them in their ecstatic state) and the ordinary devotees encouraged to 'kill' their desires in forms of castration more or less literal. Gnosticism is the most Greek movement within Christianity and it postulates the clearest separation between spirit and flesh. Whilst orthodoxy always resists this movement it nonetheless contains it within itself. The attempt to separate oneself from the sickness of life which finds one root in philosophy thus is given another in Christianity (and the fact that this is also true in Judaism can be seen from the recurrence of the same 'heretical' patterns, as indeed it is also possible to discern in Islam).

The battle with the demonic principle which the monotheistic faiths attempt was compromised at its root. The arrival of the project of modernity reinstalls the picture which the economies of monotheistic demonology and angelology attempted to circumvent. The postulates of modernity in denying purposive action or non-measurable aspects of the world submit everything to fate. The universal rule of fate thus banishes teleology, eschatology and freedom all at once.

With the presentation of a picture of the world which is bereft of ultimate references the economy of existence is reduced to base repetition. This repetition is what has come to be named nihilism. Whilst the analyses of nihilism presented by Nietzsche and Heidegger are now widely cited, the relationship of nihilism to modernity is not related to the problem of the recurrence of political evil in the heart of modernity. That political evil reached a peak in the very country from which these thinkers came (and with the equivocal support of one of them) underlines the question of the relationship between them.

If modernity's postulates are not merely theoretical but also supremely practical in affecting the structure of the relation of humanity to nature and the divine, then they must also constitute 'politics' as a modern phenomenon. If evil is primarily thought in political terms then the displacement of eschatology and teleology from ultimate descriptions of the world must enable their reinscription in the organization of arrangements that we term 'politics'. That this was essentially guessed early in the formation of the modern project can be seen if we turn from the investigation of nature to summary statements about politics.

Just as the postulates of modernity in theoretical form prohibit the assumption of purpose (and in an equivocal complementary move, the boundless) so do the practical postulates subordinate religion entirely to matters of state. From Hobbes's *Leviathan* to John Rawls's *Theory of Justice* the secular nature of political arrangements is a given of political theory. Alongside this first practical postulate is placed a second: the body politic's health is based on the ultimate subordination of all parts to the whole. These practical postulates of modernity are expressed in the most virulent form in Hobbes's dramatic statement that the sovereign is the only one to decide on matters religious.

If the subordination of religion to the state is paralleled by the final authority on the fate of each individual necessarily residing with the sovereign decision then there is a practical aspect to nihilism in the supremacy of executive will even over the will of God (a political 'death of God'). This practical aspect of nihilism limits the possible scope in which political decision is comprehended. It permits intrigue as a normal aspect of relations and sanctions in principle (if only in conditions of emergency) total mobilization and a cult of the state. The meaning lost in the cosmos is restored in politics but its condition of restoration is a displacement of religious hope and fear into the machinery which makes possible war. This second aspect of nihilism is therefore connected to a second change in the nature of *techne*. Political evil may be understood as a consequence of the fate which governs modernity.

What the chapters in this book rehearse in response to this circumstance is an attempt to invoke anew the principles of demonology and angelology that the theoretical postulates of modernity repel whilst having the practical consequence of installing as fates. This work is, in Derrida's apt phrase, a 'counter-conjuration'. Differently placed and in many ways in combat with each other, the chapters collected here probe the possibility of speaking about spirits. The history of modernity needs to be revisited in the recognition that forces not subsumable under the names of the 'human' and the 'natural' work in the world, that Satan is, in fact, the Lord of this world.

Chapter 1 is organized around the figure of Satan and uses this figure to forge unexpected and radical connections. Opening as a response to the recent work of Derrida it becomes an extended meditation on themes drawn from Walter Benjamin which are subsequently related to the thoughts of Kant and Freud. In boldly defending the thought of eschatology the author, Gary Banham, forces onto the agenda a new set of questions about the meaning of thinking in terms of ends. Joanna Hodge in Chapter 2, by contrast, traces a different Derridean trajectory which is based on the pseudonymous writing of 'Kierkegaard'. Recovering the distinct registers of the aesthetic, the ethical and the religious, Hodge outlines a diabolism of ambiguity which raises questions about the practice of authorship and the anxiety of influence. In making an ethical claim about indirect communication this chapter radically questions the Nietzschean thought of nihilism.

In Chapter 3 Alphonso Lingis investigates the prosthetic origin of religion, recovering the supplementary relation to finitude that is practised in burial rites. Following in the wake of Nietzsche and Bataille, Lingis traces patterns of economy as formed around the relation to death. Gallows, mourning and ritual slaughter are revealed as connected to the original wound suffered by mechanisms of sense when faced with the problem of finitude. Lingis's disturbing chapter indicates the necessity for a religious organization of war and ritualized processes of slaughter and expulsion. Charlie Blake in Chapter 4 also offers a response to Bataille but, unlike Lingis, organizes this response around an appreciation of Bataille's gnosticism. Focusing upon the nature of this gnosticism Blake plots differential economies and suggests new insights into the processes of contemporary scientific theorization. Blake concludes that the theoretical postulates of modernity are no longer plausible.

Jill Marsden in Chapter 5 revisits the nature of Nietzsche's account of nihilism to suggest the possibility of a demonic thought as present within the account of eternal return (a thought itself communicated to Zarathustra by a demon). Connecting Nietzsche to Freud, Marsden elaborates a libidinal thought of affirmation. Attempting affirmation the other side of meaninglessness, this chapter is resolved to celebrate will to power as the condition of life. Diane Morgan, like Jill Marsden, initiates a libidinal investigation of Nietzsche. Unlike Marsden, however, Morgan locates her investigation (in Chapter 6) around questions of sexual inversion. Revisiting questions about transsexuality in relation to blasphemy and irreligion, Morgan celebrates and intensifies the dissolution of the body in inversion which is contrasted with the nostalgic Nazi appropriation of Nietzsche in order to refashion the body politic. Morgan sets against the Nazi Nietzsche a figure which can be allied with Djuna Barnes and in which the affirmative resonances of will to power are pared down to organs without bodies whose replication permits the multiplication of plural desires.

In Chapter 7 James Williams turns to Deleuze for his thought of nihilism. Suggesting an idealist reading of Deleuze that accords primacy to the formative power of ideas, Williams attempts to refine the thought of multiplicity. In a cautious and wide-ranging discussion of Deleuze's work Williams reveals a more nuanced relation of thought to its objects than is presupposed in many other accounts of Deleuze. The necessity of experiment as the basis of thought re-evaluates the notion of science and promises for Williams a differential future. Keith Ansell Pearson, like Williams, responds to the challenge of Deleuze but, unlike Williams, does so in relation to the thought of Derrida. Relating Derrida's thought of the supplement to the Deleuzian thought of rhizomatics, Ansell Pearson presents in Chapter 8 a new philosophical response to the questions of life and death. Refusing the Platonic thought of death Ansell Pearson brings out the border line between life and death as residing in spectrality. Both revising our understanding of Deleuze and suggesting unexpected connections between his work and Derrida's, this chapter radically challenges the reception of both thinkers.

Antony Easthope in Chapter 9 traces two stories about Freud's relation to the spectres of the past, both the enlightened Freud and the uncanny Freud. Situating psychoanalysis in relation to modernity, this chapter complicates the question of the nature of modernity. Resisting the Deleuzian critique of psychoanalysis and suggesting the importance of cinema for staging the relation to ghosts, the chapter concludes with an apposite and unexpected conjuncture of Freud with Rilke and Pynchon.

In Chapter 10 Dan Conway produces a response to Heidegger in many ways akin to Easthope's reading of Freud. Conway revisits the question of Heidegger's relation to nazism in the guise of an extended commentary on the interview in *Der Spiegel*. He probes beneath the surface of Heidegger's account of ontology to reveal the existence of an unexpected 'shadow'. In this process of retrieval he suggests new answers to the question of how Heidegger was able to ally himself with political evil.

Howard Caygill in Chapter 11 responds to the notion of spirit by elaborating a relation between Joachim of Fiore, Hegel and William Blake. In reinterpreting the notion of the philosophy of spirit Caygill revisits the questions of allegory and presentation. In a dense reading of Blake's *Marriage of Heaven and Hell* Caygill relates the text to the plates designed to accompany it. In the resulting opening to the visionary qualities of Blake he discerns a futurity in an affirmative philosophy of spirit that reintegrates representation into the concept. Graham Ward, like Caygill, insists on returning to the figure of Joachim of Fiore but places this figure in relation not to Blake and Hegel but to Irigaray, Serres and Wim Wenders. In recovering hybridity Ward complicates the understanding of Christianity and recovers a gnosticism internal to orthodoxy. Tracing the elaborate angelology of Serres and relating it to the angelic redemption figured in the films of Wim Wenders, he concludes Chapter 12 with an analysis of the body of the angel in the thought of Irigaray. In thinking sexual difference as angelic Ward opens the way for a new future for a Christianity that reclaims its inherent feminism and in the process suggests the highly political stakes of eschatology.

Beginning with Satan, then, this book concludes with angels. Whilst the spirits invoked in the work are far from harmonious with one another and many an *agon* is fought within the pages of this volume, all the contributors agree on the vital necessity of questioning anew the attempt of modernity to exorcize all spirits. Whether diabolist or angelic the need for the thought of spirits is urgent and represents the eschatological imperative of the future.

Gary Banham and Charlie Blake

gary banham

MOURNING SATAN

A Klee painting named 'Angelus Novus' shows an angel looking as though he is about to move away from something he is fixedly contemplating. His eyes are staring, his mouth is open, his wings are spread. This is how one pictures the angel of history. His face is turned toward the past. Where we perceive a chain of events, he sees one single catastrophe which keeps piling wreckage upon wreckage and hurls it in front of his feet. The angel would like to stay, awaken the dead, and make whole what has been smashed. But a storm is blowing from Paradise; it has got caught in his wings with such violence that the angel can no longer close them. This storm irresistibly propels him into the future to which his back is turned, while the pile of debris before him grows skyward. This storm is what we call progress.[1]

This citation from the so-called 'Theses on the Philosophy of History' is interpreted by Gillian Rose in relation to the contrast between mourning and melancholy. She suggests that the mournfulness that the angel conveys is expressive not of 'the work of mourning but [of] its eschatology'.[2] This interpretation emerges from her general argument that Benjamin is caught in a state of '*aberrated* mourning' and is unable to reach the fulfilment of '*inaugurated* mourning'. This reading of Benjamin is reached by applying to him the terms of both Freudian psychoanalysis and Christian orthodoxy.[3] Its organizing theme is however the necessity for a remembrance of the local nature of Talmud Torah and the upholding of this against what Rose terms 'exilic' attachment to the Messiah.

The setting of the Talmud against the messianic yearning of Benjamin enables Rose to confidently set aside the eschatology of mourning in favour of its 'work'. This diagnostic relation between psychoanalysis and Judaism is quite at variance with the position advanced by Derrida in *Spectres of Marx*. The reason for the opposition between Derrida and Rose here is partly to do with the fact that their analyses begin at opposite ends. Where Rose starts from an assumed contrast between distinct forms of mourning (those that have failed to begin and those that have succeeded in beginning), from which she can disallow appeals to eschatology, Derrida, by contrast, starts from the eschatological in order to determine the sense of mourning. He writes the following: 'in the same place, on the same limit, where history is finished, there where a certain determined concept of history comes to an end, precisely there the historicity of history begins, there finally it has the chance of heralding itself – of promising itself'.[4] This is the eruption of the last judgment from the end of history, a judgment that will be last by opening out something beyond all judgment: the historical itself. This corresponds, I will suggest, to the importance of the figure of the angel that Benjamin introduces as a sign of the messianic. Beginning from this side will allow a new sense to be given to the 'work of mourning', a sense which will harmonize with (rather than simply opposing) the eschatological.

The necessity of evil

Both Derrida's and Rose's accounts can be supported through readings of the way the baroque is presented in *The Origin of the German Trauerspiel*.[5] For Rose, the account of the baroque supplied there indicates the basis for the impossibility of Benjamin's accession to 'inaugurated mourning' (Benjamin remaining on this analysis caught within the baroque world). For Derrida, however, the baroque could be taken to reveal the catastrophic end of history which presents the possibility of the opening of historicity.

Benjamin suggests that the baroque was 'haunted by the fear of catastrophe' and points to the reason for this as being:

> The baroque knows no eschatology; and for that very reason it possesses no mechanism by which all earthly things are gathered in together and exalted before being consigned to their end. The hereafter is emptied of everything which contains the slightest breath of this world, and from it the baroque extracts a profusion of things which customarily escaped the grasp of artistic formulation and, at its high point, brings them violently into the light of day, in order to clear an ultimate heaven, enabling it, as vacuum, one day to destroy the world with catastrophic violence.[6]

The baroque's lack of eschatology provides the most frightful possibilities with their chance. Because the hereafter has had emptied from it every trace of the secular world, that world absorbs entirely internally to itself the violence of heaven and is thus set on a destructive course. This is why Rose suggests that fascism arises from the spirit of the baroque. This precise designation of a connection between the *Trauerspiel* study and the analysis of fascism can easily be supported from Benjamin's texts. In the *Trauerspiel* study Benjamin writes:

> Spirit – such was the thesis of the age – shows itself in power; spirit is the capacity to exercise dictatorship. This capacity requires both strict inner discipline and unscrupulous external action. Its practice brought to the course of the world an icy disillusion which is matched in intensity only by the fierce aspiration of the will to power. Such a conception of perfect conduct on the part of the man of the world awakens a mood of mourning [*Trauer*] in the creature stripped of all naive impulses.[7]

This account of the baroque is evidently of a piece with the account of fascism which is given in 'The Work of Art in the Age of Mechanical Reproduction', where Benjamin writes:

> Mankind, which in Homer's time was an object of contemplation for the Olympian gods, now is one for itself. Its self-alienation has reached such a degree that it can experience its own destruction as an aesthetic pleasure of the first order. This is the situation of politics which Fascism is rendering aesthetic. Communism responds by politicizing art.[8]

Whilst Rose's analysis is quite easy to support, however, the very sources which do this most clearly also suggest problems. First, Benjamin's account of the baroque is that it was an age *without* eschatology. It is the absence of eschatology which leads spirit to be determined as power. If this is so, then the way beyond the mourning produced by this situation would surely be through access to eschatology rather than through continued opposition to it. But if that is so, then the counter to fascism is necessarily the messianic.

This, I will suggest, is the logic of Derrida's move. To examine this will require us to turn from Benjamin's explication of the 'spirit' of the baroque towards his account of 'fate' within it. Benjamin determines the arrival of the drama of fate in the baroque period as concerned with the fact of the Reformation and the necessary reaction to it. He describes Lutheranism as an 'excessive reaction which ultimately denied good works as such, and not just their meritorious and penitential character' and suggests that there was contained in this 'an element of German paganism and the grim belief in the subjection to fate'.[9] One's course is determined, one can set nothing against it, there is only grace. Against this vision of demonic fate, Calvinism and the Counter-Reformation develop as two responses which attempt to reintegrate human action with the course of the cosmos. But both carry within them the hopelessness which Luther brought into the world. Both can only reconnect a sense of action with a vision of redemption by emphasizing the necessity of worldly success. This is the reason why the spirit of the baroque is one which leads to an emphasis on power.

It is also why Benjamin describes the baroque view of history as Satanic: concerned, that is, only with political intrigue. The image of the court thus becomes one with the image of hell, both of which are in their turn mournful in the extreme (and Benjamin does not hesitate to identify the 'Trauergeist' with Satan himself). We can illustrate this nexus of themes together with a citation from the work with which Derrida is so concerned in *Specters of Marx*: *Hamlet, Prince of Denmark*, where at the close of Act 2, scene 2, Hamlet himself states:

> The spirit that I have seen
> May be the devil; and the devil hath power
> To assume a pleasing shape; yea, and perhaps
> Out of my weakness and my melancholy,
> As he is very potent with such spirits,
> Abuses me to damn me. I'll have grounds
> More relative than this: the play's the thing
> Wherein I'll catch the conscience of the king.

Here we see the devil himself suspected as prowling the court, and as possibly making play with the melancholy of a prince. Hamlet, naturally, decides to resolve his difficulties through the device of drama. But Hamlet is also, as we know, indecisive, and this trait of his character is illuminated by Benjamin's suggestion that the resignation of the prince followed from what he terms 'the genuinely theological concept of melancholy': *acedia*, the deadly sin of sloth. The rise of this temperament corresponds to the new importance given to the astrological sign of Saturn, the figure recovered by the Renaissance. This figure was the one who would provide secret knowledge which would permit the possibility of escape from the satanic round of history. But Saturn's effect would itself fortify and strengthen this reign as it rendered ineffective the grasping for significance of the prince who became compelled to remain in the realm of contemplation and debarred from action. (Benjamin suggests that Hamlet alone Christianized the Saturnine to the extent of offering an action which would transform rather than a contemplation that would leave in place.)

Saturn points us to an understanding of Satan. Satan is the figure who presents the greatest paradox: the spiritualization of matter and the materialization of spirit joined into one unity, which is the possibility of modernity. Evil is thereby experienced as the ultimate and absolute form of spirit which is the negation of spirituality as such.

Here we must proceed cautiously and take each step of Benjamin's analysis with care. He links the figure of Satan with both magic and allegory. Of magic he states that it threatens the adept with 'spiritual isolation and death'. But this fact about magic is connected also to the rise of the allegorical and Benjamin concurs with the verdict that Satan is the 'original allegorical figure'.[10] Satan is the first to represent by his very appearance a reference to a message which he both is and is not identical with. Magic and allegory are not linked fortuitously as necessarily allegory must transform everything it touches into something other than it is. Allegory is the greatest form of the satanic because it must impose a vertiginous investigation which lacks any limit or goal. This is its absolute character, which is utterly material in its wanderings through spectacular displays which can lead only to other displays. This is why Benjamin states that mourning is at once the mother of allegories and their content. This leads Benjamin to two decisive moves: he presents first the transcendental illusions of Satan and then the false synthesis which is the basis of satanic consciousness. Both of these moves are worth noting in full. First, the transcendental illusions: 'What tempts is the illusion of freedom – in the exploration of what is forbidden; the illusion of independence – in the secession from the community of the pious; the illusion of infinity – in the empty abyss of evil.'[11] The three illusions are united in that all depend upon an absolute and unbounded relation between the actor and the world. The freedom allowed lacks any discernible limit, the independence given is constrained by no one and the infinity which one then explores is that of a boundless nature of evil. To each, however, is attached a price. For the sake of the freedom gained, the loss of soul; for the independence, absence of contact and isolation; for the infinity, the loss of redemption. This gives rise to the false synthesis that is a satanic consciousness: 'The purely material and this absolute spiritual are the poles of the satanic realm; and the consciousness is their illusory synthesis, in which the genuine synthesis, that of life, is imitated.'[12]

So the false synthesis is deathly. It is the consciousness of an end to the one who is surrendered to Satan. But this is what constitutes the satanic as a ruin. It cannot survive its own triumph because the consciousness which would affirm itself as found here must thereby clasp death as its own truth. This is recorded allegorically in that the blackest of arts has always been regarded as necromancy to which every black art bears some relation. And at this moment of the destruction of the world by the satanic synthesis, the world asserts itself in producing what Benjamin terms 'beauty': subjectivity falls, 'like an angel' towards heaven in its sense of beauty. This transfiguration – which ends *The Origin of German Trauerspiel* – is perhaps the most mysterious and difficult aspect of the whole work. And the truly difficult question which it opens is: how can the knowledge of the good know itself to be such? What prevents it again being led astray by the satanic? This question strikes at the heart of the question of the messianic.

The symbol which Benjamin left us as an answer to this problem is Klee's *Angelus Novus*. This symbol is explicated not only in the 'Theses on the Philosophy of History' but also in what is known as the 'esoteric fragment' of Ibiza. This fragment exists in two versions, one dated 12 August 1933 and the other dated 13 August 1933. Both versions have as their head the title 'Agesilaus Santander' (a curious conjunction of the name of a Spartan king and a Spanish town). Both versions tell us that Benjamin was given two secret names by his parents which he determined not to use. Both versions also tell us that Benjamin was born under the sign of Saturn. But there is a central difference between the fragments which manifests itself at the point of closest proximity between them: in relation to the character of the angel. The first version determines this in the following fashion: 'The *kabbalah* relates that in every instant God creates an immense number of new angels whose only purpose is, before they dissolve into naught, to sing His praise before His throne for a moment. Mine was interrupted in doing so; his features had about them nothing resembling the human.'[13] The parallel section to this in the second version contains here a very significant variation. In this second version Benjamin writes:

> The *kabbalah* relates that in every instant God creates an immense number of new angels, all of whom only have the purpose, before they dissolve into naught, of singing the praise of God before His throne for a moment. *The new angel passed himself off as one of these before he was prepared to name himself.* I only fear that I took him away from his hymn unduly long.[14]

The importance of this difference is heightened when we note that in the second version another new attribute is attached to the angel: he resembles 'all from which I have had to part: persons and above all things'. The angel is not what he appeared. He is not a fleeting angel created only for a moment of praise but one who has hidden his name. This hiding of the name is connected somehow to his new appearance as one who resembles everything from which Benjamin has had to part.

What is the name of the angel? Gershom Scholem alone has presented us with an answer thus far. His suggestion is that the title 'Agesilaus Santander' is an anagram. He writes: 'Agesilaus Santander is, sealed as it were with a superfluous "i", an anagram of The Angel Satan (*Der Angelus Satanas*).'[15] This identification has much in its favour, not least the fact that the angel is described in both versions as 'clawed' and the fact that Satan is the embodiment of that strangest of doctrines: the fallen angel. The angel is a 'messenger' etymologically but Satan's position is more direct: he accuses. The angel in the second version here given resembles loss. This resemblance to loss is a message of accusation. But the fact of resemblance itself is noted by Benjamin in his earlier fragment 'On the Mimetic Faculty' to have declined from the time when ('for the ancients') it was given form in the newborn child, who was 'perfectly modelled on cosmic being'.[16] Massimo Cacciari gives this figure of Benjamin's angel sense in his explication of the new angel as a figure of 'young Melancholy'.[17]

This transition of the new angel from Satan to the young melancholy of the infant redoubles the perplexity of the transformation of baroque allegory from the absolute spiritual materialism of Satan to the shining image of beauty with which the *Trauerspiel* study closed. And now the mystery of this transformation of Satan into an image of redemption can be given a clearer questioning form: how can Satan be opened up to a spirit which is not fateful? Or, put another way, is there a presentation of redemption which enables us to be free from the world of necessity?

It is these questions which lie at the heart of Baudelaire's Satanism. In 'Satan's Litanies' he writes:

> Who even to lepers and such outcast scum
> by love inculcates all we know of bliss,
> > Satan, take pity on my sore distress!
> Who gave to Death, your oldest paramour,
> a child both lunatic and lovely – Hope!
> > Satan, take pity on my sore distress!
> Who grants the criminal's last look of pride
> that damns the crowd beneath the guillotine,
> > Satan, take pity on my sore distress![18]

Here we see Satan appealed to as the intercessor for the poor, the wretched and the despised, the ones forgotten by the church.[19] Satan is now the one who will take pity on distress and is the one who (in union with death) gave birth to hope. That hope is an infant is consonant with the picture we have compiled thus far.

Baudelaire is thus the successor of the baroque in presenting an image of the necessity of Satan. This necessity is now understood to be the one source of hope in the world. The paradoxical situation thus arises that necessity is implored to free us from itself. But this imprecation is as fleeting in its presentation as the song of the angels of the *kabbalah*. Baudelaire's poem fades with the coming of the totalitarian politics that arises, as Rose puts it, from the spirit of the baroque. And against such politics Baudelaire's quest for the beauty of the diabolical fades into a still appeal without resonance.

More lasting is the dilemma which Baudelaire's work gave voice to: how to incorporate a new sense of Satan, how to mourn the passing away of the world before its own violence in a way that will hasten the arrival of the promise of the divine? This question is rightly understood by Rose as arising from 'exilic' Judaism. It is after the exile in Babylon (the place which is the strictest antithesis forever afterwards to Jerusalem) that the figure of the angel erupts into the sacred texts and perpetual memory of Judaism. Angels are the figures through which the idols of Babylon live on within the sanctum of Judaism itself. They are what mourns the captivity into which the chosen people fell. The Talmud Torah's local law to which Rose appeals against the eschatological significance of the angel is the place where the rabbinate attempted an allegorical cleansing of the angel on behalf of an anterior law and for the sake of a memory of the first order of the divine. Rose in repeating the gesture of the rabbinate attempts thereby to utilize the allegorical response of the local law to eschatology, a response which has since been rendered inoperative through its irreducible contamination by the presence of the idol within the angel.

This fact about the angels does not merely concern their seasonal placement (Cacciari points out that from the first angels ruled over days of the week, months of the year, and seasons, to the extent that they are identifiable with astrological signs); it also applies to the fact that what the Babylonian idols represent is the same as that which angels represent: fates. The Babylonian idols (in this being one with the Greek gods) represent circles of necessity, the wheel of fortune which follows precise laws which are determined with the capriciousness of lots. The angels by contrast appear to be free, but their freedom is manifested at only one point, the one where, as Cacciari puts it, 'the adventure of the universe opens': the point where the split within their ranks opens between the decision for God or for Satan. This decision once made, what choice is left for them? They now circle incessantly around the orbit of the one decision made. The angels are thus *all* creatures of an instant: an instant of decision whose resonance is eternal.

The fateful character of this decision brings the angels before us anew as the reception into the post-pagan world of Moira, whose reign is above the gods of Greece and now above the angels and demons of the Judeo-Christic-Islamic world. It is the conjunction of eternity with the moment which produces an angelic dimension of time. In this dimension of time the accumulation of instants that we call the historical is reduced to a single dimension: an unending catastrophe. This catastrophe is the repetition of the eternal mythical pattern of fateful action, the endless spectacle of the decision made once and for all being repeated endlessly in the instants that we determine as epochs of history. As Cacciari puts it: 'The Angel incessantly searches for the *just* representation of a new time: present-instant, interruption of the continuum, *Jetzt-Zeit* (now-time). *Every* Jetzt can represent this new time.'[20] Allegory presents a possible time which is no longer ruled by the persistent pattern of a series of presents. It does this in the form of a memory: a memory of a time which has never been. This memory must point beyond the allegorical fact of the experience of the world. Within allegory there is contained therefore an access to something which is not allegorical: the symbol of life (where symbol is the union of the beautiful and the good). This presents the synthesis that is opposed to the false synthesis of satanic consciousness but does so through the medium of that consciousness: allegory. As Benjamin puts it: 'Allegory established itself most permanently where transitoriness and eternity confronted each other most closely.'[21] But the allegory's existence is possible because of the separation between the angels. It is because they have divided into two camps that the light of heaven has turned into something other than itself: evil. This dissension points towards its own solution in a newly unitary time which we figure under the sign of the Messiah. But this newly unitary time, messianic time, must inaugurate a new revolution within the ranks of the angels. This revolution has two possible ways of being understood, both paradoxical.

The first way of understanding the revolution which will be installed by the Messiah is that of most forms of Christianity: Satan will be completely vanquished and overcome, the torment of the damned will reach its pitch before all the damned are cast into an eternal night. This most orthodox of visions has the great problem that victory over the realm of hell is carried out on hell's own terms. Those who are the active agents of damnation are simply themselves damned. God seems therefore unable to save them from themselves. Christianity thus concedes ultimate reality to Satan and absolutizes his power, a power which is not conquered by God but merely cancelled. This has the consequence that Christianity fails to escape from the charge of simply performing a transcendent judgment process which lacks saving power (which is what leads the Reformation to its de-eschatological position). In evacuating from the cosmos the possibility of the redemption of evil Christianity thereby imperils its own message of good news.

To avoid these consequences of the failure of Christianity it would be necessary to affirm that Satan himself can one day be received once more into the light of God. This would be tantamount to understanding the fall of Satan as being what must be overcome if the cosmos is to be set once more in order and would therefore displace the centrality of humanity from the story of creation. On this interpretation the post-pagan promise is the overcoming of fate. But for fate to be overcome requires that evil be integrated once more into the divine light. This is the vision of the opening of the historical into the true event of historicity itself.[22]

But how could evil be overcome? Through itself. This occurs through a logical understanding of the satanic. What is presented in the satanic is – on Benjamin's construction – the empty knowledge of contemplation separated from the determination of action. Cacciari's account is that Satan represents the self-blinding of light such that separation of one part from the whole comes to seem a possibility. For Cacciari, as for Benjamin, this is a product of 'intellectualism'.

The separation of this part into a position of radical alterity is what must cancel itself in the reconciliation that is the true Parousia which was only announced but not performed in the Resurrection (or the giving of the Law for Judaism or the appearance of the Prophet for Islam). But what this amounts to is asserting (and this is the reason for Benjamin's constant references in the *Trauerspiel* study to 'natural history') that the life of the cosmos has divided to the extent that it has permitted death. Death is thereby indicated to be connected intimately (as with both Baudelaire and St Paul) to the satanic rebellion against God (but Satan's rebellion contains now also the image of the reintegration into one that is the sign of hope).

To pose the problem of satanic evil either as one of the relation between wholes and parts (as Cacciari does) or as the relation between life and death (as with Benjamin) is however to reveal the conceptual grid through which the whole problem is thought to be Kantian. Kant is the one who understands the opposition between whole and part as synonymous with the opposition between life and death. This is the point of his dialectic between teleology and mechanism. But to insist on the necessity of death as part of the furtherance of the possibility of life is to open this Kantian problematic out to a further determination by means of the Freud of *Beyond the Pleasure Principle*. It is this meeting of Freud and Kant in the messianic which constitutes the Derridean sense of 'the work of mourning'.

Death and purpose

The baroque *Trauerspiel* meets its perfect consummation in the corpse, the figure which provides the perfect material for the allegorical meeting of the eternal and the ephemeral. But if this is so – and Benjamin is clear about this point – then would not the perfect death be the death of allegory itself, that is, the death of death or of Satan? But to envisage this would be to have death yield a purpose and this is what would ensure that the baroque had been entered by a spirit alien to itself. This alien spirit was presented in Germany by the work of Kant.

Kant's distinction between mechanical and teleological ways of understanding the presentation of objects in cognition is rooted in the notion that we perceive by relating the whole datum we apprehend to the assessment of its parts. In understanding the object as made up only of parts interacting to produce a whole more than themselves we only cognize the object mechanically (we take it to be a machine). If we view the whole and the parts as mutually interactive however (both in terms of cause and effect), then we understand what we perceive as a natural purpose, that is, as an organism, or a living being. That which can only be perceived (or is at some point for some purpose only perceived) through apprehension of parts alone is not vital but only mechanical; that which can be understood as a mutual nexus of parts and wholes is living. The distinction between mechanical and teleological is then precisely correlated to that between living and non-living.[23]

On a Kantian construction therefore what has been presented by both Cacciari and Benjamin is that the satanic consciousness is self-contradictory because the synthetic unity appealed to in it must be one of an organism understanding itself as mechanical. This is the basis of the satanic separation from the order of heaven. Satan comes to understand himself as separate from himself, as divided into distinct active principles which however do not yield to a unitary action of himself or only do so in a way which does not involve an apprehension through consciousness but only by reference to effective causation (indicating that Satan is thus purely mechanical in his moves, i.e., as already suggested, non-free or fated).

This lapse of Satan into a non-living life is mirrored by the fall of nature into a general wishing for death. This at least is what we can garner from Freud. In *Beyond the Pleasure Principle* Freud presents himself as an *advocatus diaboli* and reminds us that: 'The notion of 'natural death' is quite foreign to primitive races; they attribute every death that occurs among them to the influence of an enemy or of an evil spirit.'[24] Freud's own inclination in the analysis of death is to suggest that the original unification of living substance was torn apart at origin and has ever since endeavoured to reunite, but that this reunification can only be brought about by the cessation of the individual units, a process which is attempted through the two conflicting methods of reproduction and death. (An explanation which, he admits, takes him close to the position of Schopenhauer.)

These considerations are carried further in Freud's analysis of 1922–23, 'A Seventeenth-Century Demonological Neurosis', in which his discussion of the manuscript *Trophaeum Mariano-Cellense* leads to the conclusion that the 'possessed' artist Christoph Haizmann 'made no sharp distinction between the powers of the Evil Spirit and those of the Divine Powers. He had only one description for both: they were manifestations of the Devil'.[25] The reason why Haizmann adopts this position is that for him the operations of both procreation and renunciation were equally the presence of the diabolical in the world and that therefore the most divine action would be to deny. This final *imitatio de Christi* brings Haizmann to the position correctly attributed to Schopenhauer in *Beyond the Pleasure Principle*: that the purpose of life is death.

Freud's diabolism when conjoined with the Kantian distinction between living and non-living indicates that the organic (whose teleological principles Kant attempted to elucidate) contains within itself a tendency to the mechanical (a fact never denied by Kant). This division within the organic – the striving to reach unity with other life through the paradoxical path of death – is what manifests in man the satanic condition. Benjamin described this in political terms as early as the 'Theologico-Political Fragment': 'nature is Messianic by reason of its eternal and total passing away. To strive after such passing, even for those stages of man that are nature, is the task of world politics, whose method must be called nihilism.'[26] It is the end of this nihilism that is announced in its self-proclaimed (recently reiterated) consummation of an end of history (the siren song of a certain Hegelianism from 1840 to 1991 and beyond). This self-consummation of nihilism in a world-wide celebration of the decadence that passes itself off as 'democracy' calls us to a remembrance, a memory of the future. This memory calls us to another time, the time of the messianic. This time is what the eschatological work of mourning would commemorate.

But how would mourning be determined by it? As a waiting without end for the end of the end. The figure of Satan is the presentation in one scheme of both the historical catastrophe and its interruption. That which the new angel would like to mend, to help, to make whole, would be itself. It would like to mend itself. But the rending itself apart in the endless catastrophic presentation of moment upon moment is the condition of possibility of the reunification that would constitute redemption.

Derrida writes:

> One must always remember that the impossible ('To let the dead bury their dead') is, alas, always possible. One must constantly remember that this absolute evil (which is, is it not, absolute life, fully present life, the one that does not know death and does not want to hear about it) can take place. One must constantly remember that it is even on the basis of the terrible possibility of this impossible that justice is desirable.[27]

What the work of mourning must be is the destruction of the world of death by immersion into the necessity of death. This is the same as saying that what has to be mourned is the fate of Satan. Satan's fate is one with his spirit: absorption into the ruin of the body, its corpse, is the location for him of the greatest weight of matter, a weight he carries again and again. This eternal return of death is the basis of the possibility of a spirit that rests entirely in negation. Death burying death, the impossible itself, and the most everyday.

Destruction of death by mourning for Satan is the imprecation for his release from his burden of burying himself. But to mourn Satan means to hope for the birth from death of the transfiguration of the world. This hope is a despair and a taste for death. This taste for death is what Benjamin himself expressed as the most necessary political attitude when in the 'Theses on the Philosophy of History' he wrote: 'Only that historian will have the gift of fanning the spark of hope who is firmly convinced that *even the dead* will not be safe from the enemy if he wins. And this enemy has not ceased to be victorious.'[28] This immersion in death is close to Satan to the point where he becomes the one who we expect to cleanse himself. The basis for this expectation is that his inner struggle with the desire of life to reunify is the struggle we each have with the other. Satan is every other Other.

Kant's division between the living and the non-living, the purposive and the mechanical is complicated by the fact that the living wishes to be (and becomes) mechanical. It thereby moves ineluctably towards its end. This end, understood by Freud as the internal movement of all life, is the purposive orientation which transcends teleology or consummates it in an end that Kant would correctly have termed demonological. This is what the satanic movement of life amounts to, a movement which world politics celebrates and wishes for to the point of holocaust (the baroque ethic of fascism). But this celebration of the satanic victory of the death principle within life is itself expressive of a move towards a new unification which can only be thwarted through perpetual birth. These perpetual births are themselves signals towards the hope which is born from death, the hope for a time transcending the present in memory of the mournful work that is the satanic past, a mournful remembrance of mourning that is the only possible gift of the future.

But if this is the Derridean response to Rose (and I believe that it is) then how can the satanic recreation of catastrophe ever be brought to an end? Only through a wrenching away of Satan from the fixation on the absolute decision of rebellion that tore the universe into parts that fail to recognize themselves in the wholeness of life. Wrenching Satan away from this fixation is the political task of a remembrance of the need for the supersession of fate. This supersession of fate was promised by the post-pagan religions but they have been unable to accomplish it. This is finally because in their fixation on the good, in their betrayal of evil (which they have left to itself), they have committed the greatest evil (the one which enables the absolute fixity of Satan to be repeated eternally). Only by turning away from the prospect of eternal life towards an absorption in the necessity of death (thereby to destroy its necessity) can we begin to open ourselves (and Satan himself) to the possibility of an existence of a good which is not fixed in the stars but capable of manifesting itself in us.

But this is finally to say no more than what is said in the aspiration of the messianic movements: that what must be conquered is death and that it can only be overcome by absorption into it. Each movement previously has taken this task as completed and simultaneously postponed it into the future. To understand the future as contained within the eternality of each moment is to open ourselves to a mourning which, paradoxically, is the true hope of life.

Notes

1 Walter Benjamin (1940) 'Theses on the Philosophy of History', thesis 9, in Walter Benjamin *Illuminations*, trans. Harry Zohn (London, Jonathan Cape, 1970), pp. 259-60.

2 Gillian Rose (1992) 'Walter Benjamin – Out of the Sources of Modern Judaism' in Gillian Rose *Judaism and Modernity: Philosophical Essays* (Oxford: Basil Blackwell, 1993), p. 207.

3 The distinctions here all point back ultimately to Sigmund Freud (1915) 'Mourning and Melancholia' (included in volume 11 of the Penguin Freud Library, Harmondsworth: Penguin, 1984). The notion of 'aberrated mourning' however is derived from Laurence A. Rickels *Aberrations of Mourning: Writing on German Crypts* (Detroit: Wayne State University Press, 1988) and the term 'inaugurated eschatology' derives from Kallistos Ware's Introduction to John Climacus *The Ladder of Divine Ascent*, trans. Colin Luibhied and Norman Russell (London: Society for the Promotion of Christian Knowledge, 1982), p. 30. Climacus is a premier example of Orthodox mysticism.

4 Jacques Derrida (1993) *Specters of Marx: The State of the Debt, the Work of Mourning, and the New International*, trans. Peggy Kamuf (London: Routledge, 1994), p. 74.

5 Walter Benjamin (1925) *The Origin of German Tragic Drama*, trans. John Osborne (London: Verso, 1977). The rendition of *Trauerspiel* as 'tragic drama' seems to me inadequate, so I will refer to the work throughout by using the German term.

6 Ibid., p. 66.

7 Ibid., p. 98.

8 Walter Benjamin (1936) 'The Work of Art in the Age of Mechanical Reproduction' in *Illuminations*, p. 244.

9 Ibid., p.138.

10 Benjamin, *Trauerspiel*, p. 228.

11 Ibid., p. 230.

12 Ibid.

13 Benjamin 'Agesilaus Santander', version 1, in Gershom Scholem (1972) 'Walter Benjamin and His Angel' in Gershom Scholem *On Jews and Judaism in Crisis: Selected Essays*, trans. Werner Dannhauser (New York: Schocken Books, 1976), p. 205.

14 Walter Benjamin 'Agesilaus Santander', version 2, in Scholem *On Jews and Judaism in Crisis*, p. 207 (my emphasis).

15 Ibid., p. 216.
16 Walter Benjamin (1933) 'On the Mimetic Faculty' in Walter Benjamin *Reflections: Essays, Aphorisms, Autobiographical Writings*, trans. Edmund Jephcott (New York: Schocken Books, 1978), p. 334.
17 Massimo Cacciari (1987) *The Necessary Angel*, trans. Miguel E. Vatter (Albany, NY: State University of New York Press, 1994), p. 33.
18 Charles Baudelaire (1857) 'Satan's Litanies' in *Les Fleurs du Mal* trans. Richard Howard (London: Picador, 1982), pp. 143–4. The French original is given on pp. 321–2:

> Toi qui, même aux lépreux, aux parias maudits,
> Enseignes par l'amour le goût du Paradis,
>
> O Satan, prends pitié de ma longue misère!
>
> O toi qui de la Mort, ta veille et forte amante,
> Engendras l'Espérance, – une folle charmante!
>
> O Satan, prends pitié de ma longue misère!
>
> Toi qui fais au proscrit ce regard calme et haut
> Qui damne tout un peuple autour d'un échafaud,
>
> O Satan, prends pitié de ma longue misère!

19 Compare here the sentiments of Arthur Rimbaud's poem, 'Evil':

> There is a God, who smiles upon us through
> The gleam of gold, the incense-laden air,
> Who drowses in a cloud of murmured prayer,
> And only wakes when weeping mothers bow
> Themselves in anguish, wrapped in old black shawls –
> And their last small coin into his coffer falls.

(From Arthur Rimbaud *Complete Works*, trans. Paul Schmidt, New York: Harper Colophon Books, 1976, p. 54.)
20 Cacciari, *Necessary Angel*, p. 51.
21 Benjamin, *Trauerspiel*, p. 224.
22 For a fuller discussion of this theological dilemma see Cacciari, *Necessary Angel*, 'Apokatastasis'.
23 For a fuller discussion of Kant's account see Gary Banham *Kant and the Ends of Aesthetics* (Basingstoke: Macmillan, 2000).
24 Sigmund Freud (1919) *Beyond the Pleasure Principle* in Penguin Freud Library, vol. 11, p. 317.
25 Sigmund Freud (1922–3) 'A Seventeenth-Century Demonological Neurosis' in Penguin Freud Library, vol. 14 (1985), p. 423.
26 Walter Benjamin (1921) 'Theologico-Political Fragment' in *Reflections*, p. 313.
27 Derrida, *Specters of Marx*, p. 175.
28 Benjamin, 'Theses', thesis 6, in *Illuminations*, p. 257.

joanna hodge

KIERKEGAARD'S WRITING MACHINES: EPISTEMOTOPOLOGY OF THE DEMON

Preliminary orientation

The diabolical is not limited to the wickedness popular wisdom ascribes to it and whose malice, based on guile, is familiar and predictable in an adult culture. The diabolical is endowed with intelligence and enters where it will. To reject it, it is first necessary to refute it. Intellectual effort is needed to recognise it. Who can boast of having done so? Say what you will, the diabolical gives food for thought.[1]

There is a presumption lurking between the lines of the texts of the history of philosophy that there is, as Socrates surmised, a connection between virtue and wisdom, such that great philosophy must be authored by the virtuous. The quotation given is taken from Levinas's essay on Heidegger's not so secret connection with nazism, 'As if to horror consenting', and it both retrieves this philosophical prejudice in favour of the moral standing of the philosophers and indicates a basis for its dubiety – a power also attributed in the tradition to the diabolical. The surmised connection between virtue and wisdom is held in place alongside an equally important surmise concerning an indiscernibility between divine and demonic power. In the writings of Soren Kierkegaard, the problem is to distinguish divine from diabolical silence. In this chapter I shall arrive at a reinterpretation of diabolism provided by Derrida in his reading of Kierkegaard in *The Gift of Death* (1992) by passing through two other registers: the question of a historical variability in construals of a relation between the divine and the demonic; and the problem raised in the thematization of the demon in Kierkegaard's writings, a problem which is covered over in a series of distinctly odd responses to Kierkegaard's writings in the twentieth century, in the writings of these two otherwise fiercely opposed thinkers, Adorno and Heidegger. It is Walter Benjamin who identifies the potential of the demonic forces in Kierkegaard's writings and who perhaps transmits that understanding to Derrida.

The capacity of Kierkegaard's writings to disturb the more usual certainty of these two readers suggests that some powerful force is at work, to which the title 'infernal writing machines' might be given. The term 'epistemotopology of the demon' is designed to capture the disruptions at work in three distinct movements: the movement, in epistemology, from a universal, divine view from nowhere to a human stance via the thinking of a demonic movement and interruption; the movement within Kierkegaard's writings, putting in question the possibility of both reading and writing; and the puzzling effects these writings have had on some twentieth-century readers. The term 'epistemotopology' presents a form of homage to Derrida's notions of topolitology, exemplorality and philopolemology. Derrida responds to Kierkegaard's *Fear and Trembling* (1844) in his *The Gift of Death*, an extended, four-part essay which begins with a reflection on the writings of Jan Patocka, and on a passage from the democratic to the totalitarian, and moves through a narration of the encounter between Levinas and Heidegger on the question of death to the reading of Kierkegaard's discussion in *Fear and Trembling*, not directly of the demonic, but of Abraham's encounter with the divine. The theme is Levinas's resistance to Kierkegaard's radical disruption of any affirmation of ethical responsibility, while the lesson of Kierkegaard for Derrida appears to be the indispensability of the oblique.

Derrida considers Kierkegaard's insistence on the redoubled anxiety at work in trembling: 'What does the body mean to say, by trembling or crying, presuming one can speak here of the body, or of saying, of meaning, and of rhetoric?'[2] This question emerges in the third part of this extended essay, which in its first section has arrived at the following conundrum:

> What is implicit yet explosive in Patocka's text can be extended in a radical way, for it is heretical with respect to a certain Christianity and a certain Heideggerianism but also with respect to all the important European discourses. Taken to its extreme, the text seems to suggest on the one hand that Europe will not be what it must be until it becomes fully Christian, until the mysterium tremendum is adequately thematised. On the other hand it also suggests that the Europe to come will no longer be Greek, Greco-Roman, or even Roman.[3]

This thought explodes into high relief once Derrida has located the paradoxes of the use within the Christian tradition of the Jewish distinction between the people of the Lord and the Gentiles, the *ethnikoi*, who solidarize only with their own kind: 'And if you salute your brethren only, what do ye more than others? Do not even the Gentiles do so?'[4] There would no doubt be further essays to write on the differences between Jewish and Christian demonology, but this is not one of them. Derrida indicates his transposed demon, at the beginning of the third part of this extended essay, in the context of his response to Patocka, as though forestalling the idea that there might be a direct response to Kierkegaard:

> Contrary to what is normally thought, a technological modernity doesn't neutralise anything; it causes a certain form of the demonic to re-emerge. Of course it does neutralize, also by encouraging indifference and boredom, but because of that – and to the same extent in fact – it allows the return of the demonic. There is an affinity or at least a synchrony, between a culture of boredom and an orgiastic one. The domination of technology encourages demonic irresponsibility, and the sexual import of the latter does not need to be emphasized.[5]

I propose to turn to Kierkegaard and his pseudonyms to reveal the process of writing itself to be a demonic process, held in check only by a rehumanising process of reading.

The problem with the opening citation is that having suggested that the diabolical is the result of an unfettered intellectual activity, it then seems to suppose that by mobilizing intelligence it might be possible to combat these unwelcome results. By contrast, in the writings associated with Kierkegaard and Heidegger there is an analysis of the danger of supposing that the source of the difficulty, the articulations of intellectuality, separated from living, can provide the resources needed to turn the danger around. For Heidegger, technology is the result of the development of calculative thinking held separate from its condition of possibility, the existence of an entity for which being is an issue. For Heidegger, technology is the form of metaphysics which conceals that it is metaphysics, thus erasing the erasure of being which takes place in metaphysics. Thus technology in the form of the *Gestell* is a demonic force, which, in its diabolical severing of intellectual construction from the constraints of living, sets loose forces in the world which if left unchallenged must result in destruction.[6]

The question of the demonic in Kierkegaard's writings then permits a rethinking of Heidegger's question of technology, for which the being beyond beings has been reduced to nothing. This is the second aspect of the epistemotopology of the demon named in my title: the disruption of the later text by the earlier. The reversal of temporal sequence involved in starting out from Levinas and ending up with Kierkegaard corresponds to a necessity in thought: that the phenomena in question are to be read first retrogressively, back to their various divergent sources, and then progressively from those sources back into the present-day context in which they have first presented themselves for inspection. Through the thematization of demons in Kierkegaard's writings it is possible to retrieve the question of agency which is erased almost beyond the point of retrieval in the articulations of technology. Kierkegaard's demons are suspended between the link back to the mediaeval figure of Faust, sustained into the modern world through Goethe's grand non-drama, and Benjamin's discovery of the demonic within the modern projects of rationalization and automation. Here then are two further figures of the demonic: Mephistopheles as the despair of an intellect without agency; and the destitution of automatism, Benjamin's chess-playing automaton as an agency without subjectivity. This is a very Hegelian version of the demonic, positing a divided concept but lacking its speculative reintegration, since the thematization of demons in Kierkegaard's writings disrupts the possibility of any such reintegration of elements. The question of the demon thus becomes antinomic.

Historical differences

The condition of the possibility of evil is the separability of principles in a being, the separability of ground and existence.[7]

Heidegger's lectures *Schelling's Treatise on the Essence of Human Freedom* (1936) flag up the contradictory thought that, despite the prejudice that great philosophy should be morally sound, it may all the same have made some kind of Faustian pact with powers of evil. They pose a problem about the relation between the demonic and thought, between philosophy and evil. If demonic work is the mark of an incomplete appreciation in human beings of the workings of the divine, then the demon is the sign of all human activity and the notion of evil becomes indistinguishable from a non-communication between the human and the divine. Such a separation is marked up by Heidegger in his diagnosis of the modern age as one in which the gods have departed, in which a relation between the mortal and the immortal is unthinkable. His diagnosis of a resulting destitution has implications also for theories of knowledge, with a contrast between an epistemology, as veridical theory of knowledge, available to the divine or the immortal, distinct from the partiality arising from the specific location of the human, as divided from the universal, from divinity and immortality. Thus there emerges a distinction between an epistemology as such and the partial epistemologies of the human. The term 'epistemotopology' then picks out the partiality and occasionality of the epistemologies of human beings. This form of epistemology takes into account a trajectory of its emergence in thought as predicated on a separation from the divine and as therefore already thematized as the working of the demonic. The task is to identify the different valencies of a thinking of the demonic, made available in the writings of and responses to the writings of Kierkegaard, by contrast to a thinking of the divine, thematized by Kierkegaard and by Heidegger in their very different ways, as lacking.

It is worth recollecting that the demonic has not always been marked up as opposed to the divine. The demonic forces invoked by both Aristotle and Plato, for example in the opening of the *Phaedo*, are of course pre-Christian and are not structured through an opposition between good and evil. Descartes's demon by contrast is inscribed as evil and as explicitly contrasted to a conception of a just and righteous divinity. In *Meditations on the First Philosophy*[8] Descartes opens out his thought experiment in the following way: 'I will suppose therefore not that God, who is supremely good and the source of truth but rather some malicious demon of the utmost power and cunning has employed all his energies to deceive me. I shall think that the sky, the air, the earth, colours, shapes, sounds and all external things are merely the delusions of dreams which he has devised to ensnare my judgement.'[9] The following citation from Aristotle's *Nicomachean Ethics*, about Thales and Anaxagoras, shows an intriguing contrast between the daimonic as inspirational and the evil spirit of Descartes's thought experiment:[10] 'It is said that these thinkers indeed know things which are excessive, astounding, difficult, and demonic; and in addition that this knowledge is useless, for they are not seeking what is, according to ordinary common sense, good for human beings.'[11] This then sets up two quite distinct notions of the demonic, one pre and the other post Christian: as the transgression beyond the bounds of the human in the direction of a Greek conception of the divine; and as a falling short of the compass of the human, in what Heidegger, following Holderlin, calls the time of the departed gods.

I propose to reverse Aristotle's suggestion that the demonic occurs when human beings go beyond themselves in the direction of the divine, and suggest instead, under Kierkegaard's guidance, that the demonic occurs in the absence of the exercise of this human capacity for self-transcendence, which is a transcendence of an immediately given horizon, in the direction of a thinking of a variability of the relation between the human and the horizon. This is thematized by Heidegger as the unthought relation between the mortal and the immortal, the sky and the earth. Part of the task of this chapter is to show that in order to think the humanity of the human it is not necessary to think either divinity or immortality: this would be to affirm the resurgence of a demon as disowned activity. It is necessary only to think the horizon as temporally open. In Heideggerian language, the *Gestell*, as a framework in which the horizon has become a fixity, can be understood as setting up a demonic thinking without human perspective and without divine delimitation. In order to release the thinking of the horizon from this fixing, it is necessary to retrieve a thinking of the human, in the Aristotelian form of a daimonic self-surpassing, a self-overcoming in the Nietzschean rewriting. There is no need to endorse the Heideggerian move, of surmising 'Only a god can save us now'.

The relation between the demon and the divine then has a long history in western philosophy. Here I have emphasized a difference between an Aristotelian daimon and the demon of Descartes's *Meditations on the First Philosophy*, which impacts on responses made in the twentieth century to the invocation of demons in Kierkegaard's various writings, which, like his writings, shifts with disruptive fluency between the registers of aesthetic appreciation, moral disapprobation and religious ecstasy. My hypothesis is that the Kierkegaardian distinctions between aesthetics, morality and the two versions of religion assist in distinguishing distinct layerings in the articulations of the daimon, the demon and diabolical. The move from daimonism to diabolism and back is too swift and benefits from the interruption imposed by invoking a curious preinscription in Kierkegaard's writings of the movements of hesitation and precipitation characteristic of the writings of a latter-day demon, Jacques Derrida. Thus there is a question of disentangling at least three distinct registers in a thinking of the demon, those of the aesthetic, of the moral, and of the religious or indeed Christian register; there is the possibility of deploying Kierkegaard's distinctions in order to unpick the collapse in modern thinking of these distinctions, especially but not only in relation to a thinking of the demonic; and there is the diagnosis of a thematization and enactment of these demonic movements in the writings of Derrida.

My hypothesis is that a second dimension of the relation between Derrida and Kierkegaard is this concern with the diabolism of thought and of writing; and a third a curious process whereby when Derrida writes about Kierkegaard directly, as in *The Gift of Death*, he is less able to mark the sophisticated nature of his response to Kierkegaard than when the reference is oblique or indeed unmarked altogether. Thus the notion of epistemotopology also captures the thought of an inverse relation between the directness of an approach to reading Kierkegaard and its capacity for responsiveness. Various other aspects of this diabolism in epistemology will emerge in the course of the following remarks. One which emerges in the context of Heidegger's thought is the detachment of the thought of the demon from a residual Christian theodicy and its reintegration through a thinking of the disowned processings of technology. As a way station from the one to the other, Kierkegaard's complex articulation of his contempt for the lack of seriousness in the deployment of the threat of diabolical doubt, temptation and delusion in the writings of both Descartes, whom he describes as encouraging teachers of philosophy 'to doubt by the hour', and, more importantly, Hegel, show that even within the Christian tradition of thinking there is a failure to take seriously the truly disruptive, destructive workings of an unfettered diabolism. The invocations of demons in Kierkegaard's writings suggest an understanding of human experience in accordance with the unpredictable and morally ambiguous workings of the demonic rather than in accordance with the model preinscribed as an imitation of Christ, which reveals the more usual gesture of solemn moralism in philosophical writing.

Practices of reading

The destructive character knows only one watchword: make room; only one activity: clearing away. His need for fresh air and open space is stronger than any hatred.[12]

The themes of the demon and of epistemotopology then are juxtaposed in my title to indicate a preoccupation with their destabilizing effects on a central philosophical prejudice in favour of stable objects of enquiry and a stable stance from which these objects are supposed to be viewed. Demonic figurations in the text of philosophy mark out an anxiety induced by a sudden unpredictable shift in position resulting from a movement of thought. The notion of epistemotopology is here deployed in part to permit an articulation of this anxiety and of this irreducible unpredictability of movement. A central strategy for my discussion is to play off the relation between Benjamin and Adorno on the question of how to read Kierkegaard. Benjamin and Adorno, to put it mildly, have utterly opposed erotics of reading, which their contrastive approaches to Kierkegaard make abundantly clear. Adorno seeks to identify his own unease with what he diagnoses as a bourgeois preoccupation with interiority in philosophy, by diagnosing it in Kierkegaard.[13] By contrast, Benjamin's essay on Karl Kraus reveals his responsiveness to the working of the demon in Kierkegaard's writings;[14] and his reception of Kierkegaard is one of the many obstacles which come between Benjamin and any free exchange of thought with Adorno:[15] Benjamin, as always, oblique, sensitive to an extreme degree, almost intuitively miming the gestures of the writer under discussion; Adorno, for all the systematic syntactic complexity, in the mode of full-frontal brutal assault.

Adorno, in utter disregard for Kierkegaard's wider ambitions, diagnoses the Kierkegaardian aesthetic as merely a name for an exquisite exploration of interiority, and seeks instead to retrieve aesthetics to provide a new name for articulating a dialectics under duress. Adorno makes use of Kierkegaard to challenge the adequacy of Hegel's conception of absolute knowledge; and in this Heidegger has much in common with Adorno: making use of Kierkegaard as support against German idealism, rather than reading him in his own right. Such use of course does not just distort the writings of Kierkegaard: it renders them illegible. Thus the name 'Kierkegaard' raises the question of a non-communication between Adorno and Benjamin, as, more generally, it poses the claim that essential communication is necessarily indirect. The lines of communication between Benjamin and Adorno and between Benjamin and Heidegger have to be indirect because of the manner in which Adorno and indeed Heidegger reduce everything with which they come in contact into elements within their gigantic refutations of Hegel. Between Benjamin and Kierkegaard there may be a more direct route; but the connection between Adorno and Kierkegaard, and between Heidegger and Kierkegaard, requires disruption and dislocation.

The question for this chapter is to diagnose the nature of Derrida's responses to Kierkegaard. Do they fall on the side of Benjamin or on that of Heidegger and Adorno? Or indeed does Derrida enact a diabolism shown as possible by Kierkegaard; shown as actual by Benjamin; and then shown as necessary by Derrida? The writings of Benjamin and Kierkegaard are infinitely at work to deepen their receptivity to otherness, to the echo of the divine in the word, thus dangerously multiplying themselves to a condition beyond that of effective action and self-preservation; the thought of Heidegger and Adorno monologically drags along in its wake the whole history of philosophy, the history of being, concealed within a supposed history of philosophy and a supposed history of the world, cast in chains behind the chariot wheels of their triumphal progress to the podium reserved for master thinkers. In this process, the thought of others is traduced, dismembered, misremembered and brought screaming into the crisis of the various contexts of unintelligibility which mark the present day, its thought and experience. The thought of the other in the writings of Kierkegaard and Benjamin by contrast is taken up, turned around, and revealed as more exactly itself than ever before: Kierkegaard on Hegel, Benjamin on Kant. Each mode of reading arrives at a thought of crisis, but by very different routes.

The groupings Adorno and Heidegger, Benjamin and Kierkegaard set out two quite distinctive, contrastive ethical modes: modes of responding or not responding to otherness and to the other, with distinctive effectivities, preconditions and consequences. There are two very different kinds of violence involved here: there is the violence of Heidegger's and of Adorno's readings through which the other is dismembered in the service of some higher cause, constructing desperately needed contexts of intelligibility. Here the reading takes priority over the text. Then there is the violence to self, at work in the writings of Kierkegaard and of Benjamin, through which they systematically wrench apart whatever is precarious in identity and meaning, thought and reception, denying themselves even the false security of self-importance. Here, the text produced as a result of reading takes priority over both reading and initial text, with especially paradoxical results when the initial texts are those of the writer, under the bar of pseudonymy. This then provides a place to assess Benjamin's practice of unacknowledged self-citation. The former, the gestures of Adorno and Heidegger, is the more obvious as violence, the latter, the practices at work in the writings of Kierkegaard and Benjamin, much more alarming. The contrast maps on to Benjamin's distinction between constitutive, law-sustaining and originary, order-creating violence, from the essay 'Critique of Violence', and my remarks here are in some sense a commentary on that essay.[16]

I suggest that there is a third form of violence at work here, inaugurated by Derrida's writing, through which the identity of the reader is disrupted in favour of affirming an identity for the writer. Here, the text produced through reading releases a demonic identity, which might be called 'deconstruction', or worse still 'deconstructionism', to which Derrida on occasion satirically refers, transcending resulting text, reading and initial text; and indeed erasing the differences between them. This is cultural production in the mode of an erasure of meaning, which inaugurates a new and more thoroughgoing nihilism than any conceivable in the nineteenth century. Central to the argument of this chapter is a concern with a distinction between the energetics of writing and those of reading. There is a dissociation of energy from agency in writing which gets temporarily reintegrated in an instant of understanding produced in reading. The operations of this dissociation are analysed by Derrida in his responses to Freud's analytical and writing practices, in the practice and theorizing of psychoanalysis.

These movements are also emphatically at work in Kierkegaard's texts, which are characterized by their insistent transposition of an auto-affection of thought into a hetero-affection of pseudonymous writing, whereby Kierkegaard enacts processes of recuperating a self-to-self relation as an outcome of exploring in the writings the diverse aspects of a self for which the conditions of integration are not yet or perhaps never will be given. The process of self-reading appears momentarily to overcome the processes of self-dissociation enacted in writing, and at the moment of composition. The gap between the self who writes and the selves produced in writing is not one which lends itself to easy reintegration. Thus the relation of hetero-affection can be seen as the basic structure of self-relation of which then auto-affection is a special case, as a derivative and reduced form. There is then a relation to be marked up between the writings of Kierkegaard, as a process of self-constitution and of questioning the possibility of an integrated self-relation, and those of Derrida, which draw attention to the manner in which Kierkegaard's writings put themselves and the identity of Kierkegaard in question and which therefore must do likewise to those of those who read them.

Indirect communication: writing and violence

When the Eleatics denied motion, Diogenes, as everyone knows, came forward as an opponent. He literally did come forward, because he did not say a word but merely paced back and forth a few times, thereby assuming that he had sufficiently refuted them.[17]

The role of Kierkegaard's insistence on reading himself while he writes his pseudonymous personae into existence requires close attention. This process of writing is quite distinct from either Derrida's or Heidegger's self-interpretative gestures, and I suggest puts them in question. The remobilization of the demon in Kierkegaard's writings permits Aristotle's demon to disrupt Heidegger's reading of Kierkegaard, and to show Descartes's demon as disrupting Derrida's readings of Kierkegaard. Heidegger's relation to Kierkegaard's work is set out in a couple of footnotes in *Being and Time* (1927), in which there is more than an echo of Jasper's treatment of Kierkegaard in *Psychologie der Weltanschauungen* (1919), as psychologist not as philosopher. Heidegger remarks in *Being and Time*, that Kierkegaard misses the existential/ontological dimension of his own thought. The more I think about it, the more extraordinary this claim seems to me to be, for the multiplication of stances and voices within Kierkegaard's writing charts the impasse in which Heidegger finds himself when he tries in the final non-concluding pages of *Being and Time* to explain what the self-constitutive moment of *Entschlossenheit* might be like. Heidegger reads Nietzsche as a crypto-theologian; I suggest that he would have done well to read Kierkegaard as a crypto-nihilist, as I propose to do, by affirming the despair beyond anxiety enacted in *The Sickness unto Death* (1849).[18] This despair takes on in Kierkegaard's construction a profoundly religio-theological tone; but through Benjamin's reception of theology, and indeed of Kierkegaard, it is possible to reveal an emancipatory, redemptive force in this affirmation, through which the dead weight of tradition can be shifted to reveal the possibility of a redoubled affirmation. This work presupposes the possibility of settling accounts with both theology and its twin, the automatism of revolutionary politics figured by Benjamin in *The Theses on the Philosophy of History*[19] as the chess-playing automaton.

There is in Kierkegaard's writings an interpretation of symptomatic gesture and a thought of repetition which brings Kierkegaard's thinking into uncanny proximity with that of Freud on the return of the repressed; and brings Derrida's responses to Kierkegaard into proximity with his responses to Freud. This proximity is marked by a displacement at work in Derrida's readings of Kierkegaard. As a marker for the problem there is the strange repetition of the phrase from Kierkegaard's *Philosophical Fragments*, 'The Instant of the decision is madness',[20] which occurs both early and late, as an epigraph to the essay on Foucault, 'Cogito and the History of Madness',[21] and in the middle of the 1989 essay on Benjamin, 'Force of Law: 'the Mystical Foundation of Authority'. The question of retrieval through repetition is coupled by Kierkegaard to a question of the reversibility of time. In *Repetition* the following contrast is drawn: 'Repetition and recollection are the same movement, except in opposite directions, for what is recollected has been, is repeated backwards, whereas genuine repetition is recollected forward.'[22] In a more direct approach there seems to me to be a danger of a recurrence of a demonic commitment to the powers of reason, rather than coming to terms with whatever has gone missing in the European notion of reason, to which the figure of the demon and that of irrecuperable antinomy have been assigned. There is a remark in *The Sickness unto Death* which exposes the impossibility of such reintegration, while proposing a rewriting of the Cartesian resolution of the encounter with the malign demon:

> By thinking sin, does a person himself perhaps become 'sin' – *cogito ergo sum*? A splendid suggestion! however, there need be no fear of becoming sin in this way – pure sin – precisely because sin cannot be thought. Even speculative philosophy would have to admit that, since sin in effect falls below the level of the concept. But, not to prolong this discussion *e concessis*, the main difficulty is something else. Speculative philosophy pays no heed to the fact that sin involves the ethical, which always points in the other direction from speculation and takes directly opposite steps; for the ethical does not abstract from actuality, but absorbs itself in it, operating essentially by means of the speculatively neglected and scorned category of the individual.[23]

Kierkegaard's demons occupy a privileged place between speculation and ethics, between theology and technology, between literature and philosophy, between writing and the nihilism to which Heidegger gives the name technology.

My reading then is to bring into view three themes: a relation between demons and technology; a question about reading and writing; and a struggle for philosophical hegemony waged by Heidegger first against others within the phenomenological tradition, and then against all comers, the philopolemology diagnosed by Derrida in *Geschlecht 4*.[24] Through these themes it is possible to articulate a relation between demonology, nihilism and writing, which should lead to a clarification of the current relation between philosophy, theology and religion, without which no reading of Kierkegaard is really possible; and without which Levinas's relation to Heidegger remains opaque. From Kierkegaard it is important to retrieve a notion of the aesthetic as a question of the place of human experience, of a topology, of the shape and location of human thought and existence. From Heidegger it is important to retrieve a thought of technology as the practices of human self-production which have become obscured through the self-evident failure of self-interrogation in the tradition of humanism. This mobilization of a distinction between aesthetics, as a question of topology, and technology, as a question of what it is to be human, disrupts the framing of thought through the now anachronistic distinctions between science and the arts and between ethics and epistemology. This is the place of Derrida's thinking.

Either/or: nihilism beyond subjectivity

Don Juan consequently is the expression for the demonic determined as the sensuous; Faust its expression as the intellectual or spiritual.[25]

Derrida then is to be positioned as both aesthetic and ethical, in Kierkegaard's terms: that is the point of the thought of undecidability. Derrida is both the traducer of texts and the reader who returns truth to its source: his is both a mode of self-interpretation, and in the same gesture one of a recuperation of the ambiguities of the texts of the tradition. His recurrent gesture of self-recuperation is an ambiguous one, putting the onus on the reader to determine the impact of the thought cumulatively at work in the writing. The manner in which his and Kierkegaard's texts move off in some direction unanticipated by its supposed author, through which its author is created, is a theme close to the heart of Derrida's and Kierkegaard's concerns. This movement of the text, the third form of epistemotopology, sets out a truly uncanny demon whose function is to make way for an affirmation of human identity, which all the same may not come. This is the demonic nihilism which on another occasion I have juxtaposed to the residual subjectivisms and anthropocentrism to be found at work in the active and passive nihilisms, suspended between the writings of Nietzsche

33

and of Heidegger.[26] Demonic nihilism thus poses a challenge to the thinking of passive and active nihilism, by displacing the notions of value and identity in favour of the question of writing.

Thus the strategy is to mobilise Benjamin and Kierkegaard against Adorno and Heidegger; and Derrida and Kierkegaard against Nietzsche and Heidegger, in order the better to reveal a demonic nihilism at work in Derrida's writings, as obliquely inherited from Kierkegaard. The demonic nihilism which I find in Kierkegaard's writings wrenches apart the stance from which any such distinction between an active and a passive nihilism might be made. For the distinction between passive and active nihilism depends on a distinction between a doubly affirmed will to power and one which, failing to affirm itself, all the same prefers to will nothing. But what if, as Derrida insists with Bartleby the scrivener,[27] one would prefer not to? What if there is no positioning and therefore no making of distinctions? The question about the indistinguishability of divine and demonic silence is opened out by Kierkegaard in the following passage from *Fear and Trembling*, not, it should be noted, in relation to the narration of Abraham's expedition to Mount Moriah, but apparently in quite another context:

> Despite the rigorousness with which ethics demands disclosure, it cannot be denied that secrecy and silence make a man great simply because they are qualifications of inwardness. When Amor leaves Psyche, he says to her: you will bear a child, who will be divine if you remain silent but will be human if you betray the secret. The tragic hero who is the favourite of ethics, is the purely human; him I can understand and all his undertakings are out in the open. If I go further, I always run up against a paradox, the divine and the demonic, for silence is both. Silence is the demon's trap, and the more that is silenced, the more terrible the demon, but silence is also divinity's mutual understanding with the single individual.[28]

The encounter with Kierkegaard opens out a question to Heidegger's privileging of a moment of silence in language as the source of its truth: for who can tell the silence of the demon from that of divine revelation? This possibility of disturbing Heideggerian certainties with Kierkegaardian doubt is one central strategy for this discussion.

Kierkegaard goes on to locate a certain demonic power at work in evasion: 'However, human beings are not willing to think eternity earnestly enough but are anxious about it, and anxiety can contrive a hundred evasions. And this is precisely the demonic.'[29] The violence at work with Kierkegaard and Benjamin is the experience of that encounter when meaning bends, as it does, identity is dispersed, and all that remains is a writing in process.[30] While Derrida is not in the mode triumphant of Heidegger and Adorno, nor is he in the mode self-destruct of Benjamin and

Kierkegaard, for there is an apparently interminable process of self-regeneration at work in the name 'Derrida', through the contemporaneous, world-wide reception of his thinking. Derrida, as many-headed hydra, receives his identity back from this immense and complex process of reception. It is we who have created him. This is a case of a demonic writing machine, which writes its identity into existence through its reception; but in Derrida's writings it is not so much Derrida's identity which is at issue, but that of European culture; hence the significance of his work. Thus, Derrida seems to me to occupy contrary positions in the process of transmitting European culture, one affirmative and one in the mode of overcoming: but overcoming what? Here it is necessary to align Nietzsche's self-overcoming with Heidegger's overcoming of metaphysics and measure the angle of difference.

In a long review from 1846, written after the completion of *Concluding Unsystematic Postscript*, Kierkegaard sets up an opposition between a logic of a revolutionary age, in which many of his contemporaries supposed themselves to live, and a logic of the present age.[31] This contrast runs in parallel to a contrast between the ideals of Christianity and the fact of Christendom, and it finds a contemporary resonance in the distinctions set out between Marxism and its distortion in Stalinism; and between European cultural ideals and the fact of European destructiveness. Kierkegaard's diagnosis of the current condition runs as follows:

> A passionate tumultuous age will overthrow everything: pull everything down; but a revolutionary age, that is at the same time reflective and passionless, transforms that expression of strength into a feat of dialectics: it leaves everything standing but cunningly empties it of significance. Instead of culminating in a rebellion it reduces the inward reality of all relationships to a reflective tension which leaves everything standing but makes the whole of life ambiguous: so that everything continues to exist factually whilst by a dialectical deceit, *privatissime*, it supplies a secret interpretation that it does not exist.[32]

This diagnosis of the present age as self-deludingly self-important can be used to good effect not just to refute Adorno's reading of Kierkegaard and his appropriation of the aesthetic; but also to disrupt Heidegger's gesture of supposing himself to have surpassed Kierkegaard. For Kierkegaard, but not for Heidegger, the first and only question is: who is speaking; who is writing; what is the locus of meaning? Kierkegaard's presumption is that unless the who is speaking, writing and meaning from a stance in which existence itself is affirmed, there is no meaning, writing or speaking. Because Kierkegaard supposes this to be the question for everyone, he is continuously bewildered by the absolute lack of resonance for his writings among his contemporaries: he cannot grasp that the self-preoccupations of the moment prevent most people from grasping the unavoidability of this set of questions.

Concluding unsystematic postscript

A man in our day who exists with as much energy as a mediocre Greek philosopher is regarded as a demon.[33]

Derrida, like Kierkegaard, asks continuously: who? who? how? But, unlike Kierkegaard, he receives a superfluity of answers, for the reception of Derrida is marked by chatter as firmly as that of Kierkegaard by silence. In *The Gift of Death* (1992) it seems to me that Derrida is in the same kind of difficulty in relation to Kierkegaard as that in which Heidegger finds himself in relation to Kierkegaard: borrowing so much from the writings that their capacity to read them is impeded. This difficulty is carried over from *Spectres of Marx* (1993), which poses questions to Marx inflected by a reception of both Heidegger's and Kierkegaard's questions: the question of the forgetting of being; the question, why is there something rather than nothing? the question, how can Abraham tell the voice of God from the voice of the devil? how can we tell demonic from divine silence? how can Marx tell the true revolutionary spirit from a spectral mockery? are revolution and divinity still thinkable, or has the thought of revolution departed with Holderlin's gods? This retrieves in a critical form the question of Derrida's relation to the texts he reads, raised by Robert Bernasconi in 1977 in relation to Derrida's reading of Levinas,[34] raised by Claude Evans in a very different tone[35] in relation to Derrida's reading of Husserl; and to be raised here yet again in relation to Derrida's readings of Heidegger and Kierkegaard.

I suggest that with Derrida and curiously with Kierkegaard, but differently, because of their different relations to the divine, there is a demonic nihilism which destroys value by accepting a gift of meaning from a source external to its writing and then subverting that source and that meaning. This then is the notion of a demonic writing machine, to be used to characterize Derrida's mode of writing, which absorbs and destroys meanings while creating an apparently infinite demand for more of the same. This can work only if a process of reception maintains the momentum of an oscillation between opening out to that external source and then rejecting and destroying it. Kierkegaard's oscillation takes place between the chatter of the marketplace and the silence of the divine. Derrida's oscillation appears to take place between an attempt to accept the gift of tradition and the chatter of the academic market place.[36] Here, an encounter with Derrida's thinking of negative theology is needed, in order to assess the basis for contrasting the different logics of destruction at work in the writings of Derrida and Kierkegaard. An analysis is needed of Kierkegaard's reaffirmation of meaning by providing his own process of reception, in, for example, *Concluding Unsystematic Postscript*, as a basis for assessing Derrida's gestures of self-interpretation and self-affirmation, in his retrieval in current work of themes and citations from previous work. For there is here at work a parallel process of destroying identities and meaning, while reaffirming them again, through the effects of a heterogenized auto-inscription.

Derrida introduces a notion of legitimate fictions in a citation from Montaigne's *Essays*, in his paper 'Before the Law'.[37] It subverts the distinction in theories of the state between mythical foundation on one side and legitimation on the other. The difficulty with this supposed subversive gesture is that it has already been undercut in advance by Benjamin's more catastrophic move, in 'Critique of Violence', of juxtaposing the human registers of mythic and positivist notions of law on one side, to a moment of divine violence in which the possibility of order is simultaneously announced and withdrawn. Benjamin takes up and elaborates a figure of the demon, now informed by notions of a Freudian and indeed an Edgar Alan Poe-based notion of the uncanny, which then recurs as the angel of history whose wings are opened by a wind above and beyond its control. The demon too is fallen into history and is revealed as the messenger, inaugurating an undesirable future, transmitting but not producing the message it bears. This then would suggest a new relation between technology, demons and history: the figure of the demon shows that technology does not reveal a termination of history but the vanishing of the nineteenth-century dream that history might be thought of as some single structure, through which a discrete process, the emancipation of human beings, might be thought to take place. Thus, as with technology, human beings are to be thought of neither as in control of history nor as subservient to history: neither history nor technology is centred on human existence at all. However, human destinies are inextricably intermixed with both sets of processes, named the historical and the technical, such that it somehow might seem as though history as a distinct process has come to an end. This is to misunderstand the nature of the shift of emphasis; it is not history but humanity which is now definitively unthinkable in isolation from the forces within which it is enmeshed. This is the significance of the transition from the active nihilism of will to power to the demonic nihilism of writing machines.

Notes

1 E. Levinas, 'As if to Horror Consenting', in *Critical Inquiry, Special feature on Heidegger and Nazism*, 15:2 (1989), 488.

2 J. Derrida, *The Gift of Death*, trans. David Wills (Chicago: University of Chicago Press, [1992] 1995), p. 55.

3 Derrida, *Death*, p. 29.

4 Matthew, 5.46.

5 Derrida, *Death*, pp. 36–7.

6 There is a connection here to T. Adorno and M. Horkheimer, *Dialectic of Enlightenment*, trans. John Cumming (London: Continuum, [1948] 1973).

7 M. Heidegger, *Schelling's Treatise on the Essence of Human Freedom*, trans. Joan Stambaugh (Athens, Ohio: Ohio University Press, [1936] 1993), p. 7.

8 R. Descartes, *The Philosophical Writings of Descartes*, trans. John Cottingham, Robert Stoothoff and Dugald Murdoch (Cambridge: Cambridge University Press, 1985).

9 Ibid., vol. 2, p. 15.

10 I am grateful to Dr Simon Ross for bringing this remark to my attention.

11 J. Barnes (ed. and trans.), *Aristotle Complete Works* (Princeton: Princeton University Press, 1984), p. 1802, translation modified.

12 W. Benjamin, 'The Destructive Character', in *One-Way Street and Other Writings* (London: New Left Books/Verso, [1931] 1979), p. 157.

13 T. Adorno, *Kierkegaard: Construction of the Aesthetic*, trans. Robert Hullot-Kentor (Minneapolis: University of Minnesota Press, 1989). This is volume 61 of the Theory and History of Literature series from the University of Minnesota Press. It is dedicated to Siegfried Kracauer and was first published in Germany on 27 February 1933, the day Hitler as incoming Chancellor of Germany declared for himself emergency powers.

14 W. Benjamin, 'Karl Kraus', *One-Way Street*, pp. 258–90.

15 Christopher Thornhill, now at King's College, London, has written a fine piece on demons, Kraus and Benjamin, first presented at the Benjamin Conference at the University of Lancaster in 1992 and printed in *New Comparison: A Journal of Comparative and General Literary Studies*, 18 (Autumn 1984), to which I am indebted.

16 Benjamin's essay is to be found in translation in *One-Way Street and Other Writings* (London, Verso, 1979). Derrida's discussion of this text is to be found as 'Force of Law: The "Mystical Foundation of Authority"' in *Deconstruction and the Possibility of Justice*, ed. Drucilla Cornell, Michael Rosenfeld and David Gray Carlson (London: Routledge, 1992).

17 Soren Kierkegaard, *Repetition* (Princeton: Princeton University Press, 1983), vol. 6, p. 131.

18 The full title of this is *The Sickness Unto Death: A Christian Psychological Exposition for Edification and Awakening, by Anti-Climacus*, ed. S. Kierkegaard. Here cited in the edition by Alastair Hannay (Harmondsworth: Penguin, 1989).

19 See Walter Benjamin, *Illuminations*, ed. Hannah Arendt (New York: Harcourt, Brace & World, [1940] 1968), pp. 255–66.

20 See Soren Kierkegaard, *Philosophical Fragments KP 7*, p. 52, where it is translated as 'And the moment of decision is foolishness', with footnote to Corinthians, 1.23.

21 See J. Derrida, *Writing and Difference*, trans. Alan Bass (London: Routledge, [1967] 1978), p. 31.

22 S. Kierkegaard, *Repetition*, p. 131.

23 S. Kierkegaard, *Sickness Unto Death*, p. 153.

24 See Jacques Derrida, 'Heidegger's ear: *Geschlecht* IV: Philopolemology', in John Sallis, ed., *Reading Heidegger: Commemorations*, (Chicago: University of Chicago Press, 1993).

25 Soren Kierkegaard, (*Either/Or*, Princeton: Princeton University Press, 1987), vol. 1, p. 89.

26 See Joanna Hodge, 'Monstrous Rebirth of Nihilism', in Diane Morgan and Keith Ansell-Pearson, eds, *Monsters of Energy* (Basingstoke: Macmillan, forthcoming, 2000).

27 See Jacques Derrida, *The Gift of Death*, trans. David Wills (Chicago: University of Chicago Press, [1992] 1995), pp. 74–5. The reference is to a character called Bartleby in the story by Herman Melville.

28 Soren Kierkegaard, *Fear and Trembling* (Princeton: Princeton University Press, 1983), vol. 6, p. 88.

29 Soren Kierkegaard, *The Concept of Anxiety* (Princeton: Princeton University Press, 1980), vol. 8, p. 154.

30 Yes, there is here a reference to Kristeva, *Revolution of Poetic Language* (1974); no, I am not quite sure what its dimensions are.

31 Part of this review was translated by Theodore Haecker into German and published in *Der Brenner* in 1914, under the title 'Kritik der Gegenwart'. This and other of Haecker's translations were published in book form in 1922. It is almost impossible that Heidegger should not have been aware of them. Indeed, Heidegger's remarks on the relation between silence, chatter and language in *Being and Time* come close to replicating Kierkegaard's words as translated into German. Haecker also wrote a book on interiority, *Soren Kierkegaard und die Philosophie der Innerlichkeit* (Munich 1913), which is cited by Adorno in his study of Kierkegard.

32 Soren Kierkegaard, *The Present Age* (Princeton: Princeton University Press, 1978), vol. 14, p. 77.

33 Soren Kierkegaard, *Concluding Unsystematic Postscript* (Princeton University Press, 1968), vol. 13, 1, p. 255.

34 See Robert Bernasconi, 'Levinas, Derrida and Differance', in David Wood and Robert Bernasconi, eds, *Derrida and Differance* (Coventry: University of Warwick/Parousia Press, 1985).

35 J. Claude Evans, *Strategies of Deconstruction: Derrida and the Myth of Voice* (Minneapolis: University of Minnesota Press, 1991).

36 For a discussion of the relation between tradition and philosophy, see the *Journal of the British Society for Phenomenology* 26: 3 (Oct. 1995).

37 A description of the publishing history of this piece can be found in Jacques Derrida, *Acts of Literature*, ed. Derek Attridge (London: Routledge, 1992), p. 182. The citation occurs on p. 183.

alphonso lingis

THE GOD OF EVIL

He who kills one is a murderer.
He who kills many is a hero.
He who kills all is a god.

What experience of evil originally separated the sacred from the profane? In what thing did evil lurk? How did sorcery launch murder in the human animal? When gods had made their appearance, how did these gods take away evil from men only to become evil themselves? How did evil enter into humans and become spiritual? Are not incarceration, torture and execution, even when practised by institutions of justice, religious practices? Does not the death penalty, as well as torture and incarceration, function to reconstitute and retain the zone of the sacred? Did not the separation of excess force from sorcerers, and its constitution into gods, implant the dialectic of wars in the human species? Did not the development of modern industry dedemonize the world, rendering it completely material? Was not evil completely spiritualized? Could evil be henceforth located anywhere but in the will of individuals – a will craving nothingness? Does not the spiritualization of evil in individual wills render unintelligible the materiality of evil? Do we not confront now the massacring and alienating forces of industry, forces which also convert individuals into images of images, as an evil wholly material God – the face of a mute idol?

Corpses

A corpse is the object of our most intense abhorrence. And it is the sight of corpses, Georges Bataille said, that made humans murderers and warriors.

How is it that the human species does not, like the other animals, see a corpse as what it is – an inert thing, from which the fellow-creature that once was is gone? Penguins fight fiercely the scuas and leopard seals that attack their chicks, but once these chicks are dead, they trample over them with indifference. In nature every organism eats, and is destined to be eaten. Some predator animals will eat one of their own kind, once dead. Bataille argues that it is in the world of work and reason that a corpse has become the object of extreme horror.

A human primate detaches something – a loose stone, a branch, a pipe wrench – from the continuity of the natural or fabricated environment about him or her. He detaches himself with his implement, and shifts his view from the environment continuous with his body to goals or results beyond it. Between the goals or results and his tool he sees a relationship of means and end, cause and effect. The identification of distinct substances, and the understanding of a relationship between means and ends and between causes and effects, is the core of reason. Everyone who works is rational.

We work in order to maintain, secure or acquire what we take to be a good. Goods contribute to the refurbishment and protection of those who acquire them. Something acquires value by being promised in the future, and by withstanding, and helping us withstand, the passing of time, by enduring.

The human primate makes of himself a tool; he inserts himself into the field of work and reason as an implement that can be used to reach ends, a cause that produces effects. The order of means and foreseen results, of causes and effects, enters into him. His mind turns into a place where his limbs and senses are subordinated to purposes, where his present consciousness is subordinated to an anticipation of the future. What has come to pass in his body – his strength, his skills – and in his mind – his memories – are subordinated to the future. His enterprise, all his efforts require the future to make sense.

The one who works maintains a sense of individual identity by envisioning himself in the future. He identifies what he is doing by specifying what he shall be doing. It is tomorrow that gives its sense to whatever he does today; it is tomorrow that gives its sense to whatever he is today.

The one who works envisages the others as collaborators, or as obstructors. Our workspace, however much it is our own, inevitably finds itself surrounded by the workspaces of others whom we have to count on, at least as unthinking accomplices. Like implements, they stand detached and destined for results and products, for a future. The results and products they are working for, their futures, give them individual identities.

But death strikes. Death suddenly strikes down a collaborator. Death does not annihilate her; the body is there and takes up as much space as before. But death violently and at one blow destroyed this worker's future and stripped of their meaning not only the undertaking she was engaged in when it struck, but retroactively all the projects she had undertaken and which had this task as their result. Death strikes in the now, and immediately drives its shock wave into the future and down the past of that life, rendering not only inoperative but senseless the order and system that had come to pass, whose endurance and momentum was shaping the emergence of goals and results. Death struck, reducing to nothing the instrument she had made of herself in the world of work, reducing to nothing her individual identity. She, a student nurse, died from an infection picked up while working in the emergency room. He fell from the scaffolding of his half-built house. Her half-completed medical education, his half-finished house, appear as intensive efforts that, had this outcome been known, would never have been made. In the world of work and reason, the human corpse becomes the locus of the triumph of the absurd.

Some force of nature fell upon or swept away a fellow-human, or some microbe attacked him from within. In a corpse laid out, we see the abrupt and irreversible immobilization of all the forces of movement that were someone's life. But the apparent stillness and state of rest in the corpse is seen to be teeming with a continuing violence: the blood, biles and gases break out, the bacteria and funguses proliferate and decompose the organs and muscles, the putrefying corpse pollutes the ground and befouls the air with its stench.

It was primarily to protect the living from contamination, Bataille thinks, that tool-making *Homo habilis*, who had begun to elaborate a world of work and reason, first began to bury the dead. Burial places were the first sacred places–zones separated from the profane world of work and reason, outer zones where violent forces hold sway. Religion begins.

But the sight of corpses also induces vertigo. The evidence of the indomitable power of violence tempts the onlooker. The more intensely one feels the absurdity and violence death has brought to a life of a co-worker, the more vertiginously one feels the compulsion to make oneself the place and agent of this superior violence. Out of the corpse rises a bloodthirsty spirit which takes possession of the living. The power to murder one of our own kind is felt inwardly as a supreme power, a divine power.

It was also to protect the living from this fascination with the violence in corpses that corpses were surrounded with prohibitions and taboos.

Black Magic

There are diseases, there are crippling accidents, there are earthquakes, floods and droughts. Every sufferer, Friedrich Nietzsche wrote, seeks a cause for his suffering – more exactly, a conscious agent to whom malice could be attributed, and against whom he could take revenge. The one who discovers he or she has a cancer blames enemies, employers who have inflicted debilitating stress, blames friends and relatives and family members. In how many cultures do anthropologists find the conviction that there are no deaths from 'natural causes', that every death has its cause in some individual of our own species! In order to sustain the belief that the one who is fevered and dying is being killed by some human enemy, religion supplies the instruments and the theory of sorcery and black magic. Other things besides corpses come to possess the power to contaminate and strike with death.

This kind of religion removes from death something of its invincibility. The cause of death can be identified and neutralized. In addition, Philippe Descola writes, 'this carefully managed determinism makes it unnecessary for them to pile mental torment on top of physical ills, since it protects them both from the sense of sin inculcated by religions of salvation and also from the feeling of unfairness experienced by more secular spirits when they are inexplicably struck down by illness.'[1]

Then every death suffered within the group results in another death inflicted. Descola reports that half of the Achuar Jivaro men die at the hands of other Achuar Jivaro men.[2] To gloss on Nietzsche: humans prefer to double the deaths rather than to die by mindless accident.

Gods

These religions of sorcery and black magic gave rise to religions that identified deities and separated them from the bodies of sorcerers. Constellations of separate deities were set up by the religions of ancient India, Egypt and Greece, among them evil deities or deities with a malicious side to them, who could take the blame for the disasters that befall humans. Deaths caused by evil gods would no longer give rise to unending vendettas among humans. Even the harm one does to oneself or others through one's ineptness or outbursts of wrath could be attributed to the meddling or inspiration of a malicious deity. Nietzsche saw that this religious fatalism freed humans from revenge and from guilt. One will no longer be accused of causing the death of someone by black magic. Further, one will not accuse oneself of responsibility for the harm one does to oneself. Yet the attribution to the figures of deities of malice in the workings of the universe casts a dark shadow on the human mind. The oldest gods of humanity are the great animals – bison, rhinoceroses, bears, aurochs, tigers – and they are appeased with flesh and blood. The most archaic religious act of the Hindus, Greeks, Hebrews and Mayas was the killing of humans or other animals, conceptualized as offerings for the gods. A community of humans itself selects its firstborn to throw to the gods in order to gain respite from their voracity. Sacrifice becomes the cardinal religious practice. Eventually wars will be fought in order to acquire sacrificial victims for the gods.

In a corpse, that of Jesus, the Christian religion identified God. But this religion attributed to one sole God both benevolence and the omnipotent management of the universe. Sorcerers were denounced as impotent impostors. Then the sufferer is left with no alternative but to find all the blame for his miseries in his own deeds. The sufferer discovers in his corrupt will an ultrahuman force to produce sickness in his body and failure in his enterprises – a properly demonic agency. The cause of her feelings of worthlessness and depression, of his AIDS, is the demonic urge inside her and inside him that perverted her and his will and turned it from God. To the suffering of sickness is added the torments of guilt. The soul becomes a place where to the external violence of sickness is added the violence of self-laceration. Such a religion compounds debility and suffering and produces a will that longs only for peace, a will to die.

But every sickness spreads by contagion, and guilt too infects others. In addition, Nietzsche thinks that the feelings of aggression intensified against one's own demons eventually erupt into hatred and vindictiveness turned against others – against those whose health looks like a power over sickness and a power to inflict sickness in others.

The religion of the gallows

Are not incarceration, torture, and execution, even when practised by institutions of justice, religious practices?

For our juridic institutions to execute someone is to declare both that he or she is completely responsible and that he or she is unredeemable. If it can be shown that the killer was forced to act by another, or that he killed in self-defence, or that he was insane, there is no criminal responsibility. Having been severely traumatized in infancy, by brutalization or sexual molestation, or having been kept captive by a tyrannical spouse or father, diminish or eliminate responsibility. The jurisprudence that admits mental torture as a mitigating factor when a woman shoots her abusive husband cannot logically ignore the abused childhood of that husband. Then to decree execution is to declare that an absolute responsibility is in the individual who pulled the trigger, and that the responsibility of a family that tormented him in childhood and of a society that oppressed him and left him desperate in adulthood was nil. The agency that decrees the absolute punishment, Albert Camus argued,[3] must logically be in a position to determine absolute responsibility.

And that is why in former times executions were decreed in the name of God. God alone can plumb the mind and heart of the accused, and it is his ministers who, in his name, declare absolute guilt and decree absolute punishment. Moreover, in their action they continue to leave the judgment to God: the condemned man on the gallows will be offered the sacraments, and the absolute punishment that God's ministers decree will soon be ratified or abrogated by God himself.

But Camus argues that the secular state has no coherent justification for carrying out the absolute punishment. Camus insists that he is not arguing that human nature is intrinsically good and that all criminals are reformable; on the contrary. He instead argues that the institutions of the state – and modern psychology and social sciences – have no means of determining sole responsibility. And indeed in recent decades capital punishment has been widely renounced in secularized states. Where the death penalty is retained, God is retained and invoked in the actions of the state.

Whether God is retained and invoked or not, the death penalty, as well as torture and incarceration, function to reconstitute and retain the zone of the sacred.

Capital punishment is an expulsion by the society of one who was born and raised in that society; he or she is now expelled as waste product and excrement. But the execution of the guilty or of the just, even if it is decreed as a surgery on a cancerous growth on the body of the society and carried out by the rational machinery of the judicial system, induces the notion of sacrifice. To sacrifice, *sacrum-facio*, is to make separated, to make sacred. Sacrifice makes something sacred by separating it from the world of work and reason, separating it definitively from the world of work and reason by destruction.

What is separated from the world of work and reason is delivered over to its own violence. The lawbreaker, delivered over definitively to the realm of the demonic and sacred by execution, becomes a spectre haunting the laborious and rational citizens. There he or she remains in storms of fire and blood. One cannot think of him or her without thinking what he or she would do – and these appear as deeds of violence shaking again and again the walls of the society from which his or her body has been expelled. In our society, the execution of convicts maintains about the confines of the ordered daylight world of work and reason an underworld population of irrational and incorrigible individuals, monstrous and demonic.

The imprisoned and the executed are never more than a sample of the lawbreakers. This also marks each as a sacrifice. 'Since nobody could hope to prosecute or execute all those involved, the convict became an expiatory sacrifice who suffered his life for all.'[4] Twenty million people died in the Second World War; twenty-nine individuals were condemned for crimes against humanity and executed by the Nuremburg Commission. Eight hundred thousand people died in Rwanda; twenty-two individuals have been executed in the war crimes tribunal. There is even a specific grandeur in being singled out in this way, in being attributed responsibility for so many crimes done by others. There is a specific sacredness in the expiatory sacrifice.

The religion of war

Religions of sorcery and black magic break up the natural attraction humans have for members of their own species and make the human animal murderous. But the religions that separated out deities from the sorcerers and then put these deities, good or malicious, into commerce with humans have made the human species genocidal. Nietzsche does not see this, because he takes the human animal to be by nature a beast of prey who becomes gregarious only in sickness. He does not appreciate how profoundly unnatural it is for human animals to kill their own kind.
Do we today understand species-recognition and species-attraction? How is it that for an insect, a fish, a bird or a mammal to recognize one of his own kind is to be attracted to him or her? Even solitary animals – octopods, hawks, leopards, orang-utans – recognize members of their own species, and this recognition involves not killing them. Predatory animals do not prey on their own kind: wolves do not feed on one another, eagles do not hunt other eagles for food.
Species recognition-attraction does not exclude aggression – even gregarious fish, birds and mammals will, with threats or with blows, seize food from one another, and in many species individuals defend territories from other individuals of their kind. The aggressor typically drives off other individuals, and does not set out to exterminate them. When food is scarce, the weakest or last-born baby bird in the nest may be left to die, or be pushed out of the nest by its siblings. A lion that takes over a pride may kill the offspring of the prior alpha male. When moving to another territory is difficult or impossible, a colony of bees or a tribe of chimpanzees may kill the rivals. Thus ethologists ordinarily do not speak of murder and war in animal species other than our own; they generally explain killings of a member of one's own species as a side-effect of some other biologically purposive activity.

Species-recognition and species-attraction have not been adequately credited or understood in the human species. It comes as a surprise to us to learn that the great majority – 85 per cent – of soldiers in the First and Second World Wars did not kill and did not shoot to kill. Even on the front lines, a great percentage of soldiers shot in the air or in the ground rather than directly at the enemy. In the Vietnam War, more than fifty thousand bullets were fired for every enemy soldier killed. This was known to the military authorities, and special training methods were instituted to implant a will to kill in the troops. And indeed in the Vietnam War a much larger percentage of the soldiers did shoot to kill than had in the First and Second World Wars. But level of the post-traumatic disorder among the survivors was correspondingly greater than in the two world wars.[5]

Wars cannot be understood as extensions of the natural territoriality of many animal species including the human. Notwithstanding the development of military science and the disciplining and professionalizing of soldiers, every war produces extravagant excesses of violence. The wars of our time – the Cold War readying Mutual Assured Destruction and economically ruining the societies of the adversaries; the wars in Rwanda, Ireland, ex-Yugoslavia and Israel – have made commonplace the conviction that the victor wins nothing. But a study of the wars of feudal and modern Europe would show that the great majority of princes who extended their territory did so at the cost of tens of thousands of their own subjects and the ruin of their economies.

Informed calculation of utility would not have motivated so many hundreds of thousands of men and women to go and lose their lives in war. War is not a simple unleashing of subrational drives like those that make individuals commit violent crimes; it does not devolve simply from some destructive instinct. It was religion that supplied the missing ingredient: the absolutization of the cause. Indeed, present-day nation states, in the measure that they are becoming secular and mercantile, are finding it harder and harder to justify war to their subjects unless attacked.

Religion is the production of transcendent experiences. There is a religion within war. War does not only give rise to enthusiasms for killing and looting; it gives rise to courage, generosity, a sense of community and submergence in a great cause. It gives rise to the ecstatic urge to heroism, the exultation of taking part in great events, of victory, and the ecstatic feeling of overcoming the pain of death.

Religion is also practice and ritual. Is not sacrifice the most ancient and most fundamental religious practice? Religion sacralizes the act of killing, surrounding it with ritual and awe. Religion makes killing in war into something sacred, into sacrifice. The call to war enlists men and women less to become killers than to make the 'supreme sacrifice' of one's life for the cause.

The desacralization of the world

An industry that has harnessed ever greater sources of power – animal, water, wind, combustive, hydroelectrical, nuclear – recognizes in principle no constraints on its transformations of forms, functions and substances. Whatever meaning and significance a resource or product posses will have been bestowed on it by the manufacturer – or by users and consumers. Hence there is no meaning in a product that has power over the mind. Commodities are means, for human ends. All resources and products are innocent. More than innocent. For capitalist marketing requires that consumers see in products the satisfaction of their desires. Carbonated drinks, automobiles, cellular phones, and computer software produce happiness. Media advertising demonstrates how many products induce a frenetic euphoria.

The desorcerization and dedemonization of the world both in industry and marketing, and in the representations of nature and culture produced by empirical science, have resulted in a dematerialization of evil. The baleful fetishes, sinister amulets and accursed talismans of sorcerers are dismissed as so much hocus-pocus. If evil exists, it can only exist in the immateriality of a will. (Guns don't kill people; people kill people.) An evil will is attached not to material objects, but to nothingness.

The notion of a criminal is the notion of an individual in whom the explanations for aggression in hungry and territorial animals are excluded. The victim, whether another citizen or a property or institution, is deemed innocent; the criminal act produced only destruction.

The desolation itself, the void, nothingness is taken to exercise a fatal attraction on the sovereign individual of modern godless civilization. Thus, when dealing with an adolescent mass murderer we invoke Raskolnikof; when dealing with Gilles de Rais and Pol Pot we invoke Sade, Blanchot and Klossowski. Evil is not aggression or greed (accumulation and profit are innocent), but cynicism, cruelty and indifference to suffering.

Sovereign and Luciferean individualism

The end of feudalism and the ideology of a Holy Roman Empire gave rise to the notion of the sovereignty of nation states, and in the European enlightenment this notion of sovereignty was ascribed to the individual in those states. In Kant sovereignty was ascribed to the rational individual, a sovereignty exercised in obeying no laws but those he legislates for himself – but with a rational legislation that consists in promulgating the universal and necessary laws of nature.

The writings of the Marquis de Sade, Goethe and Dostoevski have located evil in the figure of the Luciferean prince of darkness. Evil would be the work of individuals whose hubris puts them above the human lot and above human norms, and evil would be the act by which they constitute their suprahumanity. 'Dehumanizing myself is my own most fundamental tendency,' Jean Genet wrote. 'Abjection must intoxicate us if we are not to be killed by its intensity.' The act that dehumanizes is selling out on people. To attack one's enemies is to affirm solidarity with one's friends. To betray one's friends is to separate oneself entirely from humankind.[6]

The evil one would have a kinship with the madman, since Aristotle conceived him as one who does not live in the common world but in a world of his own fabrication. At the same time he would have a kinship with sovereign reason, source of sovereign power.

In Sade, the sovereignty of the rational individual is exercised by recognizing the arbitrariness of instituted political, religious and ethical laws, and recognizing nature as a Saturn ceaselessly devouring his own children. The sovereign individual recognizing no one and nothing to respect and obey, faces nothing. And he exercises that sovereignty by purely destructive activity. The evil will is then completely disconnected from all goods, all materiality, and is the purest form of spirit. The evil gods are now found within.

The Marquis de Sade puts before us, as pedagogue of evil, the libertine great lord. Nietzsche, Ortega y Gasset and Hannah Arendt locate evil instead in the ordinary man. It is striking that each time a tyrant is overthrown, he continues to command the allegiance of a third of the nation he had tyrannized for a generation. See Pol Pot. See Pinochet in Chile, who was recently voted to a lifetime seat in the Senate. See Ferdinand Marcos, who has just been buried in the Heroes Cemetery and his children elected to the Senate. What kept these men in power and keeps for them the allegiance of so many still are not individuals of exceptional power and ambition, but instead the mediocre, grubby, parsimonious, cautious, self-righteous moral majority. Does not all the force of evil lie in what is petty in little people – the greedy, the lazy, the self-indulgent, the brutal, the cynical, the venal?

Institutional malice

Malice is located in the individual will for nothingness, and evil is completely dematerialized, spiritualized. Yet is there not a materiality of evil in the forces of contemporary industry?

Massive extermination of peoples is endemic to our civilization. Today eight hundred billion dollars are spent annually world-wide on arms. An expenditure of forty billion dollars would put an end to poverty world-wide. Weapons are in large measure sold to and used in regional conflicts in the poorest areas. The populations of the rich countries are unwilling to risk lives of their men to impose their will on other countries; instead the rulers of rich countries now substitute economic blockade–starvation. With Haiti declared 'not worth the life of a single American soldier', blockade produced three years of reduction to starvation of the population of the poorest country in the American hemisphere. The thirty-year policy of reduction to starvation inflicted on Cuba has recently been intensified. Seven years now on Iraq. Refugee camps are now a permanent feature of our planet.

Brutal labour and mass unemployment are reimposed on populations by the regular shifts in focus of wealth in the globalized economy, against which national and regional barriers are impotent. It is badly understood how globalized mercantile civilization rekindles religious and ideological fury and racial, national and tribal hatred.

Through hunger and fear, but also in existence subjected to salary, saving and accumulation, individuals become the instruments or objects of a production, a history, a process, a comminatory. Individuals are expropriated of their force, their labour, their bodies, their meaning, the here and now of their individual existence. Technological devices are invented and massproduced and superseded before they can be integrated into the purposes of individuals and groups. Speedboats and snowmobiles are massproduced before their destructive impact on the environment can be understood; campaigning through televised sound bites and election by electronic voting are there before the effect on public understanding of the issues can be gauged; genetic engineering is there before its effect on the significance of an animal or a child can be understood. The juggernaut of technical progression produces a helplessness of individuals.

Participation in society is replaced by attendance at a spectacle; individuals cannot accede to meaningful functions but purchase images of and for themselves. The most vigorous sector of industry is devoted to producing forms, images, games, spectacles.

We do not understand how these forms of destruction of ourselves work, and we do not understand how they can be resisted. Jean-Luc Nancy[7] speaks of our essential misunderstanding of alienation, positing a self-production of the individual in Marx, of an essential misunderstanding of technology in Heidegger. But behind these misunderstandings, is there not a long process of desacralization, dedemonization, neutralization of the physical world?

The malice, being seated in material processes and institutionalized structures, is outside us, with an exteriority that has kept it from our understanding, as well as from our action. Because we do not understand, because the massacring and alienating forces of industry, forces which also convert individuals into images of images, are irrational, they appear to us as an evil god inhabiting the machinery of industry. But this god itself is not a spirit, is wholly material. What is there is the face of a mute idol.

Notes

1 Philippe Descola, *The Spears of Twilight* (New York: New York Press, 1966), p. 235.
2 Ibid., p. 64.
3 Albert Camus, Ibid. 'Reflections on the Guillotine', in *Resistance, Rebellion, and Death*, trans. Justin O'Brien (New York: Vintage, 1995), pp. 209-27.
4 Theo van der Meer, 'Sodomy and the Pursuit of a Third Sex in the Early Modern Period', in Gilbert Herdt, ed., *Third Sex Third Gender* (New York: Zone, 1996).
5 Lieutenant Colonel Dave Grossman, *On Killing: The Psychological Cost of Learning to Kill in War and Society* (Boston: Little, Brown & Company, 1995).
6 Jean Genet, *Our Lady of the Flowers* (New York: Grove Press, 1963), p. 82.
7 Jean-Luc Nancy, *Une pensée finie* (Paris: Galilée, 1990), pp. 32ff.

charlie blake

THE GRAVITY OF ANGELS: SPACE, TIME AND THE ECSTASY OF ANNIHILATION

Revolt – its face distorted by amorous ecstasy – tears from God his naive mask, and thus oppression collapses in the crash of time. Catastrophe is that by which a nocturnal horizon is set ablaze … it is time released from all bonds; it is pure change; it is a skeleton that emerges from its cadaver as from a cocoon and that sadistically lives the unreal existence of death.[1]

What do we talk of one devil? There is not a room in any man's house but is pestered and close-packed with a camp-royal of devils … In Westminster Hall a man can scarce breathe for them; for in every corner they hover as thick as motes in the sun.[2]

I tell you, the race of human kind is matter, I have torn myself asunder, I have brought them the mysteries of light, to purify them.[3]

In his essay 'Time and History: Critique of the Instant and the Continuum' from his 1978 collection, *Infancy and History: Essays on the Destruction of Experience*, the Italian philosopher Giorgio Agamben distinguishes in general and heuristic terms between three ways in which the understanding of history, and by inference the experience of the conscious subject in and of history, is determined by a particular conception of time. These are the linear, the cyclical and what he describes as the gnostic conceptions of time, elements of the latter of which, as he puts it, 'lie scattered among the folds and shadows of the Western tradition'.[4] While this tripartite distinction might arguably be viewed as reductive, it does, nonetheless, have a valuable explanatory power when applied to questions of contemporary nihilism, on the one hand, and those relating to what I shall here describe as the occluded discourse of the angelic and the demonic in modernity, on the other. These are two series of questions which, it will be argued, are inextricably linked by the manner in which time and temporality figure in both discursive domains as a way first, of *giving voice* to a covert or explicit longing for an originary absence, and second, of providing a means whereby that longing might then be reconfigured, ecstatically and meta-temporally, as both a conversation with spirits of various designations and, concomitantly, as what Deleuze and Guattari might once have described as a becoming-demonic/becoming-angelic,[5] understood here, however (and with some divergence from the Deleuzian models of time and temporality which figure in *Difference and Repetition* and elsewhere[6]), as an interwoven series of lines of charge and intensity, generated by and from an age and a pathos in which the devaluation of all values, the fundamental prerequisite for all genuine nihilisms, has effectively been achieved. For an unnoted by-product of the division of models of time identified by Agamben is that relations between the human and the angelic/demonic, which I am treating here as the most deeply repressed ontological relation of modernity, have been inescapably diversified and reinscribed along planes of consistency determined by visions of the future as both a concept and a continuum, and more specifically, by the dominant linear conception's repression of the future as a spatial extension of the present from whence information, in direct contradiction to notions of 'time's arrow',[7] may travel back to that perceived present in the form of visions, voices, prophesies or precognitions.

One of the most important effects of this repression has been to silence the conversations of and with the future on the grounds that the future, whilst its outlines might be scientifically or stochastically or theologically outlined, can have no conversations as such, because to allow for them would be either to promote a literal notion of eternal recurrence, extrapolated perversely from that invoked by Nietzsche's notorious demon of repetition, in which the cycles would be able to intersect asynchronically, or, alternatively, to allow for a linear notion in which predetermination was so absolute and fatal that notions of agency would cease to have meaning beyond being effects of that predetermination itself. The former extrapolation conjures up a multiplication of phenomena so extraordinarily complex and futile that the conventional human reaction, as Nietzsche suggested, is to recoil in horror and despair at so outrageous a notion. In this reaction, however, as in its more affirmative and libidinous alternative, the *amor fati*, both the demon of Nietzsche's darkest moment, and the diabolical entity glimpsed smirking behind the supposedly 'scientific' evasions of Freud's speculations on the death-drive, may be deemed less as metaphors than as the spectral and inversely projected images of virtual-to-actual entities engaged in a process of hypostisization, in which they encounter the human with ever greater intensity as we, in the process of becoming-demonic/becoming-angelic ourselves, of traversing and map-

53

ping our multiple futures as a species and beyond, orient ourselves with ever greater precision towards the strange attractor identified, by various designations and conceptual systems, as the end of time. And it is in this sense, also, that the peculiar coincidence of repetition attending both Nietzsche and Freud's speculations on the thanatropic intensities which emanate in the forms of the demonic and the angelic should be considered as indicating something far more substantial, more material and more intrusive than mere philosophical or literary embellishment; as substantial, that is, as the sentient flesh of the human itself.

To begin to make sense of these chimerical, ontodaemonological and teleological assertions, and their relation to what I have described in my title as 'the ecstasy of annihilation', it is important to grasp first the macro- and micro-eschatologies which tend to be generated by Agamben's distinction. In preliminary terms, for example, the cyclical vision of time may be said to embrace a range of perceptions of the trajectory of human consciousness and material existence, from the experience of the daily, monthly and seasonal cycles associated with biological and ecological rhythms to the parabolic curves of economic theory, or from the Platonic 'Great Year', and the Hindu and Buddhist notions of the Yugas and the wheel of Samsara, to at least some interpretations of the doctrine of eternal recurrence famously postulated by Nietzsche, as well as the degenerative historical visions of Spengler or Toynbee. The linear vision, particularly as derived from the western monotheistic traditions of Judaism, Christianity and Islam, on the other hand, lends itself more readily to messianic and apocalyptic visions of the human and post-human trajectory. Thus macro-eschatologies and teleologies tend to be implicit and dominant within the linear conception even in its most secular forms. The third vision, the gnostic, however, suggests to Agamben a more curious and enigmatic trajectory for the human and its legacy. The time of gnosticism, as Agamben puts it, is:

> an incoherent and unhomogenous time, whose truth is in the moment of abrupt interruption, when man, in a sudden act of consciousness, takes possession of his own condition of being resurrected ('*statim resurrectionis compos*'). In keeping with this experience of interrupted time, the Gnostic attitude is resolutely revolutionary: it refuses the past while valuing it, through an exemplary sense of the present ... expecting nothing from the future.[8]

Agamben goes on to discuss, through reference to Kafka, Benjamin and Heidegger, the way in which the most revolutionary challenges to traditional philosophical and metacritical thinking in the West in the twentieth century invariably centred on an attack, primarily, on the notion of continous time. In reference to the concept of *Ereignis*, for example, which he suggests 'designates both the centre and the extreme limit of Heidegger's thought after *Sein und Zeit*', Agamben retreats from detailed discussion of this elusive notion, but is willing at least to assert that: 'it allows the Event to be conceived no longer as a spatio-temporal determination but as the opening of the primary *dimension* in which all spatio-temporal dimensions are based.'[9] This may well be wishful thinking on the part of Agamben (as, arguably, on the part of Heidegger also). It is not, however, my intention here to discuss the finer points of Heidegger's later thought in relation to time and the Event; rather, what is of interest in Agamben's account of figures such as Heidegger or Benjamin is the manner in which he seeks some kind of hyper-ontological basis, and, within his own terms, concomitant ontological innocence, from whence a new kind of materialism might be enacted, and that he does so explicitly through reference to an idea of gnostic time as a kind of plenum moment, akin in his reading to both Heidegger's *Ereignis* and Benjamin's *Jetzt-Zeit*, which breaches conventional spatio-temporality and in doing so gestures provocatively towards something beyond rather than beneath or within that primary coordination of thought, moment and subjectivity which comprises the conscious self. An experience of emancipatory or mystical possession, in effect, in direct contrast to the empty and fleeting instant of linear time, in which we are mere slaves of vacuous temporality, the 'in vain' of Nietzsche, or a relentless, mechanical, historical progression. Thus: 'Just as the full, discontinuous, finite, and complete time of pleasure must be set against the empty, continuous and infinite time of vulgar historicism, so the chronological time of pseudo-history must be opposed by the cairological time of authentic history.'[10]

Although Agamben's meditation on time and history in modernity tends, for the most part, towards a quasi-ecstatic materialism, whilst being strongly informed by certain Heideggerian lines of speculation, his use of gnosticism as illustration is extremely selective, inasmuch as it also tends to promote an image of gnostic time as signifying a foundational ontology for the future based on a turning away from that future and the sense of futurity itself, and an immersion instead in the disconnected present, and in doing so ignores or suppresses the far more radical and negative ontology at the heart of gnostic tradition. It is almost as though the diabolical voices which undoubtedly haunt the shattered dwelling of gnosticism have been either silenced or secularized – which perhaps comes to the same thing – and the 'moment of abrupt interruption' which Agamben celebrates here has been domesticated to allow for a more positive ontology which, in subverting linear time, indicates a ground for the subject beyond spatio-temporality, and hence beyond being and becoming, which will, as if by some unexpected and libidinous enchantment, grant us a kind of primordial, rather than a merely provisional, authenticity.

This is not, it should be pointed out, an unreasonable interpretation within the tradition, and has a number of respectable precedents, in particular in the work of the Heideggarian scholar of gnosticism, Hans Jonas.[11] But there is an alternative and more provocative, and one could argue, more pessimistic, reading available. For what gnostic time might also be said to represent is an aspect of a more general soteriological vision which, in a manner roughly comparable with a number of secularized expositions of the pathos of postmodernity, considers time as having become, or rather as having revealed itself as, a process of bifurcation, fragmentation and ultimately of dissipation in space. But it is also, and more particularly in its negative rather than its positive mode of expression, a decidedly heretical soteriology in terms of the dominant western metaphysical, scientific and theological traditions, inasmuch as it involves a spatialization of the axis of time which, once experienced vertically (and vertiginously) by the subject, uncovers the simultaneous multiplicity of origin, preservation and the illusion of end in the moment of annihilation itself, as signified by the light as a paradoxical becoming-virtual-becoming-nothing of matter. It signals an abrupt redemption, that is, in which the subject is, and always was, and always will be, nothing at all.

In its more positive mode, for example, Agamben's 'moment of abrupt interruption' can be traced through the frozen moment of annihilation and continuity/discontinuity indicated in Georges Bataille's ostensibly paradoxical vision of ecstatic catastrophe and skeletal sovereignity in the epigraph given above, and is implicit also, albeit in a perverted form, in two of his essays on or connected with materialism and gnosis.[12] Or, and to trace it to one of its several points of origin in the fragments of the second-century Christian gnostic theologian Valentinus (who, characteristically amongst gnostics, distributes a spatial eschatology to the chosen ones, or *pneumatikoi*; these being individuals blessed with the possibility of redemption, and who therefore attend with requisite fervour to the demonic nature of matter, on the one hand, and to the spark of the divine imprisoned within that matter as it comprises the human, on the other), it is the fire of true gnosis: 'From the beginning you are immortal and children of eternal life. You wished to distribute death amongst yourselves so as to consume it and annihilate it, and so that death might die in and through you. For when you dissolve the world, you yourselves are not dissolved and rule over creation and over the whole of corruption.'[13] These two fragments, ostensibly separated by nearly two millennia, are cogent for several reasons to Agamben's classification of models of time, as well as to the problems inherent in that classification when referring to 'the moment of abrupt interruption' as a characteristic of the occluded status of gnosticism[14] in western thought. On the one hand, they both exemplify a tendency in the more positive forms of gnostic spatio-teleology to valorize the continuity of selected elements of being as the result of annihilation itself, not merely in terms of individual or collective death understood as a passive and unavoidable transition between the temporal and the metatemporal state of the soul, but also as an active involvement in the process of annihilation through some form of non-propitiary sacrifice, whether of self or species or world or cosmos.[15]

In this sense, the linear notion of time is certainly not entirely lost in some versions of gnostic eschatology and teleology, nor in its more recent legacy, but is given instead a different kind of 'spin'. The poetics of annihilation are, in this case, intimately bound up with the idea of eschatology as *limit* and *horizon*, but a notion of liminality which is generated transversally by the *veil* and the *shadow* – a frequent pairing of images in the gnostic tradition – which are themselves the progenitors, indirectly and without a necessarily inherent linear teleology, of the illusion of life and matter which comprises the prison of the human and the cosmos.

In the extraordinarily vivid bundle of images and notions which make up the gnostic cosmogeny, cosmology, ontogeny and eschatology, for example, we find a diagram and a composition of human emergence and cosmic incarceration, and a prediction of post-human dissipation through a dehypostisization of both the prison of matter and that of the human, and indeed of time itself, which, while it certainly broaches certain compromises at certain points with the Christian and neo-Platonic sources with which it often intersects, nonetheless places an emphasis on the necessity of cosmic annihilation peculiar to the pathos of the gnostic. And while this pathos is usually and correctly identified with these earlier metaphysical and theological systems as a kind of counter-metaphysic with its own ontological and ethical ramifications, in other words, as a primarily historical phenomenon, its subterranean influence, as a number of twentieth-century thinkers noted, is far from inactive in modernity, and has permeated, also, many of the discourses which have come to be associated with the postmodern. I shall, therefore, continue with a brief exposition of gnostic themes in Bataille, by way of undicating the way in which a reflection on gnosticism can illuminate problems specific to certain modern debates on nihilism and materialism, before moving on to some of the salient aspects of the foundational myth itself, its development in terms of the demonic and the angelic, and its value as a crystal through which certain configurations of modernity and its legacy can be placed within a broader cosmological and eschatological perspective in which contemporary scientific speculation and arcane myth encounter one another in the discourse of supersensible spirits.

In Bataille, for example, and especially at the heart of his often oblique notions of expenditure and sacrifice, we find resonances of the gnostic desire for auto-annihilation expressed through a generalized frustration with the constraints of the dialectic, especially as interpreted by Kojeve,[16] and an affirmation of the notion of radical 'experience' which Bataille relates to the Hegelian rejection of the sovereignity of immediacy, on the one hand, and the flow of material desire unencumbered by lack or opposition, which he associates with the sacred, on the other. Batailles's reflections on gnosticism (written, of course, before the discovery of many seminal gnostic scriptures and fragments at Nag Hammadi in the late 1940s),[17] are both curiously enlightening and eminently frustrating in this context. In 'Base Materialism and Gnosticism' from 1930, for example, Bataille establishes his initial distance from his subject matter, or at least its more gnostical elements, in the following terms: 'I admit that I have, in respect to mystical philosophies, only an unambiguous interest, analagous in practice to that of an uninfatuated psychiatrist towards his patients; it seems to me rather pointless to put one's trust in tendencies that, without meeting resistance, lead to the most pitiful dishonesty and bankruptcy.'[18]

Such a perspective – without the implicit inconvenience of the play of transference and counter-transference which the analogy might suggest to a contemporary reader – is qualified by Bataille inasmuch as while he is concerned to indicate the ways in which dialectical materialism, as derived and adapted from Hegelian idealism, shares with its gnostic sources a concern with problems of human society which have remained fundamentally unaltered – the nexus of human values and material forces which generate violence, suffering, the concept of evil, and so forth – he is unprepared to accept the underlying process of ontological bifurcation implicit within those gnostic origins, in preference to the more modern, essentially dialectical, albeit deeply flawed vision inherited from Hegel. Bataille's underlying historical point here being that in sharp contrast to Hellenic and Christian systems wherein such negative phenomena were categorized according to notions of ignorance or lack or theodicy, the gnostic, Manichean and Zoroasterian systems evolved 'in an epoch when metaphysics could still be associated with the most monstrous *dualistic* and therefore strangely abased cosmogenies'[19] in which any kind of ontological resolution was necessarily impossible, in the absolutely final rather than the dialectical sense of that term. Bataille then goes on to indicate that what is most crucial for him, at least insofar as the fragments of gnosticism might be used to illuminate contemporary concerns, is their resemblance to contemporary materialism, on the one hand, and their flirtatious ambivalence towards the evils and excesses that an immersion in the material realm tends to propogate, on the other. He notes, for example, that: 'It is difficult to believe that on the whole Gnosticism does not manifest above all a sinister love of darkness, a monstrous taste for obscene and lawless *archontes* ... The existence of a sect of *licentious Gnostics* and of certain sexual rites fulfills this obscure demand for a basesness that would not be reducible, which would be owed the most indecent respect'. '[B]lack magic', he concludes rather obscurely, 'has continued this tradition to the present day.'[20]

Aside from his barely suppressed excitement at the prospect of the 'love of darkness' and the ritualistic licentiousness he discerns in the tradition, or at in least certain aspects of it, what Bataille seems here concerned with is the use to which gnosticism might be put, psychologically at least, to clarify the status of matter in relation to reason and the ideal. Matter for Bataille is external and limiting, but reason has the choice of either raising it to a 'superior principle' and thus abasing itself as a servile 'authorized functionary' of matter,[21] or of recognizing it as that which ultimately comprises the true 'ground' of reason, and dealing with the consequences of that recognition. Thus while he is at least partially resistant to the ontological dualism implicit in all forms of gnosticism and Manicheanism, at the same time he undoubtedly recognizes a productive and specifically evaluative tendency in the tradition, as a barbaric precursor of the kind of materialism and economism, ultimately if reservedly dialectical, which he seeks, at least at this stage, both to investigate and to promote for modernity.

Commenting on what he calls the 'dualistic materialism' of Bataille, for instance, and specifically on Simone Petrement's history and interpretation of dualism in philosophy and religion, which evidently made a profound impression on Bataille, Dennis Hollier, in his authoritative survey of Bataille, materialism and impossibility, notes that: 'Rather than a system of thought in the strict sense, dualism is an attitude of thought: dualism is not a dualist system but a will to dualism, a resistance to system and homogeneity.'[22] Such ontological anarchism must, of course, be contained, and it invariably becomes contained by virtue of a metaphysical fiction in which rather than there being two opposing principles, as in archaic dualism (God and matter, good and evil), there is instead a series of two worlds or realms in which these principles, or what is left of them, dramatize what is fundamentally a will-to-monism and homogeneity masquerading as a dualism: a 'double game [*double jeu*] of the will' which 'resides in the structure of being itself' and 'which thwarts [*dejoue*] the will'.[23] Such a perspective leads Bataille over the years to develop and to refine his notion of expenditure, a fundamentally entropic and thus thanatropic machine

whose active depletion of information and subsequent tendency to maxi-
mal disorder are set against thought; thought here being the product of a
far-from-equilibrium condition and process whose order, together with
the chaotic economy of expenditure, must be engaged with simultaneously
by human consciousness, even if such an engagement demands blindness
or headlessness or some other form of dismemberment on the part of the
subject.

Considered in this way, Bataille's materialism is undoubtedly dualistic
at heart, but it is a dualism also which he wishes to anchor in at least some
form of synthesis, so that diagrams might be drawn up of the other
dualisms that concerned him so obsessively, such as that of the sacred and
the profane. Distracted primarily, it could be argued, by his encounter
with the all-embracing pneumatology of Hegel (not to mention his more
concrete experience of the banal annihilative tendencies of fascism),
Bataille's neo-gnosticism is, therefore, and in spite of his often incendiary
provocations on death, sacrifice and perverse eroticism, of a peculiarly
bloodless variety, and especially in his more measured theoretical and fictional works, finding a more powerful expression in the early essays and
fragments, where he is unencumbered by the need to provide rational
exposition, coded or otherwise. To an extent, it could even be argued that
Bataille's atheology is an attempt at a compromise with an intuitive though
strongly resisted agreement with the gnostic worldview, on the one hand,
and an historically grounded secular epistemology, on the other, which
having its dominant root system in soil made fertile by Marxism, must of
necessity affirm certain aspects of matter – its gravity and suffiency, its
externality to both the idea and the ideal – at the expense of the light, but
which still hankers after that light as glimpsed through the radical discon-
tinuities of death and eroticism, and through the blazing nocturnal horizon
at least partially revealed in the moment of catastrophe.

Such an all-too-human evasion begins to make more sense if we turn to
the gnostic cosmologies themselves, which Bataille only knew indirectly, it
should be reiterated in his defence, through carved stone traces, diverse
hermetic texts, and the calculated bile of heresiologists as filtered by several eminent late nineteenth-century scholars.[24] To begin with, it must be
stated, as is now conventional in commentaries on the subject, that there is
no such thing as a standard gnostic cosmogeny, cosmology, soteriology or
eschatology. Indeed, one of the main attractions of gnosticism for both
nihilists and those who would aspire to become metanihilists is its inherent diversity and lack of centralized doctrine. As a number of scholars have
pointed out, the general suppression of the gnostic worldview in the early
years of Christianity and its failure to establish any kind of stable ecclesiastical authority – for reasons having at least something also to do with its

absolute rejection of the material world – meant that it has always tended to flourish underground, through a series of rhizomic systems and transcient cells, in which details of mythopoeia and practice were debated and contested without any real possibility of – or unilateral desire for – the establishment of a worldly hierarchy. Gnosticism, with its explicit contempt for the creator of the universe, was always going to be heresy from a later historical perspective in the lands ruled by that entity; yet within that heresy, and even by virtue of it, flourished a multiplicity of micro-heresies, whose points of convergence then survived through a process of largely random distribution and selection, and the resultant continuity of certain texts and subterranean traditions, to provide what we now understand as the philosophy of gnosis. Central to this philosophy, as we now reconstruct it from its remaining traces, was the notion that the matter comprising the phenomenal realm was inherently evil because the creator of the cosmos, the demiurge, sometimes called the shadow, or the abortion, or Jehovah,[25] was both radically incompetent and riddled with resentment at his/her secondary status to the absent god or 'alien' responsible for his/her existence; that biological reproduction, at least in certain gnostic circles, was therefore also inherently demonic;[26] and that redemption was possible for at least some of those condemned to the resultant human existence by virtue of their fundamentally paradoxical and thereby ultrahuman status as the progeny of an absent source, ontologically prior to creation itself. In this sense, Umberto Eco is absolutely correct when he notes that:

> The GNOSTIC views himself as an exile in the world, as the victim of his own body, which he defines as a tomb and a prison. He has been cast into the world, from which he must find a way out ... The more frustrated we feel here, the more we are struck with a delirium of omnipotence and desires for revenge. Hence the Gnostic recognizes himself as a spark of divinity, provisionally cast into exile as a result of a cosmic plot ... Gnostic man becomes an *ubermensch*. By contrast to those who are bound to mere matter (HYLICS), it is only those who are spirit (PNEUMATIKOI) who are able to aspire to truth and redemption. Unlike Christianity, Gnosticism is not a religion for slaves, but one for masters.[27]

While Eco certainly identifies two of the central and consistent traits in the pathos of gnosticism over the past two millennia – a spiritual elitism, and a contempt for the body which expresses itself either through an unbounded hedonism or a severe asceticism – any attempt to provide a synthetic account of the gnostic system is inevitably compromised by virtue of the sheer complexity implicit within that system as it has been handed down to contemporary historians, theorists, critics, aspirants or *pneumatikoi*. Of the best, from Hans Jonas's highly influential and charmingly seductive phenomenological reading, to the syncretically historio-graphical narrative of Kurt Rudolph,[28] to the more genetically inclined account of Giovanni Filaroma, the tendency thus far has been to attempt a coherent and comprehensive picture whilst at the same time picking out those elements most attractive to the commentator for whatever personal reasons might obtain at the time of writing: philosophical, scholarly, heretical, sexual or aesthetic – or even gnostic. This is a tendency towards which the present brief account unapologetically intends to retain a cer-tain loyalty, albeit tempered by the requisite scepticism appropriate to the exercise and to the age of preparatory nihilism in which it is set. The spe-cific detailing of different sects and their internal schisms and persecu-tions, the hermeneutically driven collaging of heresiological assertion with neo-Platonic and neo-Aristotelian commentary and criticism, the con-struction of the correct interpretative apparatus to deal with fragments of hearsay, heresiology, mythic illustrations and documentary evidence, is, after all, the business of scientists, scholars, academics and intellectuals, who are by definition, or at least by gnostic definition, trapped eternally and hopelessly between the realms of the *hylical* and the *pneumatical* in the unredeemable realm of the *psychical* – that ideational limbo of doomed phantoms and chattering revenants who yearn without gnosis or even the possibility of gnosis, and whose redemption, therefore, will be forever deferred.

This, at least, is the case for some of the later gnostic systems which allow for a third classification of the human between the material and the divine or proto-pleromatic. In Valentinian eschatology, for example, the hylics perish along with all that is material, while the pneumatics first ascend to the realm of the demiurge before entering the bridal chamber of the pleroma where they are reassimilated as light. The psychics, on the other hand, either throw in their lot with the hylics and simply perish, or persist in a kind of purgatory called Ogdoad, which is a place in which information is still manifest as partial knowledge rather than as truth.[29] What is most significant here is that the fundamental dualism of the gnos-tic eschatology frequently manifests a trinitarian tendency when it comes to both cosmology and human ontology. Gnostic dualism is in this sense a kind of generative binary system in which the binary code is a necessary product of the original blasphemy as that blasphemy acts as a pale reflec-tion or projection of a primordial event in the pleroma initiated by the absent or non-existent first cause. Thus in Hippolytus's account of the cos-mology of one gnostic sect, the Peratae, we discover that:

> The universe is one, having three parts. One part of their threefold partition
> is as it were a single principle like a great source, which can be divided by

the word into an infinite number of divisions. The first and most important division in their view is a trinity, and is called 'perfect goodness', a paternal power; but the second part of their trinity is like an infinite number of powers which have originated from themselves; the third is the particular. And the first is unoriginate and is good, the second good [and] self-originate, the third is originate.[30]

This tripartite division of the cosmos is useful starting point, inasmuch as it indicates the manner in which although much gnostic ontology is dualistic in its outward form, it is invariably grounded in a notion of space, time and consciousness as divided into three incommensurable realms, which find expression at various levels of the system through a series of bifurcations and tertiary emanations, from the initial series of androgynous aeons prior to the division of the pleroma, to the sub- or post-pleromatic and mimetically androgynous or sexually paired archons, each assigned a specific dominion within the hylical cosmos with its conceptual, plasmatic and material territories, as well as their attendant agents of administration, negotiation and communication: thrones, principalities, powers, virtues, intelligences, and of course, common-or-garden spirits, angels and demons.[31]

Commenting on Hippolytus's interpretation of the Peratae and their cosmology, Filaramo notes that this tripartite division is reflected not only in the classification of the human into three ontologically determined categories, but also, through a process of homology and resonance, into a threefold understanding of time: a classification of origin, emanation and eschatology which strangely pre-empts certain contemporary cosmological speculation on the singularity of the so-called 'big bang' and the chaotically inflationary universe that follows this primal event, in which both time and space, and a multitude of other more short-lived or unobservable dimensions, come into being and then move towards absolute cessation – or redemption. In relation to gnostic time, for example, Filoramo writes that: 'The mythical basic time of the Beginning is followed by an intermediate time, which affects the life of the Gnostic, a prelude (however interminable it may appear) to that final time that precedes the definitive dissolution of time itself.'[32] Beneath this division of time, as well as within the explicit dualism of gnosticism overall, Filoramo detects an underlying monism, represented by that which divides the pleromatic realm from that of matter – the veil. It is within the veil, according to Filoramo, that we can find a corollary of what we would now call mediation. As Filoramo continues:

> Beneath the dualism that (externally and on a vertical axis) separates this world from the divine Pleroma and (internally and on a horizontal plane)

contrasts pneumatic reality with hylical reality (both present in humanity) is an underlying tendency of thought that obscures its monistic inclinations, using and exalting in particular a conceptual figure ... mediation or, in Gnostic terms, image. 'The truth did not come naked into the world, but in types and images.'[33]

The gnostic argument towards which Filoramo is referring here is the cosmogenic doctrine whose variants usually if not always agree that the cosmos as we perceive it now is far from the traditional Platonic, neo-Platonic or Christian image of a perfection of geometric design, but is in fact a rough assemblage of fragments born out of chaos. A chaos, that is, of aborted materials from the sexual and ontological blasphemy of the aeon Sophia, or Pistis-Sophia, or sometimes Sophia-Barbelo or merely Barbelo, who attempted to reproduce through autogenesis and produced a monster who, initially unaware of his/her origins, assumed him/herself to be God, the prime mover unmoved, and created the universe as we now know and partake of it in his/her ignorance and loneliness. In anonymously authored tracts such as 'The Origin of the World', 'Thunder: Perfect Mind' and 'The Hypostasis of the Archons', discovered at Nag Hammadi, for example, the basic message is that: 'Sophia (Wisdom) which is called 'Pistis' [faith] wished to create a work alone without her consort. And her work became an image of heaven (so that) a curtain [veil] exists between the heavenly and the lower regions (aeons). And the shadow came into being beneath the curtain [veil] and that shadow became matter.'[34]

The shadow – or demiurge – generates matter as a by-product of the veil, of which it is both the inverse and silhouette, and which separates the brilliance of the pleroma from the darkness of the cosmos. But that matter, that resultant chaos, has no spirit or pneuma within it, and is thereby likened to a discarded placenta without a child. Initially horrified, a horror that instantly generates an archetype sometimes called the 'troubler', and later identified by the Manicheans as Satan,[35] Sophia-Barbelo partially reveals herself to the demiurge who is, in some versions, then filled with remorse and resentment at there being a deity and a realm of aeons higher than himself, and who consequently infects matter with that remorse and resentment in the form of time, as well as through the prototype, as yet without moral or intellectual consciousness, of humanity, who is both a child of and a slave to time and matter. Simultaneously, the demiurge generates archons, who then generate thrones, territories, intelligences and spirits, and so forth, in descending hierarchies beneath the thrones of the archons, who will then worship him as a partial compensation for his failure as a supreme divinity whose process of emanation is a but a risible imitation of the generation of paired aeons beyond the boundary of which he is the hypostasization, in the pleroma, and of which Sophia, the creator of the veil and the limit, and the demiurge, is the last. What follows varies enormously from source to source. But for our present purposes there are two problems or events that need to be singled out. The first is the nature of the veil created by Sophia in the moment of her blasphemy. The second is her attempt to make reparation for that blasphemy by projecting copies and versions of herself into the primordial hell of time and matter, of the cosmos, whereby the unfortunate products of her error, which are for our purposes humanity, might be offered the possibility of ultimate redemption. In other words, her presence among us is also the promise that at least some of us, though by no means all, will contain elements of the divine pneuma which she carries through her incarnations until time and space and matter cease to be and the unity of the pleroma, the emptiness signified by the light, is once more obtained through the annihilation of the cosmos and its provisional creator.

To deal with the second event first, the presence of Sophia amongst us in serial incarnations, along with the emphasis on androgynous archons and archetypes which characterize gnosticism, suggest a vision of gender and theogeny decidedly at odds with the traditional monotheistic masculinism. Gender in the human understanding of the term, however, becomes an issue only when Sophia, who is the female aspect of an androgynous pairing or code, wilfully breaks with the laws of the pleroma by initiating the process of autogenesis, and thereby precipitating a crisis in the pleroma in which time, space and matter effectively come into existence. The ontological status of the pleroma prior to the cosmos is one of pure and unconditioned virtuality, of infinite singularity, rather than either potentiality or actuality in the traditional and finite sense of the terms, and it is only with the irruption of the veil that both separates and unites the two realms that time and existence have any reality. The manner in which the veil both projects the cosmos as a realm of shadow forms and supplies the notion of limit to that cosmos is one that is, of course, rich in the kind of imagery that certain strands of philosophy and critical theory, especially since Derrida and Irigaray, have come to delight in. What differentiates this model from the foundational Platonic version as exemplified in the *Timaeus* and elsewhere, however, is that the veil, while signifying both limit and mimesis, is in no way to be identified with the original *chora*, but is rather a part of the membrane which the *chora* has discarded having failed to give birth to a universe comparable in any way to the pleroma itself, or indeed to any universe at all. The veil creates a well of darkness and chaos within the initial equilibrium, and immediately begins its train of bifurcations, generating archons and hierarchies of angels and demons with an exponential intensity and acceleration. Along with this spiritual generation, and in a desperate attempt to create something ontologically distinct from the pleromatic template, the demiurge generates matter. But matter, and especially the be-ing of matter, is necessarily unstable in the far-from equilibrium conditions of the cosmos. Existence requires becoming, in the form of time and consciousness, to make possible the atonement of Sophia's sin, and that necessary though insufficient requirement is met by the demiurge, who is, after all, a part of Sophia, though a part she has rejected as imperfect. The demiurge in this sense might be imagined as a holographic representation of the veil as it emerges from Sophia: a representation who divides from and then strives to read his mother's fear and remorse within the veil through its brutally distorted images and archetypes of pleromatic axioms, and who then projects, or rather abjects, those images into their materiality at the same instant as he sets up the possibility of consciousness, whereby space and time can order that materiality and give it direction and telos. Up until that point, direction is entirely arbitrary. After that point, the cosmos is coordinated, mathematicized, by virtue of the possibility of consciousness, and the exponential inflation of the universe that we now inhabit begins. Sophia, meanwhile, intervenes by permeating the veil and then projecting herself beyond its boundaries into the darkness of form and matter. She then breathes the pneuma into matter and establishes consciousness through the generation of its kernel, spirit, which in the manner traditional to the binary thinking of gnosticism also generates anti-matter and anti-spirit, which then become the sources of agency in angels and demons. The function of spirit manifested as human consciousness reflecting on itself is not only, therefore, to act as a measure of the cosmos in which it finds itself, but also to act as an agent through which that cosmos might eventually be understood, its fundamental laws mastered, and its existence terminated, so that the primal blasphemy might also be annihilated along with the time that gave it form in memory and design.

The ultimate forgetting in this sense is a reabsorption into the purity and infinity and absolute measure of light. But such a forgetting must first be activated by an understanding of the cosmos as error, as a deviation from pleromatic law, and it is for this reason that Sophia walks amongst us, usually in the form of a prostitute, or a humiliated woman, or in some cases a virgin queen. Whether as Helen of Tyre found in a brothel by Simon Magus, or as the Elizabeth of John Dee, Sophia has always to struggle to be recognized for what she is. Ostensibly, she is woman deprived of the power, or more dangerously for patriarchal human culture, the inclination, to reproduce, and as such, provides a reminder of both the futility of biological reproduction itself, of life, and of the original sin which brought the cosmos into being.

To suggest, therefore, as I did at the beginning of this paper, that the tripartite classification of time suggested by Agamben might in some way be comprehended as indicating both a series of lines of charge and intensity on a micro-level, functioning through a kind of perpetual quantum hesitation, and a multiplicity of spirit-becomings on a cosmic or macro-level, functioning through consciousness and desire, does not, it should by now be clear, imply that I have been either advocating or condemning a particular response to nihilism, nor even attempting a definition of that nihilism as either an assumption or a reality. Indeed, such a response, whether rationally, affectively or ethically driven, would be entirely inappropriate to both the matter and the motive under consideration. Neither, as the pluralization should make clear, has the term 'spirit' here indicated some hypostasization of a cosmic process into a singular and all embracing ontotheological design, dialectical or otherwise. Spirits, in this plural understanding, certainly have an ontology of a sort, and one that might feasibly be described; but if it can be described at all, it is an ontology which must be considered as indicating a multiplicitous angelic and demonic attraction from the far distant future, indeed from the 'end' of time itself, rather than the present or the past of our chronically recursive species. In this perspective, I have been following and adapting the broad outlines – if not the mathematical details – of the argument developed by David Deutsch in *The Fabric of Reality*, in which he demonstrates the manner in which a quantum understanding of time, deduced from physical laws, mathematical extrapolations and empirical observations, indicates a bifurcation in transdimensional space at the precise moment of any given event in any given universe, and the creation of new and multiple universes, and hence identities and attributes, at each bifurcation, each of which will almost certainly actualize its multiple, and possibly infinite, potentialities.[36] Deutsch's argument is dense and intricate, but in terms of time as a quantum concept, is admirably summarized as follows:

> Time is not a sequence of moments, nor does it flow. Yet our intuitions about the properties of time are broadly true. Certain events are indeed causes of one another. Relative to an observer, the future is indeed open and the past fixed, and possibilities do indeed become actualities. The reason why our traditional theories of time are nonsense is that they try to express these true intuitions within the framework of a false classical physics. In quantum physics they make sense, because time was a quantum concept all along. We exist in multiple versions, in universes called 'moments'. Each version of us is not directly aware of the others, but has evidence of their existence because physical laws link the contents of different universes. It is tempting to suppose that the moment of which we are aware is the only real one, or is at least a little more real than the others. But that is just solipsism. All

moments are physically real. The whole of the multiverse is physically real. Nothing else is.[37]

In this realist and notably Epicurean understanding of time, the notion of identity as self-consciousness may be pictured as each and every moment of observation that allows such consistency to arise chronically, achronically and transdimensionally, to the extent that infinite moments and events are always implicit within any apparently singular moment or event at the quantum level. Moreover, while these divergent universes may be incompossible from our current perspective, non-existent or closed off from any possibility of communication with our own, from the perspective of the end of time, what Frank Tipler describes in his controversial thesis in *The Physics of Immortality* as the 'Omega Point', absolute compossibility of all possible universes subsists in the sense that the Omega Point is understood as a metatemporal and metaspatial singularity, deduced from mathematical calculations, in which all possible information, form and expression, in all possible universes, has been stored and computed at the edge of that terminal singularity. A mirror image, that is, of the primal singularity in which all universes were, it is conjectured, born at the beginning of time and space itself, but one from which certain entities have been computed, generated and reanimated by virtue of the nature of the singularity itself – entities who then may decide (or rather, have decided, will decide and are now deciding)[38] to reanimate the whole multiverse and all that it has ever contained within that singularity.

From the neo-gnostic perspective which has been adopted here, therefore, the possibility of past, present or future human communication with such entities as we may (for there is no scientific or philosophical reason not to), describe as the angels or demons who dwell at the end of time, is in no way ruled out by the distance and directionality involved, nor even by their contemporary absence or even their non-existence, at least in our universe. For we are not dealing here with a fictional ontology in any conventional sense, but rather, with a misconfiguration of spatial and temporal understanding which has confused the fictional, the virtual, the real and the material, and entirely ignored the singularity of the spectral as generating an actualization in reverse, a mode of moving across time vertically and transversally, in much the same way that we currently imagine we move in or through conventional space. In this understanding, the archaic resonances that we tend to associate with the angelic messengers or protectors and the diabolical obstructors or inspirers that we encounter in myth and visionary literature should not distract us into imagining them as belonging merely to what Freud described as the primitive mode of thought,[39] to a more credulous age in which fabulation was the most advanced form of explanation for natural and psychological forces available, to be superseded in due course by philosophy and science. Rather, they should be understood and encountered as the traces of a deterministic spectral vanguard from the end of time, locked as both metaphor and invitation in the archaic strata of our collective and conceptual history, but momentarily silenced by the demand for linear time so central to modernity's acceleration towards its inevitable implosion at the limit of pure materialism, and hence at the limit of nihilism, which is in a larger sense the gateway to the becoming-spectral or becoming-angelic/becoming-demonic, of the human itself.

Notes

1 Georges Bataille, 'Sacrifices', *Visions of Excess: Selected Writings 1927–1939*, ed. Allan Stoekl (Minneapolis: University of Minnesota Press, 1985) p. 134.

2 Thomas Nashe, 'The Terrors of the Night', *The Unfortunate Traveller and Other Works*, ed. J. B. Steane (Harmondsworth: Penguin, 1978) p. 212.

3 From the *Pistis Sophia*, cited by Stephen Holroyd in *The Elements of Gnosticism* (Shaftesbury: Element Books, 1994) p. 75.

4 Giorgio Agamben, *Infancy and History: Essays on the Destruction of Experience*, trans. Liz Heron (London: Verso, 1993) p. 100.

5 The concept of becoming-demonic/becoming-angelic has been adapted illicitly, and with several significant alterations to their use of time and temporality, from the display of concepts, diagrams, extrapolations and memoirs set out by Deleuze and Guattari in the plateau entitled '1730: Becoming-Intense, Becoming-Animal, Becoming-Imperceptible', in Gilles Deleuze and Felix Guattari, *Capitalism and Schizophrenia Vol. 2: A Thousand Plateaus*, trans. Brian Massumi (London: Athlone Press, 1988) pp. 239–53.

6 See especially, Gilles Deleuze, *Difference and Repetition*, trans. Paul Patton (London: Athlone Press, [1968] 1994), and *The Logic of Sense*, trans. Mark Lester (New York: Columbia University Press, [1969] 1990).

7 A succinct discussion of the notion and implications of time's arrow may be found in John Barrow, *Theories of Everything: The Quest for Ultimate Explanation* (London: Vintage Books, 1988).

8 Agamben, *Infancy* p. 101.

9 Ibid., p. 104.

10 Ibid., p. 105.

11 Hans Jonas, *The Gnostic Religion: The Message of the Alien God and the Beginnings of Christianity* (Boston: Beacon Hill, 1958).

12 Georges Bataille, 'Base Materialism and Gnosticism', in *Visions* pp. 45–52; 'L'Absence de myth', *Le Surréalisme en 1947* (Paris: Maeght, 1947).

13 Valentinus, Fragment 5, cited by Robert Haardt, *Gnosis: Character and Testimony*, trans. J. F. Hendry (Leiden: E. J. Brill, 1971) p. 118.

14 A distinction has often been made in gnostic scholarship between gnosticism as a body of doctrine and gnosis as a kind of pathos towards existence and its overcoming. Where I refer to gnosticism in this essay, it should be made clear that it is the genealogy of the latter sense of gnostic pathos, rather than the historical path of its

expressions in groups or cults, that I am addressing primarily.

15 See Georges Bataille, 'Hegel, Death and Sacrifice', trans. Jonathan Strauss, in *Yale French Studies 58: On Bataille*, ed. Allan Stoekl (New Haven: Yale University Press, 1990) pp. 9–28.

16 On Bataille and Kojeve, see Jean-Michel Besnier, 'Georges Bataille in the 1930s: A Politics of the Impossible', trans. Amy Reid, in *Yale French Studies 58: On Bataille* pp. 169–80.

17 The fullest translation into English thus far is J. M. Robinson, ed., *The Nag Hammadi Library in English* (New York: Harper, 1988).

18 Georges Bataille, 'Base Materialism and Gnosticism', in *Visions*) p. 46.

19 Ibid.

20 Ibid., p. 48

21 Ibid., p. 51.

22 Denis Hollier, 'The Dualistic Materialism of Georges Bataille', *Yale French Studies 58: On Bataille* p. 27.

23 Ibid., p. 129

24 The sources mentioned by Bataille notably include Eugene de Faye and William Bousset. Bousset's emphasis on what he considered the oriental (i.e., non-Christian) origins of gnosticism was especially influential in the period in which Bataille was writing on the subject.

25 Giovanni Filoramo, *A History of Gnosticism*, trans. Anthony Alcock (Oxford: Blackwell, 1990) p. 78.

26 On Barbelognosticism and its beliefs, see Haardt, *Gnosis*, pp. 179–82.

27 Umberto Eco, 'On Hermeticism and Gnosticism' in *Interpretation and Over-interpretation*, ed. Stefan Collini (Cambridge: Cambridge University Press, 1992) p. 36.

28 Kurt Rudolph, *Gnosis: The Nature of an Ancient Religion*, trans. Robert McLahon Wilson (Edinburgh: T&T Clark, 1983).

29 Rudolph, *Gnosis* p. 86.

30 Filoramo, *Gnosticism* p. 56.

31 For a summary of and commentary on variants in angelic and demonic hierarchies within the Judaeo-Christian tradition, see Malcolm Godwin, *Angels, an Endangered Species* (New York: Simon & Schuster, 1990) pp. 23–149.

32 Filoramo, *Gnosticism* p. 57.

33 Ibid.

34 Rudolph, *Gnosis*, p. 73.

35 On the overtly satanic elements in gnosticism and Manicheanism, see Jeffrey Burton Russell, *Satan: The Early Christian Tradition* (Ithaca, NY: Cornell University Press, 1981) pp. 51–79, 163–6.

36 If the modern source of multiple universe theory is undoubtedly G. W. Leibniz in *Theodicy: Essays on the Goodness of God, the Freedom of Man, and the Origins of Evil*, trans E. M. Huggard (LaSalle, Illinois: Open Court, 1985), the most influential recent exposition has been that of Hugh Everett and Brian De Witt. For a quantum intepretation of Everett and De Witt and the multiverse relevant to this discussion, see David Deutsch, *The Fabric of Reality* (Harmondsworth: Penguin, 1998) pp. 32–54. On the implications for eschatology in cosmological speculation, see Frank Tipler, *The Physics of Immortality* (London: Doubleday, 1995).

37 Deutsch, *Fabric* p. 287.

38 Tipler's estimation of when this resurrection will occur is extraordinarily precise – between ten to the power of minus ten to the power of ten and ten to the power of minus ten to the power of one hundred and twenty-three seconds before the Omega

Point is reached. For the mathematics underpinning this figure, not to mention the complications it poses for non-differential ordinary language in the use of tense, see Tipler, *Physics*, p. 225 and *passim*.

39 On this and 'omnipotence of thoughts' see Sigmund Freud, 'The Uncanny', *The Pelican Freud Library, Vol. 14: Art and Literature*, trans. James Strachey (London: Pelican, 1985) pp. 362–76.

jill marsden

INTERMINABLE INTENSITY: NIETZSCHE'S DEMONIC NIHILISM

What, if some day or night a demon [*ein Dämon*] were to creep after you into your loneliest loneliness and say to you: 'This life as you now live it and have lived it, you will have to live once more and countless times more; and there will be nothing new in it, but every pain and every joy and every thought and sigh and everything unutterably small or great in your life will have to come back to you and all in the same order and sequence – even this spider and this moonlight between the trees, and even this moment and I myself. The eternal sandglass of existence is turned over again and again, and you with it, speck of dust!'

Would you not throw yourself down and gnash your teeth and curse the demon who spoke thus? Or have you ever experienced a tremendous moment when you would answer him: 'You are a god and never have I heard anything more divine!' If this thought were to overpower you, it would transform you as you are or perhaps crush you; the question in each and every thing, 'Do you desire this once more and countless times more?' would weigh upon your actions as the greatest burden! Or how well disposed would you have to become to yourself and to life *to crave nothing more fervently* [*um nach Nichts mehr zu verlangen*] than this ultimate eternal confirmation and seal?[1]

In the famous first communication of Nietzsche's thought of eternal return in *The Gay Science*, a devilish voice infiltrates the sacrosanct space of pure interiority. If thinking from Plato to Descartes has taken itself to be the soul's silent dialogue with itself, then the thought of eternal return irrupts into the psyche of Western philosophy with the spasm of convulsive shock. Whilst it is true that both Socrates and Descartes are attended by their 'demons', such visitations are no more than an anxious quiver in a rational discourse otherwise at ease with itself. Nietzsche's 'demon', on the other hand, is supremely malign, gleefully providing a macabre twist on the Occidental fantasy of 'eternal life'. To live 'in vain' – one of Nietzsche's most succinct definitions of nihilism – is here elaborated in its unrelenting horror: 'Let us think this thought in its most terrible form: existence as it is, without meaning or aim, yet recurring inevitably without any finale of nothingness: *"the eternal recurrence."* This is the most extreme form of nihilism: the nothing ("the meaningless"), eternally!'[2]

Some thirty eight years later in his paper *Beyond the Pleasure Principle*, Freud is given to reflect upon the emergence of a seemingly senseless thirst for repetition at the heart of self-regarding subjectivity. Commenting on the peculiar phenomenon that in their games children may 'repeat unpleasurable experiences' with as much zeal as they repeat pleasurable ones, Freud invokes the notion of 'the appearance of some "daemonic" force at work'.[3] Since this destructive impulse seemingly aggresses against the pleasure principle (that the organism seeks to avoid displeasure by reducing tension as much as possible) Freud advances the unusual hypothesis that there is *'an urge inherent in organic life to restore an earlier state of things'*.[4] Reasoning that it would be 'in contradiction to the conservative nature of the instincts if the goal of life were a state of things which had never yet been attained'[5] he speculates that the living entity is fatally consecrated to its own collapse: 'If we are to take it as a truth that knows no exception that everything living dies for *internal* reasons – becomes inorganic once again – then we shall be compelled to say that *"the aim of all life is death"'*.[6] In this sense, the compulsion to repeat one's own undoing is in thrall to the death drive and when exhibited in adult psychopathology presents its victim with a 'hint of possession by some "daemonic" power'.[7]

Despite the different context and idiom of their respective ideas, both Nietzsche and Freud invoke an accursed will to repetition which conducts thinking to the black heart of Sisyphean futility. For Nietzsche, the demonic threat of a meaningless life endlessly relived is the apogee of nihilism; for Freud, the compulsion to repeat is a manifestation of the organism's longing to die. For each, the hapless subject of modernity is traumatized by the stirring of dark forces from within, fated to aggravate its lacerated pride in its pathetic attempts at self-overcoming. Yet amidst this useless striving there is a glimmer of salvation. If it is possible to acknowledge Nietzsche's demon as a god and his prophecy as divine, what might this signal for the fate of modernity? Is it possible to *crave nothing more fervently than the eternal return* and if so, would this be to *affirm* nihilism or to *negate* it? More ominously, might this voyage into the smouldering pit of evil kindle a path for thinking beyond affirmation and negation as such, a thinking seared in the crucible of *diabolical desire*?

It is the aim of this chapter to argue that Nietzsche's diagnosis of eternal return as the most extreme form of nihilism marks the attempt to think through the energetics of diabolical desire as immanent to modernity as such. I shall begin by outlining Nietzsche's understanding of nihilism as *thanatropic* – simultaneously symptomatic of decline and its perpetual recommencement. This will serve as a precursor to exploring the potentiality for exorcizing the demonic curse of eternal return and the viability of affirmation as a 'solution'. In this context it will be claimed that what is at stake in these texts is not epistemological but *libidinal*, a point I shall illustrate by indicating how Freud's notion of the death drive consummates Nietzsche's project. I shall then conclude by exploring the notion of demonic nihilism as an attempt to rethink negation beyond good and evil.

Thanatropic nihilism

In the notes to the posthumously published *The Will to Power*, numerous definitions of nihilism are to be found, many of which appear to be in conflict with one another. This is scarcely fortuitous given that a term bearing the weight of both a historical movement and a philosophical concept is arguably in conflict with itself. As an event in European history nihilism signifies the demise of transcendent values (the 'death of God') but as a concept is coterminous with the progress and programme *of* that history. According to Nietzsche, nihilism is rooted in the Christian-moral interpretation of existence in that it both negates 'this world of becoming' by positing an extrinsic realm of value ('truth') and negates its own negation through a withdrawal of faith. It is at the hands of its own morality that Christianity finally expires: 'the sense of truthfulness, developed highly by Christianity, is nauseated by the falseness and mendaciousness of all Christian interpretations of the world and of history'.[8] Nietzsche suggests that 'truthfulness' eventually 'turned against morality, discovered its teleology': no longer able to esteem what we know, we simultaneously find ourselves prohibited from esteeming the lies we should like to tell ourselves.[9] As a psychological state, therefore, nihilism only impacts when it is realized 'that becoming aims at *nothing* and achieves *nothing*'.[10] As a corollary of this loss of aim, faith in the unity and systematicity of existence begins to fade and with that, belief in any notion of a 'true' world.

> Having reached this standpoint, one grants the reality of becoming as the *only* reality, forbids oneself every kind of clandestine access to afterworlds and false divinities – but *cannot endure this world though one does not want to deny it*.[11]

According to Nietzsche, the 'Christian nihilist' is unable to endure 'this world' of becoming because it lacks a purpose which guides it. Implicit in the Platonic-Christian idea that this world only gains its value in relation to an infinitely valuable transcendent realm is the notion that the former is 'untruthful, deceptive, dishonest, inauthentic, inessential' – in short, that it ought not to exist.[12] The categories 'aim,' 'unity,' 'being,' which were used to 'project some value into the world' are now withdrawn 'so the world looks *valueless*'.[13] This devaluation of the highest values hitherto fosters an insidious pessimism and rancorous mistrust at *any* attempt to attribute meaning to existence: 'One interpretation has collapsed; but because it was considered *the* interpretation it now seems as if there were no meaning at all in existence, as if everything were in vain'.[14] It is evident that such a nihilist *retains faith* in the value of the highest values for on finding them lacking in this world, he or she concludes that there is no value to existence whatsoever.

In a particularly subtle genealogical insight Nietzsche attributes the psychological state of the nihilist to a crisis at the level of *desire*, subtending questions of judgement and belief:

> The philosophical nihilist is convinced that all that happens is meaningless and in vain; and that there ought not to be anything meaningless and in vain. But whence this: there ought not to be? From where does one get *this* 'meaning,' *this* standard? – At bottom, the nihilist thinks that the sight of such a bleak, useless existence makes a philosopher feel *dissatisfied*, bleak, desperate. Such an insight goes against our finer sensibility as philosophers. It amounts to the absurd valuation: to have any right to be, the character of existence *would have to give the philosopher pleasure*.
>
> Now it is easy to see that pleasure and displeasure can only be *means* in the course of events: the question remains whether we are at all able to see the 'meaning,' the 'aim,' whether the question of meaninglessness or its opposite is not insoluble for us.[15]

At bottom, the nihilist suffers a disappointed passion, a love of wisdom cruelly unrequited by an indifferent object of desire. The world of becoming exhibits the reality of the Schopenhauerian 'evil, blind will' in which satisfaction is constantly frustrated, its miserable subjects skewered on the wheel of Ixion for all eternity. As Schopenhauer testily acknowledges, existence is futile because even satiation prompts fresh desires, irritating the wound of life that fails to heal. Ultimately, such a view hinges upon the notion of desire as object governed, and in the absence of a *telos*, striving is pointless and purposeless. In the light of this, it is significant that Nietzsche should divorce the notions of pleasure and displeasure from the language of teleology and pose the question of whether aim and meaning might be thought otherwise.

One potential response to the demise of 'some *superhuman authority*' might be to search for some *other* authority 'that can *speak unconditionally* and *command* goals and tasks' such as the authority of conscience, reason or social instinct.[16] Yet such a strategy appears to typify what Nietzsche terms 'incomplete nihilism' – the endeavour to escape nihilism without revaluating the values that have dominated hitherto.[17] According to Niet-zsche the nihilistic question 'for what?' is the legacy of a history within which 'the goal must be put up, given, demanded *from outside*'.[18] Formu-lated in these ineluctably passive terms, incomplete nihilism remains com-mensurate with metaphysical pessimism, a declining life force wretchedly thirsting to obey. In the language of desire, incomplete nihilism might be construed as displacement activity, the elevation of a new idol to the pedestal of the divine. Such a gesture is tantamount to the restitution of pleasure, the rehabilitation of metaphysical security in a godless universe: 'finally, *happiness* – and, with a touch of Tartuffe, the *happiness of the greatest number*',[19] but for Nietzsche, to question whether or not to invest in existence is merely the expression of physiological decadence.[20] Accord-ingly, he contends that when pessimism develops into nihilism 'opposites replace natural degrees and ranks'.[21] Ultimately, it makes little difference whether the response to the death of God is despairing or optimistic for desire remains object governed, conceptually bound within the theologi-cal matrix. If it is legitimate to describe nihilism as *thanatropic* – tending towards negation yet perpetually *repeating* its life-negating impetus – this is because loss of faith in the postulation of a final being is only to mark a limit to desire *once again*. To mourn God or to deify his surrogates is to judge a *lack* in being, born of negative desire – a craving to be fulfilled once and for all.

To think through the question of 'meaninglessness and its opposite' might plausibly entail a critique of binary logic as such and Nietzsche's text is rich with critical resources for mobilizing such a project. Neverthe-less, inasmuch as he identifies his own thinking of eternal return as the most *extreme* form of nihilism, the question might be how to *intensify* nihilism, rather than to adopt a judgement in relation to it. For Nietzsche, nihilism in its *active* mode does not simply negate former values but exac-erbates their destruction:

> Nihilism does not only contemplate the 'in vain!' nor is it merely the belief that everything deserves to perish: one helps to destroy. – This is, if you will, illogical; but the nihilist does not believe that one needs to be logical. – It is the condition of strong spirits and wills, and these do not find it possible to stop with the No of 'judgement': their nature demands the No of the deed. The reduction to nothing by judgement is seconded by the reduction to nothing by hand.[22]

Since faith in reason has augmented the human desire for knowledge the world initially seems worth less when the highest values cherished hith-erto have been devalued, yet to admit this *unreservedly* is the path via which new values might be sought.[23] It is important to be clear that in 'philosophising with a hammer' Nietzsche does not dispense with the language of 'goals' but his inflection of this idea is instructive. Since, minimally speaking, *any* goal constitutes *some* meaning, he reasons that even the 'belief' in the inexorable course of planetary annihilation sustains a moral order. Insofar as we continue to *believe* in morality – that the world ought to be otherwise – we pass sentence on existence.[24] Moreover to anchor meaning to issues of pleasure or displeasure is seen to be the recourse of the type of nihilist who 'no longer dares to posit' a will, a purpose, a meaning: 'suffering might predominate, and in spite of that a powerful will might exist, a Yes to life, a need for this predominance'.[25] In this regard, he speaks darkly of a goal 'for which one does not hesitate to offer human sacrifices, to risk every danger, to take upon oneself whatever is bad and worst', in short, *the great passion*.[26]

Faith in the veracity of metaphysical ideals having given rise to nihilism, Nietzsche poses the question as to whether it is possible to relinquish such convictions and admit to ourselves the merely 'apparent' character of existence – the 'necessity of lies'. To think of meaning and value independently of truth is to liberate desire from its constriction within the straitjacket of morality. On this basis he surmises that 'nihilism, as a denial of a truthful world, of being, might be *a divine way of thinking*'.[27] Could 'great passion' be the conduit through which nihilism might be thought *libidinally*, that is, beyond the language of judgement, an attempt to access the *sacred heart* of religion?

The value of affirmation

The note from *The Will to Power* in which Nietzsche designates the thought of eternal return as the most extreme form of nihilism concludes with the statement: 'We deny end goals: if existence had one it would have to have been reached'.[28] The next segment of the note begins as follows:

> So one understands that an antithesis to pantheism is attempted here: for 'everything perfect, divine, eternal' also compels a faith in the 'eternal recurrence.' Question: does morality make impossible this pantheistic affirmation of all things, too? At bottom, it is only the moral god that has been overcome. Does it make sense to conceive a God 'beyond good and evil'? Would a pantheism in this sense be possible? Can we remove the idea of the goal from the process and then affirm the process in spite of this? – This would be the case if something were attained at every moment within this process – and always the same.[29]

In this dense and cryptic note, Nietzsche appears to be exploring the question as to whether it is possible to conceive divinity beyond the categories of affirmation and negation. Intriguingly, *faith* in the eternal recurrence is linked to a pantheistic affirmation yet it is implied that eternal recurrence as the most extreme form of nihilism is precisely an antithesis to pantheism. It is noticeable that in both contexts the thought of eternal recurrence is placed in inverted commas, prompting a number of questions about its status here. If pantheism is the 'opposite' of nihilism might it not be by that token alone nihilism *to the second power*? To affirm that all things are manifestations of God ('an-in-itself of things that might be 'divine' or morality incarnate'[30]) is the logical inverse of affirming that all things are manifestations of his absence. The issue is complicated by Nietzsche's insertion of the word 'faith' in relation to a pantheistic eternal recurrence and his obvious interest in rethinking this notion 'beyond good and evil'. Affirming becoming beyond morality raises the question as to whether it is possible to speak of 'good' beyond 'God' and independently of the language of conviction. The danger is that a pantheistic affirmation of existence may be regarded as *redemptive* – the casting out of 'demons' as a solution to the 'problem of evil'. As Nietzsche comments in the same cluster of notes, the Christian moral hypothesis 'conceded to the world, in spite of suffering and evil, the character of perfection – including "freedom": evil appeared full of meaning'.[31] If eternal return is to be liberated from the spectre of the moral arbiter God, perhaps it is a reacquaintance with *evil* rather than good that now needs to be pursued.

Such considerations might usefully inform our reading of Nietzsche's famous first communication of eternal return in *The Gay Science*. Two possible responses to the words of the demon are envisaged. On hearing the thought that all returns eternally, one is asked whether one would prostrate oneself, clench one's teeth and curse the demon's words or whether one has ever experienced a tremendous moment which would impel one to recognize this demon as a god and celebrate his infernal teaching as divine. It seems significant that the second response to the demon hinges upon the prior condition of having experienced a 'tremendous moment'. One recalls the experiences of Nietzsche's Zarathustra who literally stands within the gateway of Moment, complete with the spider and the moonlight between the trees.[32] Such a moment is liberated from linear, historical temporality in which future redemption is promised to the virtuous but also from the terrible burden of the 'it was', Zarathustra's name for 'the will's teeth-gnashing and most lonely affliction'.[33] To experience this tremendous moment is to free desire from the penal servitude of willing and to return the world of becoming to the 'innocence' of tragic Dionysian 'wisdom'.

The plausibility of this particular interpretation notwithstanding, there is something about this second response to the demon which remains troubling. It is tempting to read the sentences directly following the affirmation of divinity as qualifying this joyous response, but the tone of the narrative voice becomes ever more ominous: 'If this thought were to overpower you, it would transform you as you are or perhaps crush you; the question in each and every thing, "Do you desire this once more and countless times more?" would weigh upon your actions as the greatest burden!' The thought might transfigure the one who thinks it but it may also be crushing. More than a hint of the cadaverous perfume of Christian gravitas clings to the question of *desire* as it is here formulated. One is reminded of Nietzsche's diagnosis of the origin of bad conscience as the reactive internalization of wild instincts. In the torture chamber of consciousness the morally subject-ed one savages, persecutes, claws at itself, like a caged animal rubbing itself against the bars of its cage.[34] To be eternally responsible – is this not correlative to being eternally guilty – a sublimation of the thirst to abase oneself before God? The 'animal man made inward' 'ejects from himself all his denial of himself, of his nature, naturalness, and actuality, in the form of an affirmation, as something existent, corporeal, real, as God, as the holiness of God, as God the Judge, as God the Hangman, as the beyond, as eternity, as torment without end, as hell, as the immeasurability of punishment and guilt'.[35] Is demonic affirmation merely divine affirmation once again?

Seen in this light it is scarcely surprising that Nietzsche's 'most abyssal thought' is frequently interpreted as an 'existential imperative' – an injunction to live one's life *as if* it were to be eternally repeated. This fundamentally *moral* response to the demon's words constitutes a relocation of authority at the level of maxims guiding action and as such constitutes a greater resignation to the inevitable than the nihilism it sought to overcome. It could even be argued that to affirm in this context is hyper-nihilistic, the second response resuscitating the desire for eternal subjection to the law: 'The authority of *conscience* now steps up front (the more emancipated one is from theology, the more imperativistic morality becomes) to compensate for the loss of *personal* authority'.[36] Submission to a self-imposed law is still tacitly recuperable within a logic of agency and stoic acceptance just as servile as the sinecures of the priest. Moreover, at the level of autonomy one can only find the eternal return of the demon and his gruesome taunts a tedious irrelevance. Such a thought could only retain its terrifying, transfiguring power if it were ceaselessly forgotten. Yet from the perspective of good sense such a possibility can only threaten to compound the insanity of this doctrine, for repetition unaccompanied by recollection remains meaningless. If a ceaseless pattern of repetition has already occurred innumerable times and has been forgotten innumerable times, the prospect of its future recurrence can scarcely induce even

the most incidental tremor of anxiety, let alone a sense of radical obliga-
tion. Since an imperative to re-will generated at the level of consciousness
would be senseless, the prejudice that Nietzsche's idea is some kind of
ethical test can no longer be entertained.

In the light of this reading we might interpret the closing statement of
section 341 of *The Gay Science* as more than merely ancillary to what has
gone before: 'Or how well disposed would you have to become to yourself
and to life *to crave nothing more fervently* than this ultimate eternal confirmation and seal?' It is possible to read this 'or' as marking a *third* kind
of question and a *third* mode of desire beyond the exclusive disjunction of
negation and affirmation. Indeed, it might be said that the two responses
to the demon are both 'affirmations' at the level of belief in that each is
predicated upon acceptance of the truth or reality of recurrence. Affirmation *beyond* good and evil would entail thinking of desire non-egoically,
non-teleologically and most of all, non-epistemologically. Significantly, the
third question drifts free from 'reaction' to the words of the demon and
reformulates the notion of the *nihil* once again. The only italicized segment
in the passage highlights a mode of desire irreducible to the tame deci-
sionistic vocabulary of 'the will'. To *crave nothing fervently*, to have 'great
passion' for the nothing, signals an enthusiasm for annihilation that is ruth-
lessly impersonal. This is not the *nihil* of logical negation but an invocation
of the non-moral, non-logical world of becoming which all attempts to pass
judgement on existence relentlessly suppress. Abandonment, wrenched
free of snivelling existential dread, is *sacrifice*, the pure matter of religion.
Perhaps too, this thinking is demonic rather than divine, but demonic in
the sense in which Freud uses the term – inaccessible to the magniloquent
chirpings of the ego. Like the silent force of *thanatos* which stealthily
unbinds, the thought of eternal recurrence resists accommodation within
the syntax of rational thought. To consider how the thought of eternal
return might impact at the level of *unconscious forces of desire* we now
return to Freud.

Demonic desire

Whilst the identification of evil with desire has a rich and abiding Christian pedigree (arguably inherited by discourses of modernity such as psychoanalysis), in acknowledging that there is an unconscious element to
desire in conflict with its own capacity for satiation, Freud deviates from
the path of striving to exorcize demons from traumatized nature. In the
scholastic tradition inherited from Aristotle, desire is conceived as that
which has already attained its potential for realization extrinsically, modelled proximally on the originary perfection of the divine. The relocation

of teleology within the practical philosophy of enlightenment rationality consummates the project of modernity as reconstructive, legislating in advance for what it will learn, harnessing the future to the apriority of the concept. Heir to this legacy, Freud frequently presents desire as the drive to attain and sustain a potential, but in his reflections on the death drive he begins to rethink desire as precisely that which violently subverts the perfection of teleological process. Tempting as it is to view *eros* and *thanatos* as oppositional concepts, agents of construction and destruction respectively, Freud's elaboration of the latter points beyond dyadic thinking to a notion of interminable intensity.

In the course of developing the infamous notion that '*the aim of all life is death*' Freud contemplates the view that all the organic instincts are conservative and tend towards the restitution of a state from which they earlier departed.

> For a long time, perhaps, living substance was thus being constantly created afresh and easily dying, till decisive external influences altered in such a way as to oblige the still surviving substance to diverge ever more widely from its original course of life and to make ever more complicated *détours* [*Umwegen*] before reaching its aim of death. These circuitous paths to death, faithfully kept to by the conservative instincts, would thus present us to-day with the picture of the phenomenon of life. If we firmly maintain the exclusively conservative nature of instincts, we cannot arrive at any other notions as to the origin and aim of life.[37]

The hypothesis of self-preservative instincts readily attributed to all living beings stands in marked contrast to the idea that instinctual life as a whole serves to bring about death. However, in *Beyond the Pleasure Principle* Freud advances the theory that the preservative drives are mere modifications of the death drive. The latter are accordingly demoted to 'component instincts' whose function is to ensure that the organism shall 'follow its own path to death' by warding off any possible ways of returning to inorganic existence other than those immanent in the organism itself.[38] This generates the peculiarly paradoxical situation that the living organism struggles most strenuously against circumstances which might enable it swiftly to attain its longed-for demise.

Embellishing this theory in finer detail, Freud conjectures that a further distinction might be made at a cellular level. It is suggested that within the higher animals, the germ cells, having acquired 'their full complement of inherited and freshly acquired instinctual dispositions', separate from the rest of the cells and reactivate the process of their evolution:

> Under favourable conditions, they begin to develop – that is, to repeat the performance to which they owe their existence; and in the end once again

one portion of their substance pursues its development to a finish [*und dies endet damit, dass wieder ein Anteil ihrer Substanz die Entwicklung bis zum Ende fortführt*], while another portion harks back once again as a fresh residual germ to the beginning of the process of development.[39]

This process of completion and recommencement impedes the organism from realizing its desire to die, winning for it what may be regarded as 'potential immortality'.[40] The instincts governing these processes constitute the group of sexual instincts which are conservative in the same sense as the other instincts in that they bring back earlier states of living substance, but they are conservative 'to a higher degree [*in stärkerem Masse*]' in that they are peculiarly resistant to external influences and preserve life itself for a comparatively long period.[41] Freud goes on to designate these sexual instincts the 'true life instincts' in that there is 'an opposition between them and the other instincts' which lead, by reason of their function, to death[42]: 'It is as though the life of the organism moved with a vacillating rhythm [*Zauderrhythmus*]. One group of instincts rushes forward so as to reach the final aim of life as swiftly as possible; but when a particular stage in the advance has been reached, the other group jerks back to a certain point to make a fresh start and so prolong the journey.'[43]

Two factors of particular importance emerge from Freud's account of the unconscious forces of desire. First, it is to be noted that the conservative life instincts are presented as stalling mechanisms within the larger, general economy of death and thus are instrumental in interminably reintensifying the desire to die. Such a notion rests uneasily with the claim that the life and death drives are 'oppositional' ('an opposition whose importance was long ago recognized by the theory of the neuroses'[44]). Furthermore, Freud suggests that there is a gradation within the conservative instincts, such that the sexual drives operate at a higher peak of intensity and hence differ both from the death drives and from themselves. In this connection, Freud accords particular prominence to the fact that the repetition function of the germ cell is only made possible 'if it coalesces with another cell similar to itself and yet differing from it'.[45] A second and related point to note in this regard is that the process of the organism oscillates rhythmically in accordance with these internally diverging forces, never achieving the nirvana of homeostasis that it purportedly craves. Thus, whilst the death drive might *appear* to resonate with the nihilistic will for nothingness, might *appear* to be goal governed and might *appear* to exhibit the hallmarks of negative desire, Freud's presentation of the energetic tendencies of the unconscious actually imply something rather different. The compulsion to repeat *intensifies* the thirst for ruination, much as it might be said that active nihilism intensifies the will to negation. This is an understanding of desire sprung loose from *telos* and if it repeats its 'evil, blind willing' again and again, this is because its desire is *insatiable*. The final irony of *thanatos* is that death is never enough.

If it is possible to remove the idea of a goal from the process of recurrence and affirm the process in spite of this then it might be argued that a thinking of divinity beyond good and evil is possible. What must be recognized in this context is that affirmation does not signal the vanquishment of demonic forces but rather their immanence to life as such. The nihilist is disaffected with the world of becoming because it offers no solace to the craving to consummate knowledge once and for all. Hence, like Socrates, the nihilist believes that only a 'finale of nothingness' can staunch the haemorrhaging wound of mortality. Inversely, for the one able to affirm the demon's words, continuing to exist means to humble oneself once again, affirmation in this sense being scarcely distinguishable from the pious self-monitoring of the Kantian slave. By contrast, what is so unique about the Freudian depiction of the death drive is its sheer immorality. Freudian thanatography immaculately illustrates the *failure of desire as design*. The potential immortality of which Freud speaks is not an eternal life of bliss purged of virulent strains of evil but an interminable repetition of the same, a constant rising and falling of intensity intrinsic to unconscious libidinal life.

Beyond good and evil

We are perhaps now in a position to reconsider what Nietzsche might intend by the 'great passion' which does not hesitate to offer human sacrifices, risk danger and take upon itself whatever is bad and worst. In the context of a note from *The Will to Power* dealing with the causes of pessimism, Nietzsche observes that 'the most powerful desires of life that have the most future have hitherto been slandered, so a curse weighs on life'.[46] For Nietzsche, the problem of evil lies not in its 'existence' but in its repression: 'Man must grow better and more evil!' For 'evil is man's best strength'.[47] 'Evil' is a term which Nietzsche employs to subvert the Christian demonization of 'great passion' by reinforcing and intensifying its *power*. In the chapter entitled 'Of the Three Evil Things' in *Thus Spake Zarathustra*, Nietzsche indicates how Christian thinking curses when it blesses, defining its virtues reactively in relation to its 'enemies'. Sensual pleasure [*Wollust*], lust for power [*Herrschsucht*] and selfishness [*Selbstsucht*] are the 'three evil things' which have 'hitherto been cursed the most and held in the worst and most unjust repute'.[48] It is worth noting that each of the three evil things is a *mode of desire*, desire which Nietzsche reconfigures in terms of an exultant physiology which has sloughed off Platonic-

Christian inscriptions like a disease, encrusted skin. Despite the harnessing of these forces by the egoic categories of modern thought, Nietzsche
presents them as unconscious, transindividual energies. For example, the
'rightful baptismal name' for the longing for power is the 'bestowing
virtue' which encompasses both erotic passion and the creative self-overcoming energy of *Selbstsucht*:

> You thirst to become sacrifices and gifts yourselves; and that is why you
> thirst to heap up all riches in your soul.
>
> Your soul aspires insatiably [*unersättlich*] after treasures and jewels,
> because your virtue is insatiable in wanting to give.
>
> You compel all things to come to you and into you, that they may flow
> back from your fountain as gifts of your love.
>
> Truly, such a bestowing love must become a thief of all values; but I call
> this selfishness healthy and holy.[49]

The thirst of which Zarathustra speaks is less acquisitive than sacrificial, an
insatiable desire to expend rather than to preserve. This glorious longing
for dissolution exhibits no weariness or dissatisfaction for it migrates freely
beyond all goal-orientated desire, compounding its craving to waste itself
interminably. Again, death fails to satiate. Counterposed to this is a hungry
selfishness which wants to steal and conserve yet it is this mode of desire
that has historically 'become body in us'.[50] This is the morally reactive
mode of being which programmes both Christian nihilism and the cosmic
optimism of the rational modern subject. Perhaps all those processes which
roam independently of responsibility, human agency and utility have been
granted the name of evil but the 'good' has always been the preserve of
'some wretched loafer of a moralist' who says 'no! man should be *different*'.[51] As Nietzsche writes in one of *The Will to Power* notes: 'one still
believes in good and evil and experiences the triumph of the good and the
annihilation of evil as a task (that is English; typical case: the flathead John
Stuart Mill)'.[52] Approached libidinally rather than metaphysically, the
'problem of evil' no longer devolves upon questions of morality or the fact
that the human animal will suffer. What matters alone is *intensity*.

To persist in *judging* existence and passing sentence on life is to com-
mute desire to the account books of good and evil, whether or not an
'affirmative' stance is attempted. Pleasure and pain do not constitute
grounds for estimating life and pronouncing upon its value, for existence
is indifferent to what helps or hinders the accidental occurrence of the
human in the flux of becoming.

> 'The sum of displeasure outweighs the sum of pleasure; consequently
> it would be better if the world did not exist' – 'The world is something
> that rationally should not exist because it causes the feeling subject more

displeasure than pleasure' – chatter of this sort calls itself pessimism today!

Pleasure and displeasure are accidentals, not causes; they are value judgements of the second rank, derived from a ruling value – 'useful,' 'harmful,' speaking in the form of feelings, and consequently absolutely sketchy and dependent. For with every 'useful,' 'harmful,' one still has to ask in a hundred different ways: 'for what?'

I despise this *pessimism of sensibility*: it is itself a sign of a deeply impoverished life.[53]

Rejecting the view that the human wants pleasure and avoids displeasure, Nietzsche insists instead that what the human 'wants', what every smallest part of a living organism wants, is an increase in power. Pleasure and pain are consequent upon this striving, not its condition of possibility. He uses the example of a primitive organism that extends its pseudopodia in search of something that resists it – not from hunger but from will to power: 'Displeasure thus does not merely not have to result in a diminution of our feeling of power, but in the average case it actually stimulates this feeling of power – the obstacle is the stimulus of this will to power'.[54] In this respect, he insists that psychologists have confused two kinds of pleasure, that of falling asleep and that of victory: 'The exhausted want rest, relaxation, peace, calm – the happiness of the nihilistic religions and philosophies; the rich and living want victory, opponents overcome, the overflow of the feeling of power across wider domains than hitherto'.[55]

The stimulation of the feeling of power describes the energetics of diabolical desire – the great passion which thirsts interminably to overcome itself. Just as Freud depicts the organism as playing out a vacillating rhythm of creative and destructive tendencies, Nietzsche supplies an account of the will to power as delighting in overcoming resistances and intensifying the process interminably.

Pain is something different from pleasure – I mean it is *not* its opposite.

If the essence of 'pleasure' has been correctly described as a feeling of more power (hence as a feeling of difference, presupposing a comparison), this does not yet furnish a definition of the essence of 'displeasure.' The false opposites in which the people, and *consequently* language, believes, have always been dangerous hindrances to the advance of truth. There are even cases in which a certain kind of pleasure is conditioned by a certain *rhythmic sequence* [*rhythmische Abfolge*] of little unpleasurable stimuli: in this way a very rapid increase of the feeling of power, the feeling of pleasure, is achieved. This is the case, e.g., in tickling, also the sexual tickling in the act of coitus: here we see displeasure at work as an ingredient of pleasure. It seems, a little hindrance [...] is overcome and immediately followed by another little hindrance that is again overcome – this game of resistance and victory arouses most strongly that general feeling of superabundant, excessive power that constitutes the essence of pleasure.

> The opposite, an increase in the sensation of pain through the introduc-
> tion of little pleasurable stimuli, is lacking; for pleasure and pain are not
> opposites.[56]

The energetics of diabolical desire are inaccessible to the logic of opposition, contradiction and sublation, for pleasure is intensified by pain just as
life is stimulated by its thanatropic passion. For Nietzsche affirmation is
achieved by virtue of evil, not by redeeming oneself from suffering. It is
only via intensified repetition, the interminable intensity of the will to
power, that desire deviates from *telos* sufficiently and bids voraciously to
overcome itself again and again. Nietzsche's notion of eternal return cancels all finalistic principles that moralize life and offers in their place a
sacred thinking of a twofold voluptuous delight, an excessive passion to
create and to destroy.

Demonic nihilism names the senseless longing upon which order and
organised religion float. The exhausted, weary yearning to die is but a wisp
of pale, evaporating smoke from the furnace of white-hot sacrificial desire
– the glowing embers at the base of religious craving. To surrender the
grounds upon which morality is instituted is undoubtedly evil but it is
through the relentless restitution of evil that a passage beyond oppositional thinking and morality is possible. Diabolical desire is the unconscious motor of modernity and only when constrained by the axiomatics of
representational thinking does it become attached to goals. The thought of
eternal return is not available as a riddle to be solved but as a goad for
thinking, divine *irresolution*. If the ends of modernity are *knowable* they
remain so insofar as they remain modern. Nietzsche's darkly cryptic
thought of eternal return resists the status of an epistemological principle
and by that very fact conducts thinking to the edge of madness. If desire
thirsts for its own oblivion this is only true to the extent that it simultaneously thirsts to escape its own destiny. We are good because we lack the
strength to be evil but we 'are' will to power and *nothing* besides.

> This world: a monster of energy, without beginning, without end […] a sea
> of forces flowing and rushing together, eternally changing, eternally flooding
> back, with tremendous years of recurrence, with an ebb and a flood of its
> forms […] blessing itself as that which must return eternally, as a becoming
> that knows no satiety, no disgust, no weariness: this, my *Dionysian* world of
> the eternally self-creating, the eternally self-destroying, this mystery world
> of the twofold voluptuous delight, my 'beyond good and evil,' without goal,
> unless the joy of the circle is itself a goal; without will, unless a ring feels
> good will toward itself – do you want a *name* for this world? […] *This world
> is the will to power – and nothing besides*! And you yourselves are also this
> will to power and nothing besides![57]

Notes

1 F. Nietzsche (1882) *The Gay Science*, trans. W. Kaufmann (New York: Vintage Books, 1974) §341, pp. 273–4 (translation modified). References to the German edition are to *Die Fröhliche Wissenschaft*, ed. Giorgio Colli and Mazzino Montinari (Berlin: Deutscher Taschenbuch Verlag, Walter de Gruyter, Friedrich Nietzsche Sämtliche Werke: Kritische Studienausgabe, Band 3, 1990), p. 570.

2 F. Nietzsche, *The Will to Power*, trans. W. Kaufmann and R. J. Hollingdale (New York: Vintage Books, 1968) §55, pp. 35–6. References to the German edition will be to *Der Wille Zur Macht* (Stuttgart: Kröner Verlag, Kröners Taschenausgabe, Band 78, 1964).

3 Sigmund Freud (1920) 'Beyond the Pleasure Principle' in *On Metapsychology: The Theory of Psychoanalysis*, Pelican Freud Library Vol. 11, trans. James Strachey and Angela Richards (London: Pelican Books, 1964) p. 307. References to the source essay 'Jenseits des Lustprinzips', will be from *Psychologie des Unbewussten* (Frankfurt am Main: S. Fischer Verlag, Sigmund Freud Studienausgabe, Band 3, 1975).

4 Ibid., p. 308.

5 Ibid., p. 310.

6 Ibid., pp. 310–11.

7 Ibid., p. 308.

8 Nietzsche, *Will*, §1, p. 7.

9 Ibid., §5, p. 10.

10 Ibid., §12, p. 12.

11 Ibid., p. 13.

12 Ibid., §586, pp. 319–22.

13 Ibid., §12.

14 Ibid., §55, p. 35.

15 Ibid., §36, pp. 23–4.

16 Ibid., §20, p. 16.

17 Ibid., §28, p. 19.

18 Ibid., §20, p. 16.

19 Ibid., p. 17.

20 Ibid., §38, p. 24.

21 Ibid., §37, p. 24.

22 Ibid., §24, p. 18.

23 Ibid., §32, p. 22.

24 Ibid., §6, p. 10.

25 Ibid., §35, p. 23.

26 Ibid., §26, p. 19.

27 Ibid., §15, p. 15.

28 Ibid., §55, p. 36.

29 Ibid.

30 Ibid., §3, p. 9.

31 Ibid., §4, p. 10.

32 F. Nietzsche (1885) *Thus Spake Zarathustra*, trans. R. J. Hollingdale (Harmondsworth: Penguin, 1961) p. 179 References to the German edition will be to *Also Sprach Zarathustra* (Kritische Studienausgabe, Band 4).

33 Ibid., p. 161.

34 F. Nietzsche (1887) *On the Genealogy of Morals*, trans. W. Kaufmann (New York: Vintage Books, 1967) part II, §16, p. 85.

35 Ibid., §22, p. 92.
36 Nietzsche, *Will*, §20, pp. 16–17.
37 Freud, 'Pleasure Principle', p. 311; p. 248 (German text second).
38 Ibid.
39 Ibid., p. 312; p. 249.
40 Ibid.
41 Ibid., p. 313; p. 250.
42 Ibid.
43 Ibid.
44 Ibid.
45 Ibid.
46 Nietzsche, *Will*, §33, p. 22.
47 Nietzsche, *Zarathustra*, p. 299.
48 Ibid., p. 206; p. 236.
49 Ibid., p. 100; p. 98.
50 Ibid., p. 102.
51 F. Nietzsche (1888) *Twilight of the Idols*, trans. Duncan Large (Oxford: Oxford University Press, 1998) p. 24.
52 Nietzsche, *Will*, §30, p. 21.
53 Ibid., §701, pp. 372–3.
54 Ibid., §702, p. 373.
55 Ibid., §703, p. 374.
56 Ibid., §699, p. 371; pp. 470–1.
57 Ibid., §1067, p. 550.

diane morgan

'AN ANGEL ON ALL FOURS': 'INVERTS' AND THEIR DOGS

In Djuna Barnes's *Nightwood* (1936), Doctor Matthew Mighty O'Connor, 'his' mouth snarling with curses, damns a fellow 'invert': 'For what do you know of me, man's meat? I'm an angel on all fours, with a child's feet behind me, seeking my people that have never been made, going down face foremost, drinking the waters of night at the water hole of the damned, and I go into the waters, up to my heart, the terrible waters! What do you know of me? May you pass from me, damned girl! Damned and betraying!'[1] O'Connor, Barnes's male-to-female transsexual *avant la lettre*, is describing 'his' unfortunate cottaging experiences. Misrecognized as a gay man, when 'he' perceives 'himself' as a someone who desires men *as a woman* (whatever that might mean), he is condemned to repeat an act which reiterates the elusive nature of his desires. The high-bosomed, big-wombed woman 'he' wants to become, may be the Marseilles girl who '[thumped] the dock with a sailor' he has memories of having been. Such a past virtually provides 'him' with a projection of the future: 'The wise men say that the remembrance of things past is all that we have for a future'.[2] The memory of past that has not been lived but which is retro-spectively postulated as the impossible destiny of one's future, is the com-plicated narrative the transsexual O'Connor invents to accompany 'his' becoming.[3]

The transsexual experiences Nietzsche's 'how one becomes what one is' more often than not as the question: 'how does one become what one is?'.[4] The answer to this question seems to present itself in the shape of correc-tive surgery. Such an intervention promises to realign fantasy and reality, to destroy the falsity of becoming, to terminate its cruelty by releasing the authentic identity of being. The young Nietzsche tells us that only being, 'being thus and not otherwise', can free us from the fickle flux of becoming.

Becoming is 'hollow, deceptive, shallow and worthy of our contempt'.[5] Whilst we are caught up in its processes, becoming is that which disperses us to the winds. Only to be as one who is buffetted by the changing elements is an unhappy existence. Nietzsche's early solution to this perilous condition is to stifle becoming (*Werden*) with the controlling assertion of being (*Sein*). No longer someone else's plaything, no longer just reacting to contingent external circumstances, the subject tests reality by separating the falsity of becoming's challenges from the clarity of being's truthfulness: 'Now he starts to test how deeply he is entwined with becoming, how deeply with being – a tremendous task rises before his soul: to destroy all that is becoming, to bring to light all that is false in things'.[6] The conviction of one's essential being – 'I am a woman in a man's body' – provides the transsexual with the teleological end to be aimed for. This end reveals the process of becoming to have been just a rectification of appearance so that it now corresponds to an *a priori* identity. Becoming just amounts to what one has always been all along. Being slips back over becoming to encompass its effects and the transformatory process fulfills itself as a complete circuit. Conventions remain untroubled as, once having crossed the gender divide, the transsexual passes imperceptibly into the traditional role s/he always desired. As Doctor Matthew Mighty O'Connor explains: 'in my heart is the wish for children and knitting. God, I never asked better than to boil some good man's potatoes and toss up a child for him every nine months by the calendar'.[7] However, the transition from one side of the gender divide to the other is not that smooth or that absolute – just as the divide itself is not that clear-cut or absolute. The transsexual becoming is often far more radical in its assumptions and consequences. Akin to Nietzsche's later philosophical formulations – discussed below – other transsexual explorations of becoming unfold a process which does not end capped by a guiding authentic principle of being.[8] In fact, the process is ongoing. The evolutionary process which is tapped within the injunction to 'become what you are' does not lead to a redemptive point, capable of recuperating any phases of inauthenticity experienced on the way. The transsexual is a damned soul, an 'angel on all fours', but also a creature awaiting a new age of classification: 'seeking my people that have never been made'.[9] The transsexual precociously belongs to a race that does not yet exist.[10] As such s/he presents the prospect of a strange and confusing hybridity which flummoxes the more conventionalized eye. The unsuspecting intruder into O'Connor's room in *Nightwood*, Nora, is confronted with an incongruent scene which she can only describe as 'a cross between a *chambre à coucher* and a boxer's training camp'.[11] The analogy jars, thereby marking a disruption of the outsider's expectations of what should and should not been seen together in the same place.

The gender performance which O'Connor stages for 'himself' at night, dressing up in 'his' feminine accoutrements, fools no one, least of all 'himself'. 'He' bluntly remarks: 'As for me, I tuck myself in at night, well content because I am my own charlatan'.[12] As a quack doctor, 'he' can only pretend to heal the dysphoria which makes 'him' so unhappy. Unable to collapse 'his' restless becoming into a self-contented being, 'he' can only console 'himself' that 'he' at least is not suffering from self-delusion. The irreconcilability of 'his' desires and situation condemn him to a life of nocturnal prowlings as 'he' joins the other marginalized 'inverts' in their desperate search for an elusive happiness:

> 'And it's the same with girls,' he said, 'those who turn the day into night, the young, the drug addict, the profligate, the drunken and that most miserable, the lover who watches all night long in fear and anguish. These can never again live the life of the day … Look for the girls also in the toilets at night, and you will find them kneeling in that great secret confessional crying between tongues, the terrible excommunication'.[13]

Banished from the light of the day, the 'inverts' at once blaspheme against religion and reinvent the gods as they confess their sins, whilst kneeling in the urinal at the altar of a revealed groin. On intimate terms with the filthiness of the night, the 'inverts' are unrelated to those 'clean races' which vigilantly police the distinction between the day and night 'for fear of indignities'.[14] However, while it is dangerous to exhibit one's desires at night in the teeming 'circular cottages',[15] equally perilous is a repression of all knowledge of the night and what it represents. Such a denial leaves one exposed to the night's revengeful return in the shape of a nightmare, a lover's treachery, or a sudden outburst of frenzied killing. O'Connor warns his visitor, Nora, to beware of her sleeping lover: 'When she sleeps is she not moving her leg aside for an unknown garrison? Or in a moment, that takes but a second, murdering us with an axe? Eating our ear in a pie, pushing us aside with the back of her hand, sailing to some port with a ship full of sailors and medical men?'[16] Even those who would never have to confess to associating with damned 'inverts' awake from disgusting nocturnal orgies, panicked and sweating, undeniably guilty of filthy deeds, without any possibility of reprieve: 'We wake from our doings in a deep sweat for that they happened in a house without an address, in a street in no town, citizened with people with no names with which to deny them'.[17]

A rare exception to the general refusal to countenance the night's truths is, O'Connor suggests, the French. Unlike the other 'clean races', the French have not tried to banish the night:

> The French have made a detour of filthiness – Oh, the good dirt! Whereas you [an American] are of a clean race, of a too eagerly washing people, and

> this leaves no road for you. The brawl of the Beast leaves a path for the Beast. You wash your brawl with every thought, with every gesture, with every conceivable emollient and savon, and expect to find your way again. A Frenchman makes a navigable hour with a tuft of hair, a wrenched *bretelle*, a rumpled bed … Be as the Frenchman … he can trace himself back by his sediment, vegetable and animal.[18]

Able to sniff the reeking scent which leads him back home after his nocutral debauchery,[19] the Frenchman has breached the conventional dichotomy between day and night, the mind and the body. Once the night is allowed to flood back in to bastardize the purity of the day, other distinctions inevitably tumble: the human can no longer hold on to its autonomy, but is concatenated with the vegetable and animal.[20] This leads to monstrous becomings, deemed by day's policemen to indicate the presence of the most noxious and 'evil spirits of modernity'.

Published in 1936, Barnes's book clairvoyantly senses the fate of her nomadic characters – queers, Jews, crossdressers and transsexuals – as they drift from one European capital city to another looking for solace. Back in the 1920s the bell was already beginning to toll ominously. For instance, in 1920 Thomas Wehrling wrote an article entitled 'Berlin is Becoming a Whore', a damning indictment of cosmopolitan nightlife. According to Wehrling, the population of Berlin has mutated into a degenerate race, sexually insatiable, gorging itself on the veneer of the modern. Indeed, Wehrling attributes urban decay to the effects of technological modernity; to blame are the cinema and glossy magazines, which unceasingly churn out luxurious image after image for drooling consumption, and the high-speed railway network which spreads the corrosive disease from city to city, disdaining the 'natural' borders between nation states. Wehrling also points to the debilitating effect the First World War had on the race stock:

> How to explain the overrunning of Berlin by whores?
> It appeared in every Western city as a result of the long period of war. The men had been gone four or even five years. An oversupply of females confronted a very sporadic demand. The competition for the men remaining behind slackened the females' reserve. The men, however, who remained here were not the most manly but the craftiest and the most corrupt, people who were accustomed to profiteering and getting what they wanted for a price. It is obvious that the profiteers who had no time to enlist and take part in the fighting ended up trafficking in women as well.[21]

Once the position of the 'most manly' men is usurped by their weaker but more insidious counterparts, the female species too becomes infected. 'Sexual chaos' is disseminated as women 'forget how to have a destiny', by artificially circumventing natural laws with 'anti-impregnation devices'. No longer obliged to carry the weighty consequences of the sexual act, women become frivolous and debauched. This degeneration is a sign of modern times 'like champagne guzzling and warm baths'.[22]

Yesterday's world view, the 'Prussian-Kantian social order' with its strong sense of incontrovertible duty and moral values, has collapsed. It has been replaced by a 'dissolute nihilism' which spreads an amorphous immorality throughout the classes. Women are particularly prone to such slovenly dissolution as by nature they require the shaping force of a virile man to protect them from themselves: 'Woman, however forms herself according to the will of man ... An overwhelming majority ... vacillates between whoredom and motherhood. If a fortunate fate smiles upon her so that such a vacillating creature acquires the strong, shaping love of an unspoiled man, then motherhood will release her from the drive to prostitution'.[23] Hence, for Wehrling, nihilism represents the overturning of essential(ist) values deemed to be natural – the mothering instincts of females, the sustaining 'force' and 'courage' of males.

As is well known, fascism presents itself as confronting such apparent moral and social dissolution with a *rappel à l'ordre*, a restitution of those values needed to put the body politic back into shape. In *Friedrich Nietzsche and the German Future* (1935) Richard Oehler affirms that, disgusted with the decadence of the 1920s, one fundamental current now flows through Germany, a yearning for 'unity of thinking, feeling and wishing'. Nietzsche and his celebration of 'something perfect, wholly achieved [*zu-Ende-Geratenes*], happy, mighty, triumphant, something still capable of arousing fear' is seen as anticipating national socialism and its recognition of the need for rigorous discipline and the elimination of the imperfect, of that which is still becoming, transitioning or in transit.[24] However, Germany itself is also still becoming. Indeed Nietzsche is quoted as stating that: 'The Germans are not yet anything, they are becoming something.'[25] But, thanks to the new regime, the end to this process is clearly in sight. Germany's essence is gradually and inevitably revealing itself. Drawing on the values of 'healthy nature', the acquisitions of the past and those of the present, new life orientated towards the future will be able to germinate.[26] This 'new life' *is* the essence of Germany – Germany is becoming what it essentially is.

As a consequence it is evident for Oehler that national socialism and nihilism are polar opposites, encapsulating the difference between that which is constructive and that which is destructive; the affirmative and the negative; the way upwards and the way downwards. Oehler embraces both Hitler and Nietzsche as providing Germany with the right solution for a robust politics of life: 'Nietzsche, like Hitler, sees that the only way to escape from the destructive will of nihilism is to be found in the renewal, the sharpening and new creation of healthy values, drawn from the original fount of large nature [*der gesunden aus dem Urborn der groen Natur geschöpften Werte*].[27] Nazism reinvigorates the past ('renewal') by combining its legacy with the dynamic forces of the present. Such a productive unification imitates the activity of nature which at once provides continuity and the resources for creative adaptation to the new. However, it remains to be shown how such an adaptation is not just a restrictive reading of Nietzsche but is also reactive, i.e. ultimately weak. This will be demonstrated in the light of the night, of nazism's refusal to think the nocturnal world and the monstrous becomings it provides cover for, as experienced by Barnes's O'Connor and other 'inverts'.

In 'Around the Gedächtniskirche' (1928) Goebbels inveighs against the 'thousands and thousands of electric lights [which] spew illumination into the grey evening, so that brightness covers the Kurfürstendamm, as if by day'. Berlin at night is as densely populated as during the day. However, those found in its bars and parading its boulevards are strangely transformed in the glare of its unnatural and artificial brilliance:

> Harlots smile from the artful pastels of fashionable women's faces; so-called men stroll to and fro, monocles glinting; and precious stones sparkle … All the languages of the world fall on the ear … There is the snobby flâneur in a fur coat and patent leather; the worldly lady, *garçon* from head to toe with a monocle and smoking cigarette, taps on high heels across its walkways, disappears into one of the thousands of abodes of delirium and drugs that cast their screaming lights seductively into the evening air.[28]

Goebbels notes a rupture with the traditions of the past as the Gedächtniskirche sticks out anachronistically, forgotten above the din of the modern metropolis. Cut off in this way from the riches of the past, this world is doomed not to survive. It greedily feasts off a pseudoculture (*Scheinkultur*), one which is not rooted in the traditions of the past and which cannot be grafted onto the 'original fount' of nature. As such, Berlin's nocturnal life teems with ultimately unsustainable life forms: 'The eternal repetition of corruption and decay, of failing ingenuity and genuine creative power, of inner emptiness and despair, with the patina of a Zeitgeist sunk to the level of the most repulsive pseudoculture: that is what parades its essence, what does its mischief around the Gedächtniskirche.'[29] The essence of these life forms, what they really are, is their transience. They represent a dissipation of all economical industry (all 'diligence' is feverishly 'squandered' in the city's bars, brothels and casinos). They cannot and are not to be saved as they do not conserve their energies but expend profligately.

Goebbels heralds the redemptive return of the day: 'The other Berlin is lurking, ready to pounce. A few thousand are working days and nights on end so that sometime the day will arrive. And this day will demolish the abodes of corruption around the Gedächtniskirche; it will transform them and give them over to a risen people. The day of judgement! It will be the day of freedom!'[30] The return to the normality of the day marks a purging of 'inverts', those whose habitation of the night turns the social order with its 'natural' binaries upside down and inside out. Day will no longer be made out of night, instead the natural separation between daylight and night will be reinstated. Once people stop using the night to prowl around and again start using it to sleep in, the health of the nation will be returned. When that happens, those unsightly nocturnal chimeras, the monocled *garçons* and the bejewelled 'so-called men', will be exposed to the glare of the day of judgment.

The other Nietzsche, the one who can be wrested from the arms of Oehler and his fellow ideologues, Goebbels and Wehrling, reads the nocturnal world of the inverts differently. Running counter to the nazi celebration of unity – Oehler's 'unity of thinking, feeling and wishing' – Nietzsche extols the benefits of all that encourages proliferation and variation:

> the weaker presses to the stronger from a need for nourishment; it wants to get under it, if possible to become one with it. The stronger, on the contrary, drives others away; it does not want to perish in this manner; it grows and in growing it splits itself into two or more parts. The greater the impulse toward unity (*Drang zur Einheit*), the more firmly may one conclude that weakness is present; the greater the impulse towards variety, differentiation, inner decay, the more force is present.[31]

Here Nietzsche is far from associating unity, a consolidated sense of identity, with strength. Strength is the exuberant expenditure of energy, not its retentive hoarding in the attempt to shore up the limits of a limited concept of what one is. Such anality whiffs of a defensive 'small-people' mentality intent on wasting their efforts on penny-pinching savings: 'the smell of the distress and overcrowding of small people'.[32] Paradoxically, such petty savings do not accumulate into a long-term investment in sociopolitical security, but rather precipitate a general cultural slide into nihilism. This situation arises because the fetishization of 'unity', along with the categories 'aim/purpose' (*Zweck*) and being (*Sein*), devalue *this* chaotic world of dispersed becoming in the name of a truer and more perfect world elsewhere. Once the self-deceptive uselesssness of such metaphysical thinking becomes clear, a potentially crushing sense of the waste (*Vergeudung*) of one's effort makes itself felt.[33] Rather than plunging into the process of becoming and even enjoying that process as an adventure into the unknown, the mean-minded, small (and ultimately weak) ideologue has tried to ride becoming, strapping an end to its back, trying to direct it to a definite destination, decided upon in advance. Once the awareness dawns that there is perhaps nowhere else to go, nothing else to get at, that becoming maybe has no overreaching principle infusing it with a unifying meaning: a debilitating feeling of futility overwhelms the exhausted toiler. Not having reached a final state of being which would in his eyes redeem him from the drawn-out processes of becoming, he can only perceive everything to have been in vain. He suffers the torture of the '*Umsonst*'. In contrast to such waste (*Vergeudung*), Nietzsche affirms a different sort of waste, that of '*Verschwendung*'.[34] Whereas the first type of waste is a squandering or dissipation of possibility in the sense of a frittering away, the second is a lavish or extravagant (*verschwenderisch*) wastefulness which explores diverse avenues of experience and outlets of energy, unafraid of coming up against dead ends or going round detours.[35]

Wehrling and Goebbels had very clear ideas about what 'dead end' outlets of energy might be. They were the homosexual relations between 'so-called men', the promiscuity of the *garçons* and the 'whorish' behaviour of women generally who diverted their sexual relations away from any inevitable reproductive outcome. All these types do not live reproductive biology as destiny. For fascist theorists, reproduction should be the guiding principle informing sexual relations as it shores up the 'essential' difference between men and women and marginalizes the un(re)productive. To mark the difference between this line in thought and Nietzsche's, we would have to understand pregnancy differently: no longer posited as a teleological end (*Zweck*), pregnancy, for Nietzsche, would have to be regarded as an event which takes one by surprise. It would have to be something which prepares itself in the deepest recesses of the person and suddenly *springs forth*, announcing itself in its 'ultimate perfection'.[36] It could not be scrupulously planned for in advance. Even if it is an event which overtakes one unexpectedly, it is to be assumed, a fate to be loved. The Nietzschean should be able to affirm: 'I do not want in the least that anything should become different than it is. I myself do not want to become different'. And an 'overflowing freshness and cheerfulness' is to accompany such an affirmation.[37]

Sometimes one could get a bit down about Nietzsche's insistence on cheerfulness and joyfulness. A bleak contrast to his world of sunshine and mountains is the desperate urban tangle of *Nightwood*, full of unhappy characters, searching hopelessly for their obscure object of desire. However, Nietzsche is not just a self-satisfied propagandist, content to broadcast his *je ne regrette rien* refrain. His idea of 'continual self-overcoming'[38] does allow a thinking of unhappiness which can still be coupled with an affirmative conception of becoming. We do not have to be happy. Becoming miserable is all right too. Nietzsche protests too insistently in *Ecce Homo* that there is 'no ripple of desire' on the calm sea of his future. Elsewhere he does reveal that a certain restless striving is inevitable when one's self is not to be found within one, as something essential and intrinsic to be unfurled as a teleological principle, but is rather placed out of immediate reach: 'for your true nature lies, not concealed deep in you, but immeasurably high above you, or at least above that which you usually take yourself to be'.[39] Any cheerfulness one might eventually find oneself enjoying, though this cannot be counted on, is the fortuitous result of a gruelling stretching of one's self in order to become oneself: 'For cheerfulness – or in my own language, the gay science – is a reward: the reward of a long, brave, industrious and subterranean seriousness, of which, to be sure, not everybody is capable'.[40] What is important is not to give up, not to resign oneself, not to compromise.[41] Much energy is needed to fuel becoming. It is a process, an action, an 'invention, a willing self-denial, overcoming of self' about which there is no mention of any guarantee of some eventual happiness.[42] Nietzsche's positive take on waste as *Verschwendung*, sickness, lack and degeneration (*Entartung*) – the buzz word for nazi purification zealots – as stimulants,[43] allows us to celebrate unhappiness and failure just as much as exuberant joyfulness, fresh mountain air, sunshine and southern cuisine. Something can still be said for northern gloom.

In *Nightwood* O'Connor compares degenerated ducks in a city park, unable to migrate to the sunny south, to the human animal's gorging itself on love's sickness:

that's why you are where you are now, right down in the mud without a feather to fly with, like the ducks in Golden Gate park – the largest park in captivity – everybody with their damnable kindness having fed them all the year round to their ruin because when it comes time for their flight south they are all a bitter consternation, being too fat and heavy to rise off the water, and, my God, how they flop and struggle all over the park in autumn, crying and tearing their hair out because their nature is weighed down with bread and their migration stopped, by crumbs. You wring your hands to see it, and that's another illustration of love; in the end you are too heavy to move with greediness in your stomach.[44]

When Nietzsche raves about parties and festivals in *The Will to Power*, he celebrates their appeal to a 'divine saying of Yes to oneself, out of animal fullness and completeness'.[45] O'Connor's image of grotesquely obese city ducks, their stomachs bursting with swollen-up chunks of bread, is probably not quite what Nietzsche had in mind by 'animal fullness' with its 'excess and overflow of blooming physicality'.[46] There is also too much *ressentiment* in their 'bitter consternation'. However, even such miserable, degenerate creatures at least lived their gluttony to the full, to the extent of morphing their otherwise streamlined bodies into monstrously distended shapes – testimonies to their insatiable desire for more. Even if the result of their appetite is a lack of flight, an evolutionary *faux pas*, Nietzsche points out the circuitous possibilities of such degeneration:[47]

> rarely is a degeneration, a mutilation, a vice and physical or moral damage in general without an advantage in some other direction. The more sickly man, for example, will, if he belongs to a warlike and restless race perhaps have more inducement to stay by himself and thereby acquire more repose and wisdom, the one-eyed will have *one* stronger eye, the blind will see more deeply within themselves and in any event possess sharper hearing.[48]

Equally, Zarathustra tells the cripples and hunchbacks, who crowd around him in eager anticipation of a remedy for their disabilities, that they need no redemption from the eye, ear or leg they lack. Such a deficiency can create its own sorts of compensation, whereas a lacking of everything bar one thing (of which one has too much) flags up a debilitating attempt to concentrate the organism. Overcultivating, for instance, the head, in a misguided attempt to consolidate, squeeze, the organism into an essence leads to the fragmentation of life:[49] Zarathustra describes his horror at seeing such unificatory fanatics who are just one ear, or one face, mere bits of humanity, parading themselves around him, full of themselves, too full of their one full characteristic.[50]

The bloated, flightless ducks condemned to remain in the northern hemisphere, to become a different sort of bird addicted to city bread, are equated with the unhappy 'inverts'' craving for love. These 'so-called' men and women, or those who are simultaneously both or neither (like Barnes's character 'Frau Mann'[51]), are lacking that which they need to be whole – whether this is to come in the shape of a complementary organ (Matthew O'Connor's yearning for a huge, fertile womb) or companion. This deficiency drives them to take part in debasing situations which aggravate their unhappiness and sense of crushing solitude. However, this inability to be 'something perfect, wholly achieved' (a *Zu Ende Geratenes*') means they become new life forms. Those that scour the nights, drinking 'at the hole of the damned' in the name of a 'god' called love, are like weirdly animated partial objects. Speaking of his 'fellow' creatures, O'Connor describes them and their malady in the following way: 'if one gave birth to a heart on a plate, it would say "love" and twitch like the lopped leg of a frog'.[52] Detached from the organism, limbs and organs are not usually fit enough to survive. However, despite the odds stacked against them, these remnants of life – incomplete, imperfect, isolated, unhappy – twitch and croak. Their radically pared-down state is a sign of the intensity of the emotion which electrifies them and is comparable to the stuffed, partial immobility of the greedy ducks and their love of bread.

For Nietzsche, the strong, vital emotion which is love does not differentiate between humans and animals, calling on both in similar ways.[53] Courtship, sexual attraction and activity feeds the invention of new, resourceful, beautiful, playful, devious pathways to attain the orgasmic goal. Nietzsche describes such alimentary emotion as 'a fever which has reasons to transfigure itself, an intoxication'.[54] It apparently makes one seem 'stronger, richer, more complete'.[55] This evocation of a certain animal plenitude, arising from a creative vigour and 'levity',[56] sits uneasily with the 'inverts'' sad experience of the degrading and debilitating search for love. Once again Nietzsche appears far too positive, far too full of exuberant (southern) sensuality – celebrating 'eternal youth and springtime'[57] – to contribute much to our concerns with the bleak decadence of 1930s metropolitan life. However, he does associate love with art and muscular activity and, as we will see, this may offer us the possibility of a reconciliation of sorts.

The radically pared-down state, intensely charged, which characterizes our 'inverts'-in-love, is a reorientation of life around the strength of cartilage and muscle.[58] The lopped-off leg of a frog and the gasping heart, untimely ripped from its protective cage, use their muscles heroically to express their grim love (of life). O'Connor recognizes the truth which is thereby graphically demonstrated by stating: 'We are but skin about a wind, with muscles clenched against mortality'.[59] As Nietzsche was aware, nature is downright stingy with her gifts, not bestowing us with much organically or genetically when it comes down to it.[60] Clinging to what little we have, making the most of it, we assume our destiny in the face of our own death. For another of Barnes's characters, the Jew 'Baron' Felix, this struggle for survival is peculiarly modern: 'The modern child has nothing left to hold to, or to put it better, he has nothing to hold with. We are adhering to life now with our last muscle – the heart'.

O'Connor reacts to 'Baron' Felix's rather apocalyptic proposition in the following fashion: 'The last muscle of aristocracy is madness ... the last child born to aristocracy is sometimes an idiot, out of respect – we go up – but we come down ... In the king's bed is always found, just before it becomes a museum piece, the droppings of the black sheep.'[61] Here O'Connor is toying with the very evolutionist theories which will be mobilized against him and his fellow 'inverts': his kind, the nocturnal prowlers – the Jews, gays, crossdressers and transsexuals – who are always either going elsewhere or becoming something else (or both), will be deemed to be unfit, doomed to extinction by the nazis. However, as 'Baron' Felix points out, these love-sick 'inverts' have scaled their organic reliance down to one last muscle, the heart. No longer just an organ and in any case completely detached from the organized system of the organism, the heart is treated as a powerful muscle with which to grip onto life.

In *The Will to Power* Nietzsche is very aware of the importance of 'muscle work'.[62] Both art and love, art having an 'organic function' in lovemaking, tune and tone the muscles.[63] The lover, whether happy or unhappy, is intoxicated with a fever which aggravates his/her capacities. Despite being stripped down to the muscular, the lover is richer than s/he who does not love.[64] The empowered muscles emit highly charged shock waves which provoke 'vascular changes' as well as affecting the appearance and psychological make-up of the lover.

> In animals this condition produces new weapons, pigments, colors, and forms; above all, new movements, new rhythms, new love calls and seductions. It is no different with man. His whole economy is richer than before, more powerful, more complete than in those who do not love. The lover becomes a squanderer: he is rich enough for it. Now he dares, becomes an adventurer, becomes an ass in magnanimity and innocence ... and, on the other hand, this happy idiot grows wings and new capabilities, and even the door of art is opened to him.[65]

The lover becomes an extravagant (*Verschwender*): energy is ostentatiously wasted – elaborately preparing one's plummage for fortuitous encounters, loitering long hours in darkened streets on the offchance – but s/he is nevertheless not depleted. Being fully geared up for love, more and more resources are galvanized into activity. The lover is mad, volatile, dangerously obsessive, reckless.

The strength of such a total mobilization can be acutely sensed in relation to Barnes's 'inverts' in ways which remain unexplored by Nietzsche, hampered as he is by rather stereotypical assumptions about sexual difference. For Nietzsche, art awakens and perpetuates an 'aphrodisiac bliss' in humans and animals alike, regardless of sex.[66] However, the creative vigour of the artist is equated with the biological male of the species. 'Semen is pumped into his blood' and this arouses the drive for copulation. Nietzsche is also blatantly heterosexual in his assumptions of courting.[67] The force of love would therefore be best illustrated without such a recourse to stock conventional imagery, highly indicative as it is of a specific and restrictive culture. Barnes's eclectic misfits provide us with illustrations which are more evocative of the potential released by such a drive.

Barnes's characters straddle the gender divide, disallowing any collapse of the celebration of love into conventional images of man meets woman. Concocting within themselves strange and wondrous hybridities – 'men' with wombs, 'women' with penises and various intersexual combinations – it is not clear what the object or aim (*Zweck*) of their desires actually is.[68] Unharnessed from the reproductive machinery, obscuring the clarity of any sexual orientation (transsexual heterosexuality remains an enigmatic concept), the 'inverts'' self-dedication to love is an invention of something new, not a reinvention of the old tradition.[69] They are in search of something, someone 'that [has] never been made'.[70] Being misfits, outcasts, nomadic thinkers of the night, they are also in touch with their ancient evolutionary past, from which they draw creative sustenance.[71] As O'Connor told us earlier, in relation to that other gourmet of the night, the Frenchman, if one does not foreclose all knowledge of the night's orifices, one can sniffingly 'trace [oneself] back by sediment, vegetable and animal'.[72] Going beyond male and female, beyond human and animal, beyond day and night, the 'inverts'' 'berserk a fearful dimension' as they straddle these divides, wild and crazily reckless like a Norse warrior.[73] O'Connor explains:"'Ah!" exclaimed the doctor. "Let a man lay himself down in the Great Bed and his 'identity' is no longer his own … His distress is wild and anonymous. He sleeps in a Town of Darkness, member of a secret brotherhood. He neither knows himself nor his outriders, he berserks a fearful dimension and dismounts, miraculously, in bed!"'.[74] By entertaining the night one exposes oneself to an unravelling of any identity generated during the day. Devoid of any affiliations, the characters in *Nightwood* – adrift in the nocturnal jungle – are like a furious Norse warrior, who is unarmoured, highly vulnerable, yet still bares himself to adversaries, dressed in his flimsy shirt.[75] Such a prospect is frightening, threatening a nihilistic overturning of values, a conflagration of traditional categories.

Nietzsche associates nihilism with a devaluation of the highest values and a lack of aim. Uncoupled from its 'because', 'why' remains a plaintive, unanswered question.[76] Becoming has to assume itself, its own necessity, whether it can generate a justification for its aimless processes or not. Nietzsche explains that 'necessity' can not come: 'in the shape of an overreaching, dominating total force, or that of a prime mover, even less as a necessary condition for something valuable. To this end it is necessary to deny a total consciousness of becoming, a "God"'.[77] However, also in *The Will to Power*, in a section already partially cited above concerning lovers and art, Nietzsche writes: 'The lover becomes a squanderer: he is rich enough for it. Now he dares, becomes an adventurer, becomes an ass in magnanimity and innocence; he believes in God again, he believes in virtue, because he believes in love; and on the other hand, this happy idiot grows wings and new capabilities, and even the door of art is opened to him'.[78] Here Nietzsche suggests that a certain reinvention of a divinity accompanies the wild facultative enfranchisement which is love. It remains for us to see what sort of god is conjured up by 'inverts' and what sort of nihilists that makes them.

Banished from the daylight, 'inverts' frequent the bars and *pissoirs* under the cover of night. On all fours and 'crying between tongues', they at once blaspheme against religion and yet invoke the gods out of a desperate need to confess.[79] However, those who inevitably violate categories, who necessarily elude contractual attempts to name and organize,[80] cannot be redeemed – or, indeed, ultimately condemned. Robin, the boyish lesbian in Barnes's novel, illustrates this point: 'She prayed, and her prayer was monstrous, because in it there was no margin left for damnation or forgiveness, for praise or for blame – those who cannot conceive a bargain cannot be saved or damned'.[81] No contract can be drawn up with them because there is no margin for negotiation. 'The Bible lies one way, but the night gown the other. The night, "Beware of that dark door!"'[82]

Exposure to the dissolution of the night – which undoes identities and certainties, releasing a process of becoming which has no end in sight – cancels out any possibility of joining the orthodox religious community. Religion is an attempt 'to dress [...] the unknowable in the garments of the known'.[83] Such an attempt is doomed to failure if one can no longer deny the lessons of the night. Whilst Wehrling and Goebbels try to reinstate daytime vigilance over the metropole, in the name of essentialist values designed to police human bodies and their functions, the 'inverts' are already becoming monstrous. The 'inverts'' prayer is 'monstrous' because it is an outward expression of the seething new shapes and forms proliferating within them. They are like flightless ducks bursting with bread; like the twitching amputated limbs of frogs; like a croaking heart on a plate: these analogies scarcely permit us to imagine what they might become. For the reactive purists, blind to the reinvigorating potentialities of deficiency or degeneration, they are just evil spirits to be exorcised. Their inversion of norms turns the knowable world upside down: angels become groin-sucking and -licking beasts on all fours in the urinals and gods are transformed into dogs.

O'Connor wisely notes that the lesbians, Nora and Robin, will always be bound together by a dog: 'Nora will leave that girl some day; but though those two are buried at opposite end of the earth, one dog will find them both.'[84] Nora and Robin do not share the ownership of a dog, do not possess a dog in common. Therefore this is not a mere question of a cherished pet dog. Rather, a dog is the only kind of god an invert may conjure up and this animal is not simply different from or identical to him/herself.[85] The animal is an expression of the pared-down muscular strength within and a manifestation of the monstrous processes s/he is undergoing. Whereas evil

spirits initially impinge from outside, the invert's 'possession' described by
Barnes is monstrous welling up from within. Instead of just reacting and
adapting to outer circumstances, they possess 'monstrous (*ungeheure*)
shaping, form-creating power'.[86] They 'berserk a fearful dimension' as they
let out the monstrous energy generated by their becoming animal, by their
unhappy yet affirmative, nihilistic becoming what they are.[87] Accordingly,
Barnes terminates her novel in the following guise:

> On a contrived altar, before a Madonna, two candles were burning. Their
> light fell across the floor and the dusty benches. Before the image lay flow-
> ers and toys. Standing before them in her boy's trousers was Robin ... Slid-
> ing down she went; down, her hair swinging, her arms held out, and the dog
> stood there, rearing back, his forelegs slanting; his paws trembling under the
> trembling of his rump, his hackle standing; his mouth open, his tongue slung
> sideways over his sharp bright teeth; whining and waiting. And down she
> went, until her head swung against his; on all fours now, dragging her knees.
> The veins stood out in her neck, under her ears, swelled in her arms, and
> wide and throbbing rose up on her fingers as she moved forward ... Then
> she began to bark also, crawling after him- barking in a fit of laughter,
> obscene and touching ... and the dog too gave up then, and lay down, his
> eyes bloodshot, his head flat along her knees.[88]

Notes

1 Djuna Barnes, *Nightwood* (London: Faber & Faber, 1985) p. 138.

2 Ibid., p. 132.

3 See S. Stone, 'A Posttranssexual Manifesto', in *Body Guards*, ed. J Epsten and K.
Straub (London: Routledge, 1991) pp. 280–304, for an interesting analysis of transsexual autobiography and the question of legibility. See also D. Beddoes, 'Deleuze,
Kant and Indifference', in *Deleuze and Philosophy: The Difference Engineer* (London: Routledge, 1997) pp. 25–43, for a more recent reading of transsexuality's potential for destabilizing the opposition 'being' versus 'becoming' in relation to
Deleuzian thought. Whilst Beddoes's contribution to transgender theory is not
claiming to be anything more than modest, she does seem to run the risk of turning
transsexuals into a mere convenient metaphor for things Deleuzian (they are 'implicated in the continual invention of a body', their bodies 'machinated by desire' (Beddoes, *Deleuze*, pp. 39–40)). This chapter is partly motivated by a wish to reinflect the
'debate' around transsexuality back to pain, unhappiness and isolation in an attempt
to break with an all too privileged and euphoric celebration of 'becomings' and the
assemblage of 'bits and pieces, partial objects' (Beddoes ibid.). 'Becomings' should
not be naively affirmed; behind them there is a history of suffering – hence my interest in this chapter in Nazi death camps – which requires recognition. Further current work which engages with transsexuality and autopoetic/retroactive transcoding
can be found in K. More's 'Limitropic Hegemony and the Third Sex' in *Radical
Deviance* 3:1 (1999).

4 F. Nietzsche, *On the Genealogy of Morals and Ecce Homo*, trans. W. Kaufmann (New
York: Vintage, 1989) p. 215.

5 F. Nietzsche, *Untimely Meditations*, trans. R. J. Hollingdale (Cambridge: Cambridge University Press, 1987) p. 155.
6 Ibid.
7 Barnes, *Nightwood*, pp. 132–3.
8 On the false opposition between being and becoming, see G. Simondon, 'The Genesis of the Individual', in *Incorporations*, ed. J. Crary and S. Kwinter (London: Routledge, 1992) pp. 297–319.
9 Barnes, *Nightwood*, p. 138.
10 Compare with F. Nietzsche, *The Will to Power*, trans. W. Kaufmann (New York: Vintage, 1968) p. 503, §958: 'I write for a species of human that does not yet exist'.
11 Barnes, *Nightwood*, p. 116.
12 Ibid., p. 139.
13 Ibid., pp. 136–8.
14 Ibid., p. 124.
15 O'Connor says that encounters in the 'circular cottages' have brought him to 'great argument' (Ibid., p. 133).
16 Ibid., p. 128.
17 Ibid.
18 Ibid., pp. 123–4.
19 The French are therefore animals, as 'animals find their way about largely by the keenness of their nose' (ibid., p. 171).
20 Hence the concluding scene of the novel, discussed at the end of this chapter, where Robin couples in a monstrous fashion with a dog.
21 Wehrling, 'Berlin is becoming a Whore,' in *The Weimar Republic Sourcebook* (Berkeley and Los Angeles: University of California Press, 1994) p. 722.
22 Ibid.
23 Ibid.
24 R. Oehler, *Friedrich Nietzsche und die deutsche Zukunfte* (Leipzig: Urmanen Verlag, 1935) p. 7.
25 Nietzsche, *Genealogy*, p. 44.
26 Ibid., p. 17.
27 Ibid., p. 18.
28 J. Goebbels, 'Around Gedachtniskirche', in *The Weimar Republic Sourcebook*, p. 561.
29 Ibid.
30 Ibid.
31 Nietzsche, *Will*, p. 346, §655.
32 F. Nietzsche, *The Gay Science*, trans. W. Kaufmann (New York: Vintage, 1974) p. 292, §349.
33 Nietzsche, *Will*, p. 12, §12.
33 Nietzsche, *Gay*, p. 292, §349.
34 See Nietzsche on furtive paths (*chleichwege*) in Nietzsche, *Genealogy*, p. 255.
35 Ibid.
36 Ibid., p. 258.
37 Ibid., p. 233.
39 Nietzsche, *Untimely*, p. 129.
40 Nietzsche, *Genealogy*, p. 21.
41 See Nietzsche, *Will*, p. 550, §1067: 'no satiety, no disgust, no weariness'.
42 Ibid., pp. 330–1, §617.
43 Ibid., pp. 343–4, §647.

44 Barnes, *Nightwood*, p. 226.

45 Nietzsche, *Will*, p. 484, §916 (translation modified).

46 Ibid., p. 422, §802.

47 For an illuminating analysis of Nietzsche's critique of Darwin's 'survival of the fittest' and his counter-model to any smart strategy of adaptation, see K. Ansell Pearson, *Viroid Life* (London: Routledge, 1997).

48 F. Nietzsche, *Human All Too Human*, trans. R. J. Hollingdale (Cambridge: Cambridge Univrsity Press, 1993) p. 107, §224.

49 As such this is a reiteration of the passage cited above which suggested that unity leads to weakness whereas variety brings strength. See, for instance, Nietzsche, *Will*, p. 346, §655.

50 F. Nietzsche, *Thus Spake Zarathustra*, trans. R. J. Hollingdale (Harmondsworth: Penguin, 1969) pp. 159–60.

51 Frau Mann is described in the following enigmatic way: 'Frau Mann, then in Berlin, explained that this person had been "somewhat mixed up with her in the past". It was with the utmost difficulty that he could imagine her "mixed up" with anyone, her coquetries were muscular and localised ... The stuff of the tights was no longer a covering, it was herself; the span of the tightly-stitched crotch was so much her own flesh that she was as unsexed as a doll. The needle that had made one the property of the child made the other the property of no man' (Barnes, *Nightwood*, pp. 27-8).

52 Ibid., p. 46.

53 Nietzsche, *Will*, pp. 426–7, §808.

54 Ibid.

55 Ibid.

56 Ibid., p. 421, §800.

57 Ibid.

58 Nietzsche espouses the same paring-down to the muscles in Nietzsche, *Will*, p. 421, §800. Such a reorientation is 'simpler' but also 'fuller' and 'stronger'.

59 Barnes, *Nightwood*, p. 122.

60 Nietzsche, *Gay*, p. 267, §267. See Ansell Pearson, *Viroid Life*, p. 19.

61 Barnes, *Nightwood*, p. 63.

62 Nietzsche, *Will*, p. 429, §811.

63 Ibid., p. 426, §808.

64 Ibid., p. 427.

65 Ibid., pp. 426–7, §808.

66 Ibid., p. 425, §805.

67 Ibid., pp. 424–6, §806, 807.

68 For instance O'Connor is described as dressing in female attire in orer 'to lie beside himself' (Barnes, *Nightwood*, p. 118). This ability to generate his/her own complement does not mean that a self-sufficient universe is created. O'Connor still presents a disjunctive picture in his environment, described as – I repeat – 'a cross between a *chambre à coucher* and a boxer's training camp' (ibid., p. 116).

69 As such they respond to the spirit of Nietzsche's sense of the value of becoming: 'Becoming must be explained without recourse to final intentions; becoming must appear justified at every moment (or incapable of being evaluated; which amounts to the same thing); the present must absolutely not be justified by reference to a future, nor the past by reference to the present' (Nietzsche, *Will*, p. 377, §708).

70 Barnes, *Nightwood*, p. 138.

71 For a clear-sighted – but notoriously misrecognized (e.g. by Lacan) and neglected – awareness of the 'ambisexual' invert's contact with 'the origin of life in ... its original, most primitive sense', preceding 'all knowledge of sexual reproduction both in the history of the individual and of mankind', see McAlpine and Hunter's 'Postscripts' to Schreber in D. P. Schreber, *Memoirs of a Nervous Illness*, ed. I. McAlpine and R. Hunter (London: Dawson & Sons, 1955) pp. 378, 394. I briefly discuss McAlpine and Hunter and their significance for transgender thought in relation to psychoanalysis in D. Morgan, '"What Does a Transsexual Want"?; The Encounter between Trans-sexualism and Psychoanalysis' in *Essays on Transsexuality at the Fin de Siècle*, ed. K. More and S. Whittle (London: Cassells, 1999).

72 Barnes, *Nightwood*, p. 124. This combining of a thinking of the new with an evolu-tionary regression into the past is a recognition – often associated with Nietzsche but here expressed by the Jewish 'Baron' Felix – that 'To pay homage to our past is the only gesture that also includes the future' (ibid., p. 63).

73 Compare with Ansell Pearson on 'transhuman desire': 'This is a desire which is not constrained by the need to realise goals, human or otherwise, but is a kind of freeplaying, nomadic singularity which traverses and cuts across the various king-doms of life, serving to render becoming "machinic"'. In K. Ansell-Pearson, 'Life becoming Body', *Cultural Values* 2 (1998): 219–40.

74 Barnes, *Nightwood*, p. 119.

75 See the *Oxford English Dictionary* entries for 'berserk': 'a wild Norse warrior who fought on the battlefield with a frenzied fury known as the "berserker rage"' and the etymologically related 'bare sark': 'bare shirt, in a shirt only, with no armour'.

76 Nietzsche, *Will*, p. 9, §2.

77 Ibid., pp. 377–8, §708.

78 Ibid., p. 427, §808.

79 Barnes, *Nightwood*, p. 138.

80 See Deleuze and Guattari quoted by Ansell Pearson, *Viroid Life*, p. 130: 'You will be organised, you will be an organism, you will articulate your body, otherwise you are just depraved'.

81 Barnes, *Nightwood*, p. 72.

82 Ibid., p. 118.

83 Ibid., p. 193.

84 Ibid., p. 153.

85 See Deleuze and Guattari, *Milles plateaux*, (Paris: Les Editions de Minuit, 1980) p. 289, on the 'correspondence of relationships' between animal and human which is not to be equated with an 'identification' or 'mystical participation'.

86 Nietzsche, *Will*, p. 344, §647 (translation modified).

87 Barnes, *Nightwood*, p. 119. See Nietzsche, *Will*, p. 550, §1067 on the 'monster of energy', and the forthcoming collection *Nihilism Now!: 'Monsters of Energy'*, ed. K. Ansell Pearson and D. Morgan (Basingstoke: Macmillan, 1999).

88 Barnes,*Nightwood*, pp. 237–9.

james williams

DELEUZE AND THE THREAT
OF DEMONIC NIHILISM

Philosophy and demonic nihilism

By demonic nihilism I understand a conscious or unconscious submission
to demons leading to nihilism, defined here as a thoroughgoing negation
of will. Nihilism is further defined as the result of a turn away from immanent powers of reason. On this count, the philosophical tradition that
stretches beyond the age of reason, through the enlightenment and on to
modernity is partly defined by a combat against demonic nihilism. The tradition's moments of reflexive critique can be seen as driven by the return
of the demonic and hence of nihilism within philosophy.

At the birth of the age of reason, Descartes banishes the Evil Demon
and Spinoza fights against the demons allowed by our finite imagination
and uncritical acceptance of opinions. Both thinkers champion a more
adequate rational understanding of the world and of what we can know on
the grounds of our own faculties. Later, Kant criticizes this moment as still
prone to illusion and hence to the return to superstition through dogma-
tism, though he fights to continue the work of reason within more clearly
defined boundaries. Nietzsche works against a Kantian nihilism that
comes out of the remnants of religious form and morality in his critique.
These remnants are demonic in the sense that they represent a temptation
to weakness and away from our most life-affirming forces – shockingly,
Christ becomes the demon.

According to Heidegger's reading of Nietzsche, the demonic returns as
the techno-scientific side of reason and as the metaphysical temptation of
philosophy; this too is nihilistic: 'Nietzsche holds this overturning of metaphysics to be the overcoming of metaphysics. But every overturning of this
kind remains only a self-deluding entanglement in the Same that has

become unknowlable.'[1] It would not be fanciful to see Derrida's development of the trope of the ghost and spirits in his later works as a response
to the demonic and nihilistic in Heidegger's thought and as the latest addition to this long tradition of philosophical self-analysis and awareness of
impurity.

Where does Deleuze fit into this rather cursory and reductive history
of ideas? More importantly, does a consideration of his case allow us to
escape the necessarily imprecise and shallow consequences of the general
thesis 'The history of modern philosophy is a dialectical struggle with
nihilism and the eternal and internal return of unreason'? A thesis that is
best left to Goya's economic expression of all its internal contradictions in
his etching with aquatint '*El sueño de la razon produce monstruos*' (The
sleep/dream of reason produces monsters) from *Los Caprichos*?[2]

Demons and nihilism in Deleuze's reading of 'Bartleby'

Owing to his philosophical genealogy, it is easier to come to terms with the
anti-demonic and anti-nihilistic side of Deleuze's philosophy than the contrary. Deleuze comes out of Spinoza, Leibniz, Kant and Nietzsche; out of
immanence, principles of reason, transcendental critique and affirmation.
Four weapons in the struggle against demons and nihilism that, arguably,
he attempts to combine in a new philosophy through his whole career.

With immanence and a rational connection to the infinite, Spinoza banishes the limits of human experience that justify appeals to mysterious
wills beyond our ken (a wilful God, and demons whose subject-like freedom is founded on an illegitimate extension of our own false sense of free
will). With principles of reason, Leibniz ensures that our reason, though
bound by a limited power of perception and hence necessarily creative, is
able to proceed securely. Kant defines the fields through which that
process may unfold as well as the proper method for drawing up those
fields and setting their boundaries. Nietzsche works against the teleological form that the process may take; he side-steps the inherent nihilism of
external goals and conscious identifications in favour of the affirmation of
what is already unconsciously driving us forward from within. Deleuze
is all this and more; he is a philosopher of and for reason as much as any
of his antecedents – but that is not the topic nor the argument of this
chapter.

Instead, despite an opposition to the three most common definitions of
demons put forward in the *Littré* implied by the positions that feed into
Deleuze's philosophy, it can still be argued that his philosophy may fall
prey to a demonic nihilism. This cannot be in the first sense of the good or
bad spirit of 'ancient polytheism', nor in the second sense of anti-angels,

the malign spirits of Christian religion, nor even in the third sense of an actual person who takes pleasure 'in tormenting others'. Each of these is too human in will and in the implied values of good and evil to fit with Deleuze's Spinozism and Nietzschean legacy. The fourth sense, though, fits well: 'The cause of inspiration, of good and bad impulsions. The demon of war, of combats.'[3] Not only does Deleuze advocate that we develop strategies to allow us to be guided by the virtual ideas, that is, the structures of forces that unconsciously set us in motion. He is also aware of the power these ideas, these demons, have in leading to our destruction in nihilism.

In perhaps his longest discussion of the demonic, in 'Bartleby, ou la formule' from *Critique et clinique*, he describes Melville's characters, men singularly driven and defined by their subconscious ideas, as creatures of a will to nothingness or a nothingness of will: 'At one pole, [there are] monomaniacs or demons who raise a monstrous preference, driven by a will to nothingness: Achab, Claggart, Babo … But at the other pole, there are those angels or hypochondriac saints, creatures of innocence and purity, struck down by a constitutive weakness, but also by a strange beauty, petrified by nature and who prefer … no will at all, a nothingness of will (hypochondriac negativism)'.[4] For Deleuze, the demonic here is not in the characters, though this is the word he chooses to use in describing them. It is in their over-developed relation to the demon or impulse that makes them demonic to our eyes and to the other characters in Melville's novels and short stories.

In 'Bartleby', this demon is expressed in the phrase 'I would prefer not to', a phrase that spreads confusion and anger wherever it is uttered, thereby allowing Bartleby to rebel against the new social order. Its nihilism runs counter to the business of the late nineteenth century. The phrase destroys Bartleby because it is allowed to engulf all other activities: 'Strangely huddled at the base of the wall, his knees drawn up, and lying on his side, his head touching the cold stones, I saw the wasted Bartleby. But nothing stirred. I paused; then went close up to him; stooped over, and saw that his dim eyes were open; otherwise he seemed profoundly sleeping. Something prompted me to touch him. I felt his hand, when a tingling shiver ran up my arm and down my spine to my feet.'[5]

Deleuze views Bartleby's life as exemplary in and for itself. It is not to be sublated into a moment of necessary and as yet absent moral or political consciousness, as Melville appears to suggest through his narrator's concluding remarks ('Ah Bartleby! Ah, humanity!') On the contrary, if there is to be humanity, it lies purely in figures such as Bartleby, that is, a humanity of singular existences driven by singular unconscious impulses with no transcendent voice to pull them together and give them a higher worth:

'Schizophrenic vocation: even when catatonic and anorexic, Bartleby is not the patient but the doctor of a sick America, *Medicine-man*, new Christ, or our brother.'[6] If an 'I would prefer not to' or a 'monstrous preference' is the demon that drives a figure to become, then there is no salvation from the Deleuzian demand to experiment with that drive and to allow it to become expressed by mirroring it in our conscious lives. Does this make him but the latest instance of the return of demonic nihilism in philosophy? Perhaps he is the most perverse heir to the tradition yet, in this invitation and affirmation of demons as vehicles of nihilism.

Ideas and becoming

How one becomes what one is. Aphorism 9 of the 'Why I am so clever' chapter of Nietzsche's *Ecce Homo* includes a succinct and precise description of the background to Deleuze's passivity with respect to our demons defined as idealism: 'In the meantime the organizing "idea" destined to rule grows and grows in the depths – it begins to command, it slowly leads *back* from sidepaths and wrong turnings, it prepares *individual* qualities and abilities which will one day prove themselves indispensable as means of achieving the whole – it constructs the *ancillary* capacities one after the other before it gives any hint of the dominating task, of the "goal", "objective", "meaning".'[7] The aphorism plays an important role in *Ecce Homo*. It repeats the subtitle of the book, a problem that Nietzsche has put off from the title page, and that he only now feels prepared to address, if reluctantly ('At this point I can no longer avoid answering the question *how one becomes what one is*').

The delay and reticence can be explained by the paradox in the subtitle and the importance of its resolution for Nietzsche's project. How can one become what one is? 'How I became what I am' satisfies common sense and a straightforward conception of linear time, as does 'How I shall become what I want to be'. But one is what one is and being can only be commented upon in terms of becoming as the end of an historical process or as the starting point for future plans. It is exactly that backwards glance and forward project, however, that Nietzsche wants to ban from any existence in the present. For him, we become badly by looking back and looking forward. Our being is misunderstood as the result of conscious plans – we become passively, and we become well by eschewing the hubris of conscious control over destiny.

But is not this to replace a paradox with a nonsense? Why give such prominence to the explanation of how one becomes what one is, if any acquired knowledge is to be redundant? If Nietzsche's turn away from the philosophical founding consciousness and free will developed in *Beyond*

Good and Evil is to be taken seriously, why does he return to the nurturing of identity in *Ecce Homo*? If projects based on knowledge of the past are detrimental, why should we pay any attention to his techniques of moral and aesthetic 'self-development'? Indeed, section 9 begins with becoming what one is, only to deny this becoming in these closing statements: 'I do not want in the slightest that anything should become other than it is; I do not want to become anything other than what I am.'[8]

The answer to the paradox lies in a distinction between an action that dreams of full possession of a goal and an action that clears the deck for a passive becoming. Nietzsche does not deny that it is possible to act as if out of free will. He denies that such action provides us with a satisfactory ideal to which we should aim, in art or morality. Full self-possession or total control over our destiny are impossible in themselves and should not be taken as limits to which we should tend: 'For assuming that the task, the vocation, the *destiny* of the task exceeds the average measure by a significant degree, there would be no greater danger than to catch oneself *with* this task. That one becomes what one is presupposes that one does not have the remotest idea *what* one is.'[9] So Nietzsche develops a practice avoiding the danger of catching oneself with the task and a theoretical account of the relation between our identity and the unconscious destiny or idea at work within us. To maintain a distance from ourselves, we must turn our attention outside to others and other things.

The theoretical basis for this practice of passive nurturing is in the distinction drawn between something that is grasped by a limited consciousness and an extended and open unconscious idea, that is, a distinction drawn between my understanding of something and that which brings together a disparate set of unconscious drives. According to Nietzsche, the former is incapable of handling the latter without destroying it: 'The entire surface of consciousness – consciousness *is* a surface – has to be kept clear of any of the great imperatives [Know thyself!] ... All of them represent a danger that the instinct will "understand itself" too early.'[10] Conscious understanding, to grasp oneself as an object directly and fully, is a source of destruction. The destructive flaw is that conscious and logical self-knowledge or self-creation seek to eliminate uncertainty and accident – the operation of unconscious drives in Nietzsche's account – in favour of a secure future and a decisive past. So differences must be resolved in favour of the polished whole and any chaotic multiplicity must be organized in reference to this whole. At the very moment where one grasps one's identity and hence one's future, another more valuable future is eliminated.

But any solution to this disaster will not lie in a straightforward avoiding of consciousness and understanding; the simple oppositions of free will and necessity, activity and passivity, are not sufficient for a resistance to the situation. Beyond the opposition of conscious and unconscious ideas, a more complex relation weds the understanding and unconscious drives in a struggle for supremacy as well as an ineluctable interdependence. In the Nietzschean attempt to let the idea work into being, the point is not to adopt a simple passivity of no-will, it is to deploy 'free will' and conscious decisions against their aggrandizement. There is therefore an active form of passivity, aimed at an unconscious becoming. So there has to be a conscious technique for allowing 'multiplicity' to occur in becoming: 'Order of rank among capacities; distance; the art of dividing without making inimical; mixing up nothing, "reconciling" nothing; a tremendous multiplicity which is nonetheless the opposite of chaos – this has been the precondition, the protracted secret labour and artistic working of my instinct. The magnitude of its higher protection was shown in the fact I have at no time had the remotest idea what was growing within me.'[11]

Deleuze's work on ideas expands upon Nietzsche's complex inter-relation of conscious ideas and the unconscious idea by providing a more explicit treatment of the relation of identity and multiplicity. For both thinkers it is appropriate to speak of ideas in a positive manner, despite their critique of them in a psychological sense, since the point is to pick up on a sense of ideas as beyond subject-based designs or plans. Like Nietzsche, Deleuze is interested in the moral and aesthetic role of passivity with respect to the unconscious idea through a critical activity against the conscious idea and ideal. His main philosophical work takes place in the rigorous definition of the unconscious idea as a multiplicity of contradictory virtual capacities – Nietzsche's drives – and in the explanation of how this virtual idea becomes actual. There is a miraculous moment in Nietzsche's account of how one becomes what one is, not so much in terms of what one should do (or not do) but in terms of the event of actualization: 'all my abilities leapt forth suddenly ripe, in their final perfection.' In describing that event rigorously, Deleuze takes away its metaphysical mystery.

But this does not mean that he escapes either the traditional problems of dualism implied by the distinction drawn between the virtual idea and the actual being. Nor does it mean that his position can avoid accusations of a demonic nihilism in the surrender of rational consciousness to an underlying and unquestionable driving force or demon. Is his idealism necessarily dualistic in the negative sense of mystical with respect to a higher realm of ideas? Is it mystical in relation to the realm of the virtual and the actual? Is it nihilistic in its active pursuit of the unconscious ideas, 'the secret labour and artistic working of my instinct'?

Reciprocal determination

Deleuze's idealism is summed up in the thesis of reciprocal determination that *all actual things are determined by ideas, and all ideas are determined by actual things*. As I will show later, what form this determination takes in both cases is all-important, as is the concept of determination for any understanding of the form of Deleuzian argument in *Différence et répétition*. His method is to provide us with the conditions for reality, defined as something both ideal and actual. He seeks to prove that a complete description of an actual thing must include a description of the ideas involved in it as well as the effect that it has on them. This supposes that he can demonstrate that every actual thing has an ideal aspect and that every idea is shaped by actual things, and that these principles – together with a principle regarding completeness – are sufficient for the complete description of any event.

However, a philosophy of becoming requires a rethink of the concept of actual thing and idea, where ideas and actual things cannot be thought of finally in terms of identity. Rather, for Deleuze, an idea is always varying, with no fixed point from whence to plot that variation, and an actual thing must be thought of in relation to varying ideas. So any actual thing is to be thought of in relation to a process of an unconscious genesis rather than an identity defined in terms of a fixed final cause. The types of teleology associated with an active pursuit of a well-defined goal are replaced by a conception of a 'passive' creative process, where the concepts of selection and drawing-up are allowed to occur free of external fixed points. Instead, the reciprocal determination of ideas and actual things becomes the site of creative experimentation and problematics.

The basis for this experimentation and problematics is Deleuze's special definition of the idea. In *Différence et répétition* the unconscious idea is defined as an n-dimensional defined and continuous multiplicity. What this means is that any idea has a set of variables, the number of which defines its dimension, and a set of ratios between the changes of those variables, that is, the continuity of the idea. For example, the idea of the city may be four-dimensional (to limit, to communicate, to divide, to collect). It will be continuous in the way the variables are related to one another (the change in communication is in ratio c/d to the change in division, say). But dimension and continuity alone are not sufficient for the definition of the idea. Deleuze needs to eliminate the possibility of a fixed idea defined in terms of specific identities, as in the case of an ideal city – that is, a representation to which all good cities must tend. He also needs to avoid the limited idea defined in terms of a set of extrinsic categories – that is, an idea that can be subjected to an evaluative judgement. This would be the case of the humane city or ecological city, where humanity and ecology provided norms for the organization of the secondary functions of collection, division and so on.

Therefore, Deleuze puts forward three conditions for the idea defined as a multiplicity:[12]

1 the elements of the multiplicity must have no assignable form, nor conceptual signification, and hence no assignable function
2 the elements must be determined, but only in relation to each other with no place for independence
3 there must be an incarnation of the ratio in terms of an actual spatio-temporal relation, and an incarnation of the elements in terms of actual terms and forms.

The first two points ensure the radical quality of his definition of ideas insofar as the varying elements cannot be thought of as well-defined with respect to a representation of them since they have no assignable form, concept or function. Neither can they be determined in relation to some external source, since any determination is solely a factor of the ratios of their elements. The third condition ensures that the ideas have some relation to actual things by insisting on a spatio-temporal relation and actual terms and forms.

The idea as multiplicity is therefore a special kind of structure insofar as the structural relation holds between variations as opposed to identities and insofar as the relevance of structure with respect to the real is not in terms of an accurate representation or analogy, but in terms of genesis.[13] As we saw earlier, in Nietzsche's account, it is claimed that the idea literally gives rise to the actual whilst evading any possible conception of the idea as well-defined. What is of interest here is the wider philosophical claim that all actual things are in relation to ideas in the Deleuzian sense. Why do such ideas exist (what is a non-conceptual, formless thing)? If they do, why are they necessary conditions for the complete description of actual things? Is there not a contradiction between conditions two and three, since the former describes an immanent determination only then to be superseded by an external determination in terms of actual things? If Deleuze can answer these questions, he has provided us with an argument 'for the necessity of the demonic', as if the ideal demonic thrust in any actual life is something necessary the influence of which we must learn to live with rather than deny.

Nihilism and the absence of justification

In order to answer these questions, it is important to situate Deleuze's study of ideas in *Différence et répétition* so that we may understand the motivation behind his description of the conditions for the idea. The study is given a chapter to itself following chapters on difference and repetition and a critical chapter on models of thought in philosophy. The key conclusions reached at this stage concern an exposition of two fundamental ontological principles: *existence is primarily difference* and *difference is expressed or given specificity through repetition understood as pure variation*. By difference in itself Deleuze understands a differential that needs no reference to identity. Difference is then neither a difference between two things, nor a variation measured in terms of a scale dependent on identities.

Rather, difference must be understood as a differing or varying; for example, a sense impression that registers a change without a comparison of states ('getting hotter', but not 'getting hotter than' or 'getting hotter by this much'). Repetition is then the way in which this differential variation can be given sense and consistency through time and space without having to refer back to identities or extrinsic forms of measurement. Sense comes about with repetition understood as a variation. As key features and ideas are repeated, that is vary, through a series of things, it becomes possible to make sense of the series and to distinguish it from others. The challenge met by the chapter on ideas and a companion chapter on sensibility is to show that the ontological conditions concerning difference and repetition apply to reality. Despite the ontological primacy of difference and repetition are they also conditions for the real? Can we say that reality is primarily difference and repetition?

There has been little critical work on Deleuze's philosophy of ideas, though three of the essays in the recent *Deleuze: a Critical Reader* emphasize the importance of ideas and sketch out the stakes and context of that philosophy very well. This work tends to concentrate on how actual things and ideas are to be related in practice, rather than on any justification of the necessity of the relation. Paul Patton, Constantin Boundas and Daniel Smith situate Deleuze's work in the context of Leibniz, Kant, Maimon and Bergson. They argue that, for Deleuze, the field of ideas is not bounded, in the Kantian sense. Which ideas are legitimate and how to define that legitimacy cannot be answered by Deleuze. Rather, unconscious ideas are to be discovered in an empirical fashion with no limit on which are possible. There is also a redefinition of empiricism as 'transcendental empiricism', that is, as a form of experimentation that allows the conditions for any given actuality to be discovered and in some sense created. It is these problems that are ideal, in the sense that the idea related to any actual thing brings with it a set of ratios or tensions that must be taken account of in any new creation. This move from legitimacy to experimentation and from pure conditions to local ones is again troublesome from the point of view of demonic nihilism, since the anti-dogmatic and anti-mystical potential of the Kantian work on proper limits is abandoned in favour of a given idea that cannot be questioned, but merely re-created.

It is surprising then that in his conclusion, Patton is the first commentator to draw our attention to the positive moral stakes of transcendental empiricism and ideas. Deleuze's transcendental empiricism allows us to discover a deeper moral existence in tune with a more important reality, in the same way as Nietzsche frames the unconscious idea within the moral problem of how to create oneself away from the illusions of consciousness and free will. Patton argues that transcendental empiricism focuses its attention on the event defined as the actualization of unconscious ideas, as opposed to an actual event. For example, that I have been wounded is not important, instead it is a question of what the wound means to me: '[Deleuze] seeks to raise the question of our stance towards the events that befall us ... It is a question of willing the event in such a manner or to such an extent that the quality of the will itself is transformed and becomes affirmation.'[14]

How to be the events that become in us is the moral dimension of Deleuze's philosophy of ideas. But, as Daniel Smith points out, this is as much an aesthetic as a moral question. Ideas are not simply discovered; instead they appear through the way in which we create works (of art, or ourselves as works of art). Thus, in transcendental empiricism the sense of experiment is less that of a test of a theory than an all-engrossing and risky way of probing into the unknown.[15] This is why Deleuze develops his philosophy of ideas within the relation of ideal problems and questions that bring about relative solutions to those problems as opposed to the relation of hypotheses to apodeictic answers: 'the movement goes not from the hypothetical to the apodeictic but from the problematic to the question'[16] For example, for Nietzsche the problem of being is already partially resolved by the special paradoxical question about how one becomes what one is.

But Smith and Patton miss the nihilistic and destructive power of this move away from a more defensive critical work of reason. It may be the case that in this work reason falls prey to an illusion about the primary role of ideas in the genesis of actual things, but this does not mean that working with such an illusion is not a desirable or even a necessary condition for ethics and life. It may be better to assign limits to the experimentation with demons on the grounds of the terminal state this experimentation may leave us in: '"I prefer not to dine to-day," said Bartleby turning away. "It would disagree with me; I am unused to dinners." So saying, he slowly moved to the other side of the inclosure, and took up a position fronting the dead-wall.'[17]

Patton and Smith describe the opposition between ideas and concepts and the way in which these ideas are revealed in art or events, but they do not explain why such ideas are necessary for a valid ethics. They do not give an account of the Deleuzian equivalent to the Kantian transcendental deduction. There is an opposition between two senses of method, here. On the one hand, there is the sense of method as how a philosophy can be applied to a set of problems or fields. On the other hand, there is the sense of method as the argument for the validity of a philosophy. Thus, although Kant uses a transcendental deduction to prove the validity of the pure concepts of the understanding, this is not the logical method used by the understanding in judging the coherence of a concept. Yet in the case of Deleuze scholarship the two are often confused. There has been much work of pure exegesis on his philosophy; this is only natural for a recent philosophy that has put into play a great number of timely and original concepts. But the validity of the philosophy tends to be deduced from its influence or from the contrast drawn with philosophies taken to be mistaken in some practical sense.

This has been taken to be an argument in itself in the sense where a possible test of a concept is its application. Indeed, at times Deleuze appears to argue that it is simply the effect of a philosophical concept or work of art that counts towards its desirability over another. Thus, the 'preferable' concept is one that allows for an extension of thought into new fields as well as an intensification of our sensations associated with a given field. The same would be true of a work of art. We ask: 'What new sensations come into play?' and 'How strong is each individual sensation captured in the work?'[18] But this argument is doubly unsatisfactory on its own terms. First, it is viciously circular, since when we ask why extension and intensification are the criteria for 'preferring' concepts or works of art we must turn back to the nature of these works, defined in terms of ideas. But it was exactly because we needed an argument for the validity of the philosophy of ideas that we turned to the criteria of extension and intensity. Second, the boundaries for the definition of extension and intensity are not set in such a way as to allow us to assess whether a particular concept or work offers a complete or coherent expression of fields and sensations. Are there less and more productive extensions of a field? What effect do these have on the intensity of sensations? For example, it could be the case that a philosophy allows for a very productive interaction of a theory of human nature and ethics, but this could be at the cost of ignorance in the field of empirical psychology. A work of art may express love with great intensity, but this could be at the cost of reducing any sensation of sexual desire. How can we respond to these questions without falling back into the circle of expecting them to be resolved by some kind of subjective reaction?

Jean-Michel Salanskis makes a similar point against Deleuze, accusing him of adopting a 'genetico-metaphysical' naturalization,[19] a form of naturalist discourse interested in the objective description of ideas as part of a natural process. This, according to Salanskis, explains why Deleuze avoids any reference to the 'destination' of ideas – that is, that they are addressed to us and that we must interpret them as forms of communication that want something from us. It also explains why Deleuze refuses the 'Kantian juridical problematic' where we attempt to formulate a priori conditions by which an idea can be said to be well-formed, since this 'is in no way an explanation of the process' of the genesis of the idea.[20] For Salanskis, the lack of either a hermeneutics or a transcendental deduction of the idea leads Deleuze into an incomplete and, in fact, arbitrary description of ideas.[21] This, though, is an incomplete reading of Deleuze's philosophy of ideas, in part attributable to Salanskis's concentration on the role of mathematics in Deleuze's work.

Deleuze's work on differential mathematics can be seen as offering a paradigm for the operation of unconscious ideas: differential equations allow us to define the singular points of another equation in the same way as the idea allows for the determination of a problem for an actual thing. But he is explicit, in *Différence et répétition*, in insisting that mathematics provides us with only an example of a broader differential calculus, a way of calculating the differential relations of ideas or their dialectic.[22] Different domains demand a 'calculus' of different ideas most of which are not mathematical. Yet Salanskis has identified a most grave philosophical problem. If we cannot fall back on arguments concerning the nature of differential equations as defining real singular points of actual things, Deleuze must provide an argument as to why ideas are real in this other calculable form.

With this calculus and conception of dialectic we begin to see an escape from the conception that ideas are the submission to demonic nihilism in Deleuze. Reason returns as a way of regulating that submission and as a way of avoiding the nihilistic and destructive impulses of a given singular idea, such as Bartleby's 'I would prefer not to'.

Sufficient reason: demons without nihilism

In order to follow Deleuze's arguments on reason, the reality of ideas and their necessary role within actual things it is helpful to follow his definition of an object. An object has two inter-related parts, one actual, the other virtual. The whole object is its actual part, what is generally understood as the object as well-defined in space and time (an ostensible thing). The complete object is the set of all the ideal elements that have determined and will determine its actual part in terms of genesis.[23] Thus the whole ship at sea is the familiar thing we can point to and inspect in terms of its decks, cabins, sails, hull and so on. But the complete ship is the open set of ideas it has come to express at a particular time, in a particular place and in a particular way; for example: to stabilize, to speed, to carry, to capture these sensations. It is essential to realize that these ideal elements are not other actual things, a particular sea or wave type, for example.

Deleuze's argument does not turn on the question of the limits of an object in terms of the problem of actual relations of cause and effect: 'Where does the ship end and the wind and sea begin?' or 'Is it the same ship in high seas and in a dead calm?' Rather, it turns on the question of what complex and problematic structure of ideas the ship responds to and recombines. The complete relation of the ship to other actual things – a storm, for instance – can only properly be understood in terms of this ideal structure. It is not so much what actually happens in the storm that matters, but what motivated the ship and storm to come together in this way (what desires and sensations in terms of movement, speed, stability, capacity).

Two important consequences for Deleuze's argument follow from this definition: 1) an application of Deleuze's argument in terms of the reciprocal determination of the actual and the ideal to the reciprocal determination of the whole actual part by the virtual part and vice versa; 2) a strict opposition drawn between potential and virtual, where the potential of an actual thing is defined as what it may lead to in terms of other actual things that do not yet exist and where the virtual aspect of an actual thing consists of the real ideas expressed in it.[24] In terms of the first point, Deleuze's argument is that the complete object is a complex differential problem – that is, a structure of differential relations (ideas as defined above). This structure is determined with respect to its elements: the differentials that it brings together. But it is not determined with respect to their exact overall relation.

This explains why Deleuze treats the virtual idea in terms of an essential problematicity. We are given a set of variables (to connect, to condense, to divide) that fully determine a problem (the problem of urbanism, for instance). But all the time that we stay at the level of ideas we cannot be given exact solutions to the question of how the problem can be resolved, given the differential nature of the elements in the structure. We know that there is a problem determined by the contradictions and tensions implicit in the structure (to connect/to divide). We also know that any solution is a false one at least at the level of ideas, since it must fix elements that are defined as variations. But Deleuze aims to show that this fixing is in some way necessary for ideas.

His argument is based on a Deleuzian version of the principle of sufficient reason taken from Leibniz and Spinoza. According to Deleuze, the
reality of a thing can be determined if and only if it is: (1) in principle
determinable; (2) determined according to a principle of reciprocal determination; (3) open to a principle of complete determination.[25] So the
Deleuzian version of the principle of sufficient reason is that thought can
only proceed towards the true if it presupposes these three principles.
This principle of sufficient reason runs through Chapter 4 of *Différence et
répétition*. It is a response to the question 'What principles are necessary
for there to be any movement towards the real and the true?' To understand Deleuze's answer we must turn to his analysis of the importance of
this principle in his major Spinoza book, *Spinoza et le problème de l'expression*.

The book contains Deleuze's most sustained study of the relation
between truth and method; as such, it belies interpretations of Deleuze's
work as in some sense anti-theoretical and disinterested in questions of
justification. It is hence important to recall that the Spinoza book is contemporary to *Différence et répétition* and *Logique du sens*; it often fills the
methodological gaps in those two works. The principle of sufficient reason
is introduced in the context of Spinoza and Leibniz's critique of the Cartesian methodology of clear and distinct ideas. Deleuze's argument is that
according to a concept of truth as expression, as opposed to correspondence, a thing is only known 'adequately' as the expression of all its causes.
Truth is therefore not a matter of having a clear and distinct idea that corresponds to the thing and that allows us to trace its causes. It is instead to
know the thing through the causes that it expresses. This means that
thought cannot start or stand on knowledge of the thing through the clear
and distinct idea, only then to extend its domain through causality.
Instead, an uncertain or 'fictional' beginning must be replaced by a study
of causes.[26] The move from correspondence to adequacy in terms of truth
is crucial for Deleuze. It allows him to move away from the essential role
of representation and identity in thought. It also shifts the focus of thought
away from the being of the thing to its genesis.[27] Thus Deleuze insists on
the Euclidian character of Spinoza's method where all the truths about a
given partially defined thing can be deduced from prior axioms and propositions that are the 'causes' of the thing being this way rather than that.[28]

The legacy of this work for Deleuze is the following definition of sufficient reason in terms of causes and effects: 'When the cause as sufficient
reason is given, so are all the properties of the thing; when it is taken away,
so are all the properties.'[29] What does this commit Deleuze to? It involves
him in an account of truth and method where method only advances
towards the true and to real things by considering things in a complete

relation to causes; that is, any method that defines the thing as independent from something that has (or has had) an effect on it must be discounted. So according to his definitions of ideas and actual things they must be considered in conjunction with one another. This is because virtual ideas and only virtual ideas allow for an explanation of the genesis or creation of the actual thing. But only actual things determine the relation of the elements in an ideal structure to one another.

So, according to the principle of sufficient reason, once we suppose that a thing is determinable, we must proceed according to a principle of reciprocal determination; that is, we must seek to fix the idea, or resolve it as a problem in an actual solution. But we must also dissolve the actual thing by tracing its genesis according to virtual ideas. The real is therefore the actual and the virtual, and they define each other under different guises: the virtual determines real genesis; the actual determines real individuality, in the sense of an individual solution for a complex problem or idea. However, exactly because any actual thing is a necessary but only a partial and incomplete solution to a complete problem at the level of ideas, Deleuze's sufficient reason also commits him to a search for complete determination (the move has to be towards 'all the properties of the thing', or nowhere at all).

Finally, reciprocal determination and complete determination lead to a progression in Deleuze's method in terms of a movement towards complete determination.[30] Any actual thing expresses an idea in an incomplete manner and can hence be made more real and more true by a new expression that captures the individual elements and the scope of the idea better. The limits imposed on ideas by the process of individualization through actualization allow for the definition of further tensions and contradictions at the level of ideas. In giving a problem an actual expression and hence a partial solution we extend it into a new structure or a new relation between structures. Thus when the problem caught in the ideal structure of urbanization is expressed in the rational grid of the modern city a further set of as yet unexpressed elements enters the equation: tensions between expansion in scale (to grow) and satisfaction of a will to individuality (to signify/to localize). But expression of these elements will itself be in need of further work in terms of its relation to the idea.[31]

So Deleuze's philosophy does involve a rational progress defined as the extension and precision of the ideas and through the reverberation from one actual thing to another through the virtual. This progress is the interweaving of the virtual and the actual at its most concrete and inevitable – so long as we accept Deleuze's principles of sufficient reason. Creation is then an experimentation in view of ideas and according to the principle of sufficient reason.

Complete determination against demonic nihilism

Deleuze's argument for the necessary relation of the ideal and the virtual rests therefore on a refinement of the principle of pure reason and on a set of assumptions regarding the nature of the virtual and the actual. It is beyond the scope of this chapter to test these assumptions; the main concern here has been to tease out Deleuze's reply to accusations of dualism and demonic nihilism. This means that only one of our leading questions can be answered with any degree of certainty: if Deleuze's account of the nature of ideas and actual things is convincing (his ontology as outlined above), and if we accept his account of truth as adequacy and sufficient reason, then he escapes the accusation of a dualism that irretrievably separates ideas and actual things. In escaping this accusation he also avoids the nihilism of the submission of reason to unconscious ideas.

However, a more rich outcome of this investigation lies in a more precise defence of Deleuze's method as it applies to ethical, aesthetic and political action. Given his tripartite definition of sufficient reason in terms of the relation of the ideal to the actual, the sense of progress and value in his philosophy must lie in a deepening and extension of the ideas or structures expressed in any given actual thing. We map those ideas and create new things to respond to new problems associated with that mapping. This is an endless task; there is no final goal to which it could tend. It is also a contingent one, in terms of the starting point of the exercise (an actual thing with its problem) and in terms of its practice (there is no perfect expression of an ideal structure nor a set of laws by which creation could be judged).[32] But creation is not senseless either. The task of creation allows for progress in terms of the idea which, as it is deepened and extended in terms of its elements through its individual expression in the actual thing, makes the actual thing more complete.

Calculation according to sufficient reason, with a view to completeness, is Deleuze's rational method against the demonic defined as a singular idea that takes over all others and all points of the actual thing in which they are expressed. The catalogue of beings possessed and doomed by their demons in Deleuze's work is then not a sign of the value of abandonment to the unconscious that lies beyond reason. It is not a sign of philosophy arriving at the most desperate nihilism of a leap into self-destruction. Bartleby, Ahab, the drunks in Fitzgerald and Lowry in *Logique du sens*,[33] Joe Bousquet and his belief that he was born for the terrible wound that slowly killed him[34] are there to show the unconscious idea as problem and as necessity; something to be included in the experimental search for a more complete life and not an end to it.

Notes

1 M. Heidegger, 'The Word of Nietzsche: "God is Dead"', *The Question Concerning Technology*, trans. W. Lovitt (New York: Harper & Row, 1977) p. 75.
2 J. Tomlinson, *Francisco Goya y Lucientes* (London: Phaidon, 1994), pp. 123–46, esp. pp. 132–4.
3 *Littré*: 1565.
4 G. Deleuze, 'Bartleby ou la formule', in *Critique et clinique* (Paris: Les Editions de Minuit, 1993), p. 103.
5 H. Melville, 'Bartleby the Scrivener', in *Bartleby and the Lightning Rod Man* (Harmondsworth: Penguin, 1995), p. 46.
6 Deleuze, 'Bartleby', p. 114.
7 F. Nietzsche, *Ecce Homo*, trans R. J. Hollingdale (Harmondsworth: Penguin, 1979), p. 65.
8 Ibid., pp. 65–6.
9 Ibid., p. 64.
10 Ibid., p. 65.
11 Ibid.
12 G. Deleuze, *Différence et répétition* (Paris: Presses Universitaires de France, 1968), pp. 236–8.
13 Ibid., p. 237.
14 P. Patton, ed., *Deleuze: a Critical Reader* (Oxford: Blackwell, 1996), p. 15.
15 D. Smith, 'Deleuze's Theory of Sensation: Overcoming the Kantian Duality', in Patton, Deleuze, pp. 48–9.
16 Deleuze, *Différence*, p. 197.
17 Melville, 'Bartleby', p. 44.
18 Smith, 'Deleuze', pp. 45–8.
19 J. M. Salanskis, 'Ideas and Destination', in Patton, *Deleuze*, p. 76.
20 Ibid., p. 74.
21 Ibid., p. 77.
22 Deleuze, *Différence*, p. 181.
23 Ibid., p. 270.
24 Ibid., pp. 272–3.
25 Ibid., p. 222.
26 G. Deleuze, *Spinoza et le problème de l'expression* (Paris: Minuit, 1968), p. 120.
27 Ibid.
28 Ibid.
29 Ibid.
30 Deleuze, *Différence*, p. 271.
31 Ibid., p. 271–2.
32 Ibid., p. 272.
33 G. Deleuze, *Logique du sens* (Paris: Minuit, 1969), pp. 180–9.
34 Ibid., p. 174–9.

keith ansell pearson

SPECTROPOIESIS AND RHIZOMATICS: LEARNING TO LIVE WITH DEATH AND DEMONS

I wish one could cease to be a human being, and be a demon.[1]

The Universe does not function by filiation.[2]

And suddenly, I am speaking with several voices: I can no longer draw the line between narrative, myth, and science.[3]

In *Totem and Taboo* (1913) Freud believes he can establish a secure grounding for the comprehension of demons: 'Neither fear nor demons can be regarded by psychology as "earliest" things, impervious to any attempt at discovering their antecedents. It would be another matter if demons really existed. But we know that, like gods, they are creations of the human mind: they were made by something and out of something.'[4] Demonic projections and projections of demons are phantasms – a prevalent view in western thought also articulated in terms of a burgeoning scientific materialism in Hobbes[5] – that can be shown to have their basis in an Oedipal complex. Indeed, in this work Freud will explain the foundations of civilization – religion, morality, the bad conscience, categorical imperatives – in terms of an Oedipal hauntology. Psychoanalysis seeks to explain the emotional ambivalence that is articulated in human practices of sacrifice, such as the mixture of celebration and mourning that characterizes the festive occasion (the totem meal, the Eucharist, etc.). Bringing together psychoanalysis and Darwin's theory on the earliest stages of human society with the notion of the primal horde, Freud evinces his notorious account of the pack of brothers who, driven out by their father, join ranks and devour him. In so doing they express their identification with him, so aquiring a portion of his strength through the cannibalistic act, but also in the process set up the foundations of morality and communal existence (acting collectively for the common good, putting an end to the war of all). The totem meal, mankind's earliest festival, therefore represents a repetition and commemoration of this criminal deed of human time that constitutes the beginning of social organization as well as the moral restrictions and prohibitions of religion. But the act reveals a complex of emotions, both love and hate, envy and admiration. As a result what lives on and haunts the repetition of civilization with its eternal discontents and malaise is the sense of guilt in which 'The dead father became stronger than the living one had been'.[6] It is out of a filial sense of guilt that the two fundamental taboos of totemism are created: the forbidding of the murder of the totem which has become the father-substitute and sexual renunciation in the form of resigning the claim to women set free from the father's dominion. The two taboos correspond to the two repressed wishes of the Oedipus complex. The sufferings of the divine goat Dionsyus and the Passion of Christ are dramas that can only be fully understood when placed in the context of this primeval Oedipal tragedy. We are, after all, notes Freud, speaking of psychic complexes and illnesses that spread contagiously like bad infections.[7]

Through the Oedipal complex Freud constructs for the human animal a 'gigantic memory' which domesticates animal becomings, as well as non-human and inhuman becomings of the human. This is accomplished through the mapping of life in terms of an arborescent schema which subjugates the line to the point, in which a point always denotes a point of origin, and in which 'man' assumes the position of the central point. This molar system of memory is defined by the points being answerable to specific mnemonic conditions of frequency and resonance (repressed 'childhood memories', for example).[8] On an Oedipal schema all such becomings amount to a displacement of a fear of the father on to an animal. But this this does not mean that psychoanalysis blocks off all escape through the line of flight. One must learn to live with certain triangular complexes and double articulations and travel beyond them, like finding the crack or faultline within the crack-up.[9] Kafka is obviously a highly instructive case here with his animal burrowings and metamorphoses in relation to bureaucracy and father-complexes. It is never, Deleuze and Guattari insist, a question of positing a simple opposition between molecular becomings and molar stratifications, but of seeking to demonstrate that every molar system (a species, a socius) has a molecular unconscious (a multiplicity or a population) which both marks its tendency to decompose and haunts its operation and organization. It would be too easy to claim that a becoming-molecular involves little more than a reaction to molar determination, so consigning it to a parasitic status, simply because rhizomatics wants to show the extent of co-implication of molecular and molar within any given assemblage. Becomings (molecular, animal, inhuman, imperceptible) always involve a 'molar extension, a human hyperconcentration, or [prepares] the way for them'.[10] The critique of psychoanalysis emerges out of this insight. Psychoanalysis is to be critiqued for reducing becomings to the *one* complex, the complex of molar determination (Oedipus, castration).[11] This is very similar to the way in which Nietzsche critiques the ascetic ideal which reduces the question of 'life' to the *one* goal and the *one* interpretation – reduces it, in fact, to the matter of the *One*.

The point, then, is not to deny that an assemblage of desire involving a becoming-inhuman is devoid of an Oedipal dimension; on the contrary, Deleuze and Guattari argue that there are many Oedipal statements entailed in such a becoming.[12] We are involved in a social formation, and we are caught up in Oedipal relations. Freud's psychoanalysis is critiqued not only because it reduces becomings solely to articulations of Oedipal desire, but rather for employing this enunciation in order to delude patients with the belief that through therapy they will be able to speak finally in their own name as unitary organisms.

In this chapter I want to explore, however, what becomes of hauntology when it is stripped of an Oedipalization as its principal determination and articulation. What becomes of demons, ghosts, beasts, things, etc. when a de-oedipalization is effected? To explore this I shall draw on Derrida's 'spectropoiesis' and, even more, on Deleuze's rhizomatics. Both Derrida and Deleuze have a concern with germinal life or the 'living on' that is deployed as a critique of the reduction of the production of life to the telos of species reproduction. Deleuze places stress on the idea that a code, which always relates to a population, enjoys a surplus value in which, for example, the DNA code contains a margin of decoding. This is due to supplements, and to single segments being copied more than once, which provide matter for free variation. In addition, fragments of code are transferred from the cells of one species to another via modes of transversal communication (modes that are crucial for understanding the phenomenon of animal becomings). In the case of Derrida, one has in mind the complex germinality articulated in a work like *Dissemination*: 'As the heterogeneity and the absolute exteriority of the seed, seminal difference does constitute itself into a program, but it is a program that cannot be formalized. For reasons that *can* be formalized. The infinity of its code, its rift, then, does not take form saturated with self-presence in the encyclopedic circle. It is attached, so to speak, to the incessant falling of *a supplement to the code*'.[13] Derrida writes of 'differance' in rhizomatic terms, as the proliferating and plural 'productive movement' which is neither preceded by nor proceeds by identity or unity, and which cannot be relieved or resolved 'by any philosophical dialectic'. One might also recall that 'dissemination' enjoys an anti-Oedipal (anti-triangular, anti-trinitarian, anti-dialectical) dimension: 'Dissemination *displaces* the three of ontotheology along the angle of a certain re-folding'.[14] Derrida's conception of writing construes the continuous and heterogeneous chain of evolution, which extends across the biological and the technological as a common praxis of writing or code, as a subset of the more general category of the trace. This means that the 'enveloping context or condition of possibility is therefore something much wider than the bio-social or the bio-anthropological, the essentializing alliance of "life" and (at the apex of evolutionary ascent) "man" being a central tenet of logocentric thinking'.[15] Ultimately, then, one arrives necessarily at a 'non-biological theory of evolution ... the supplementary *Über-leben* over and above the economy of life'.[16] This 'over-life' is another term for 'germinal life', never reproduction of the same but the invention of the new and the monstrous as the very a priori of evolution and survival. This concern with the 'living on' and 'living beyond' (the over-life) will be explored in this chapter in relation to the question of demonic powers and in relation to the matter of death.

Derrida points out that to construe a philosophy as a philosophy of life is an all too easy or simple affair simply because it is in danger of neglecting the other of life, namely death and the dead – so much so that for Derrida absolute life would be absolute evil, the life that is fully present.[17] Learning to live life is not something that can be taught by oneself but only through the intermediation provided by the other, by death, at the edge of life, at the internal or external border, speaking of a 'heterodidactics' that is situated *between* life and death, where this 'between' does not denote a simple genealogy requiring movement along a series of points from an arche to a telos (from birth to death). Nietzsche spoke enigmatically of justice as a 'panoramic power' which transcends this and that individual, as the highest representative of life, but a life that is fully implicated in death. Is it this kind of justice that Derrida is appealing to when he speaks of the life that lives beyond present life, its actual being-there?: 'not toward death but toward a *living-on*, namely, a trace of which life and death would themselves be but traces and traces of traces, a survival whose possibility in advance comes to disjoin or dis-adjust the identity to itself of the living present as well as of any effectivity. There is then *some spirit*. Spirits. And *one must* reckon with them'.[18]

Repetition needs to be freed from the material or physical model of a merely 'brute repetition' that Deleuze holds it gets trapped in with Freud's positing of the death-drive and which posits a straightforward desire to regress, or involute, to an earlier, inorganic state of things. While the pleasure principle would be limited to a psychological principle, that of the 'beyond' of the pleasure principle would be linked to a transcendental principle (not of life, but germinal life, the life and death that live on): 'If repetition makes us ill, it also heals us; if it enchains and destroys us, it also frees us, testifying in both cases to its "demonic" power'.[19] This move is not Freud's, for whom the 'daemonic power' which assails and runs ahead of neurotics like a 'malignant fate' is always to be identified and stratified in terms of a recognizable fate, a fate that is 'for the most part arranged by themselves and determined by early infantile influences'.[20] Psychoanalysis can only domesticate the demonic by placing it in the confines of regression therapy. There is something that haunts the present life, life as presence. For Deleuze this is repetition: not as regression but as originary difference, announcing not the return of the repressed (the past) but the evil spirits of the alien future; or rather, the time of Aion as opposed to the time of Chronos. This is the time of the Event (the time of eternal return). Events are not living presents but infinitives that involve a 'becoming' which in dividing itself infinitely in past and future eludes the grasp of the present. The time of events is the ghostly (virtual) time of 'incorporeal effects', effects which result from the actions and passions of bodies but which live in excess of them. The eternal return is not the time of individuals or persons but only of 'pure events' in 'which the instant, displaced over the line, goes on dividing into already past and yet to come'.[21] What makes the encounter with eternal return demonic is not the feeling of being subject to an evil fate beyond one's control or comprehension, becoming little more than the victim of the repressed; rather it is the fact that in its repetition the action is transformed into the event, in which the body is confronted with the chance to learn to communicate with ghosts and spectres of life. What is being willed in the willing of eternal repetition – in which repetition becomes the very object of willing (not mere self-destruction as in the death-drive) – is the field of forces and intensities in which the self finds itself fortuitously implicated. The eternal return turns the repetition of intensities and singularities (the mobile individuating factors which exceed the constraints of the self and live on or beyond) into the object of the highest affirmation.

Are the dead ever dead, not just at peace with themselves but at peace with us? One thinks of Birkin's anxiety and dread: the dead are never content to stay dead, they always desire something from us, they continue to live (or die), clinging on to the living and not letting go.[22] The living dead ones (who are not 'ones'; no more Ones) express in a non proprietorial way the 'monstrous Life-Substance'.[23] They live as ghosts 'of' life, testifying to the diabolical forces which ensure that the living cannot live without the non-present 'presence' of the dead, at least in a germinal sense: 'palpitating and formless within the flux of the ghost life'.[24] They live as the uninvited, the 'unseen hosts' Lawrence writes of in *Women in Love* who persist in haunting man and the gigantic molar memory he constructs of himself and for himself: 'Do you think that creation depends on *man*! … Man is a mistake, he must go. – There is the grass, and hares and adders, and the unseen hosts, actual angels that go about freely when a dirty humanity doesn't interrupt them – and good pure-tissued demons: very nice'.[25] And then there is the attraction and repulsion of the desiring-machines: 'Sometimes she beat her wings like a new Daphne, turning not into a tree but a machine … a music more maddening than the siren's long ago … They aroused a strange, nostalgic ache of desire, something almost demoniacal'.[26]

An encounter with the demonic raises, of course, the question of what it means for philosophy to communicate with death. Freud refers to a work of anthropology by Kleinpaul in which the belief in spirits found in the remnants of civilized races is said to expose a fear of the dead among the living because the dead continue to enjoy the primeval lust for murder (the lust Freud *affirms* in working through the 'disillusionment of war' in his 1915 essay), seeking to drag the living on to their train. The dead are, in actuality, living dead who live death; they are vampyres conceived as 'evil spirits' who seek to rob the living of life.[27] It is as if such an insight anticipates Freud's later preoccupation with the train of death that always leads to the same place, a regression to the inorganic that characterizes the death-drive as precisely a drive towards death as a final entropic destination: 'the aim of all living is death'. But here we encounter the essential paradox: which life is it that the so-called evil spirits seek to deprive the living of? Could it be the absolute life, the life that thinks it can dispense with death and its filthy lessons (decomposition, degeneration)? Death no longer exists for we have buried the dead once and for all; the dead are without witnesses; no survivors remain to testify against the living.

Ghosts speak and come not only from the past. Even ghosts of the past testify to the coming of the future. Within modernity it is the train that haunts life with ghosts of future metamorphoses and subjects modern humanity to the demonic power of the death-drive. In Zola's *La Bête humaine*, for example, the machine functions as the pure death instinct: 'the train was passing, in all its stormy violence, as if it might sweep away everything that lay in its path … It was like some huge body, a giant creature laid out on the ground … past it went, mechanical, triumphant, hurtling towards the future with mathematical rigour, determinedly oblivious to the rest of human life on either side, life unseen and yet perennial, with its eternal passions and its eternal crimes'.[28] Zola's aim in *La Bête humaine* was to link murder with an ancient hereditary impulse buried over by the sedimented layers of civilization, to show the 'caveman' dwelling deep within the civilized man of modernity, as he put it in a letter to a Dutch journalist. Indeed, the fact that Zola's novel, with its stress on a hereditary regression and atavistic instincts, anticipates both Freud's conception of death (1915) and his positing of the death-drive (1920) by several decades is quite remarkable. On Deleuze's reading, however, the complicated investment of the erotic instincts in destructive ones – Zola's novel was read in the precise terms of this complication on its publication – expresses not simply the noise of primal instincts caught up in an involutionary regression but rather the silent echoes of a repetition that drives us ever forward and upward. This is why for him the key actor or agent in the novel is the train itself (a field of action, a body without organs distributing intensities and producing affects). The train is a creation of modern civilization but it is also the crack which derails it, making sure that it is the 'great health' (the health that has incorporated the crack) which lives on in humanity.

In a meditation on Zola and the 'crack' in one of the appendices to *The Logic of Sense* Deleuze draws a distinction between two types of heredity: the one small, historical, and somatic; the other epic and germinal. A heredity of the instincts and a heredity of the crack or faultline. The somatic heredity might include, for example, a phenomenon such as alcoholism being passed down the generations from one body to another. This kind of transmission reproduces the return of the same; the other kind, however, that of the crack, does not; where one transmits something well-determined, reproducing whatever is transmitted, the other communicates in terms of a vital and virtual topology. In the case of the heredity of the crack 'it is not tied to a certain instinct, to an internal, organic determination, or to an external event that could fix an object'. It is thus able to *transcend life-styles* (my emphasis). The movement of the heredity of the crack is for Deleuze 'imperceptible' and 'silent'. The crack cannot be 'replicated' since its mode of transmission is diffuse and inchoate; it proceeds via an 'oblique line, being ready to change directions and to alter its canvas'.[29] The crack transmits only the undetermined crack, capable of changing directions and transforming its canvas. With the heredity of the crack characteristics are not simply acquired but have to be invented and are forced to undergo transmutation. The crack 'follows' only itself, like a runaway train destined for derailment. On the tracks of this germinal train of life there is neither beginning nor end, neither genealogy nor teleology, but only the broken middles that allow for novel intersections and cross-connections. The crack enjoys a capacity for self-overcoming, making possible creative 'evolutions', in which the creation that is involved does not offer a simple redemption but allows for the germinal becoming of the most destructive inclinations and tendencies. Deleuze wants to argue that the death-instinct constitutes the complicated 'grand heredity' of the crack. It is not tragic but epic, since it concerns revolutionary movement. But the death-instinct is retrieved from any global entropic determination or telos. 'Is it possible, since it [the death-instinct or death-drive] absorbs every instinct, that it could also enact the transmutation of the instincts, turning death against itself? Would it not thereby create instincts which would be evolutive rather than alcoholic, erotic, or financial'.[30]

Deleuze's configuration of the workings of the crack amounts, there-fore, to a fundamental reworking of Freud's death-drive. It is no longer tied to a morbid desire to regress to an earlier, inorganic state of affairs; now, the inorganic is freed from regression and has become transformed into the intensity of germinal life – the point of zero intensity – from which new fluxes and patterns of life emerge. It is in these terms that Deleuze will correct what he sees as Freud's misreading of Weissmann (on the germ-plasm) in A Thousand Plateaus.[31] The child does not come 'before' the parents but is rather their 'germinal contemporary'. The becoming-child takes place in terms of the body without organs that functions not as a memory of childhood but as a 'childhood block'. The body without organs is the site of 'intense germen'. This body is badly thought if it is mapped out in terms of a regressive egg since this egg is a milieu of pure intensity that a self always carries with it as its milieu of experimentation and its associated milieu. This egg denotes not a field of undifferentiation but a site of production 'where things and organs are distinguished solely by gradients, migrations, zones of proximity'. It is here that we can begin to think the union of cosmology and embryology. This body is not, there-fore, simply before the organism but always adjacent to it. There is always 'a contemporary, creative involution'. The body without organs conceived in these terms is never a body that can be owned or possessed; it is not a site for the production of identity but only ever becomings that involve spirits, ghosts, demons, etc. It is a site of sorcery. The error of psycho-analysis, contend Deleuze and Guattari, was to depict the phenomena of the body without organs as regressions and phantasies caught up in an 'image' of the normative body: 'As a result, it only grasps the flipside of the BwO and immediately substitutes family photos, childhood memories, and part-objects for a worldwide intensity map'.[32]

Derrida poses the question of the event precisely as a question of the ghost, seeking to comprehend the effectivity of that which is without body, as virtual and insubstantial as a simulacrum. Indeed, for Derrida a think-ing of the spectral is one that takes into account 'an irreducible *virtuality* ... virtual space, virtual object, synthetic image, spectral simulacrum, teletechnological differance, *idealiterability*, trace beyond presence and absence, and so forth'.[33] A state of affairs is haunted by the event (a ghost of time), which makes it possible to speak of a logic of haunting that is not simply larger than an ontology of being but rather denotes that which implicates life in its other as the repetition of death. Whether this haunting entails, deconstructively, a renegotiation with genealogy (a genealogical deconstruction and a deconstruction of the genealogical schema) or, more destructively, a burning of the genealogical tree, will not be decided upon here (just as Nietzsche's own project of 'on' or 'towards' a genealogy of morals does not decide upon it once and for all but leaves the matter open for the future, and as the future). We simply need note that it is not only a question of our taking up an inheritance which subjects genealogy to a heteronomous and heterogeneous determination; rather, the hereditary can be shown to enjoy an originary heterogeneity. This is what Deleuze means when he says that our only inheritance is the crack itself (the paradox of a transmission which transmits only itself). The event becomes what it is because it 'lives on'. It robs time of the present – indeed, of presence. There remains, however, a future for heredity simply because what is inherited in any passing on is the future. The 'germen' is the crack and nothing but the crack.

It cannot simply be a question of radicalizing Freud. As Derrida points out, 'radicalising' too readily gets caught up in precisely what is at stake, 'the stakes of the root and its presumed unity'.[34] It can, therefore, only be a question of uprooting Freud, of implicating genealogies and memories in rhizomes and becomings. Before saying something about the character of such becomings, I want to show the stakes of Deleuze's dis-figuration of the modern project of transcendental philosophy. This is crucial if we are to effectively comprehend the character of Deleuze's encounter with the spirit of evil and with evil spirits.

In *The Logic of Sense* Deleuze develops a new conception of transcendental philosophy by approaching the transcendental as a topological field not inhabited by the 'I', the cogito or the synthetic unity of apperception, but populated by preindividual singularities, what he calls a 'Dionysian sense-producing machine'.[35] It is this 'surface topology' made up of populations and preindividual singularities which constitutes the 'real transcendental field'. Singularities refer to 'ideal events' (ideal in the sense that they exist or endure beyond their specific individual manifestations and significations), such as bottlenecks, knots, points of fusion, processes of condensation, crystallization, and boiling. The error of attempts to define the transcendental with consciousness is that they get constructed in the image of that which they are supposed to ground, running the risk of simply reduplicating the empirical.[36] Deleuze makes a move in the direction of a non-human universe, giving primacy in the becomings of life to what he will later call with Guattari transversal modes of communication. In *The Logic of Sense*, for example, the subject is transmuted into a free, anonymous, nomadic singularity which 'traverses' humans, plants and animals by being dependent neither on the matter of the particular individuations nor on the forms of their personality. This transversality, says Deleuze, constitutes the universe of Nietzsche's 'overman'. In later work this transversal field is identified as the plane of immanence, which, starting with Descartes and running from Kant to Husserl, is treated as a field of consciousness: 'Immanence is supposed to be immanent to a pure consciousness, to a thinking subject'.[37] For Deleuze, however, immanence is only immanent to itself – that is, to a plane populated by anonymous matter in continuous variation.

Deleuze is concerned to attack the idea of knowledge that is implied in the transcendental model of modern metaphysics, which, he argues, is a model and form of *recognition* (between self and world, or subject and object, and self and other). The criticism is that construed in terms of a model or form of recognition philosophy is unable to open itself up to the aberrant, the anomalous, the fuzzy, the indiscernible, and so on. It is for this reason that Deleuze refuses to distinguish the transcendental form of a faculty from its transcendent application: 'The transcendent exercise must not be traced from the empirical exercise precisely because it apprehends that which cannot be grasped from the point of view of common sense'.[38] Ultimately, this means that the transcendental must be answerable to a 'superior empiricism', which is obviously not the empiricism of common and good sense but that of another 'logic of sense' altogether: the empiricism of the unknown, the demonic, the anarchic, etc. There is something in the world that *forces us to think*. For Deleuze this something is not to become an object of recognition but rather assume the form of a 'fundamental *encounter*' (*recontre*).[39] It has to be an encounter with the daimonic as in Nietzsche's encounter with the demon who brings him the gift and task of eternal return as an encounter with chance, the fortuitous, and the uncanny – the 'arrival' of the overhuman.

Deleuze argues that the 'I' and the 'Self' (*Je* and *Moi*) are little more than indices of the species, in particular of 'man'. By contrast, individuation is that which precedes and makes species possible. It is on individuation conceived as a field of intensive factors that Deleuze focuses as a way of reformulating the question of the transcendental. It is in this way that he hopes to 'go beyond the human condition' (Bergson) and to open up thought and experience to the inhuman and overhuman. Such a move bears witness to the power of demons and dead spirits that inform Deleuze's reworking of philosophy. Such spirits assume the form of intensive quantities or degrees which subsist even though they have lost the

extension of a determinate body and the identity of a self. They are preindividual and non-personal singularities that communicate with and pene-
trate one another across an infinity of thresholds and modifications:
'Fascinating world where the identity of the self is lost, not to the benefit
of the identity of the One or the unity of the Whole, but to the advantage
of an intense multiplicity and a power of metamorphosis'.[40] It is the open
system of the Antichrist (Hobbes's 'Confederacy of Deceivers'), 'the system of simulacra opposed to the world of identities', the affirmed power of
the decentred circle encompassing difference, diversity, heterogeneity
and so on. In such a system one never encounters gods, which are too
bound up with forms of recognition, but only demons as 'the sign-bearers:
powers of the ... intensive and instant; powers which only cover difference
with more difference'.[41]

Foucault was right to characterize *Logique du sens* as one of the most
'alien' books imaginable, amounting to an 'insolent' metaphysical treatise
that does not denounce metaphysics for neglecting being but forces it to
speak of 'extra-being'.[42] Phantasms, on this incisive reading of Deleuze, are
not to be construed as taking organisms into purely imaginary domains but
rather as providing the very materiality of bodies with a virtual topology in
which they become what they are: 'They should consequently be freed
from the restrictions we impose upon them, freed from the dilemmas of
truth and falsehood and of being and non-being ... they must be allowed
to conduct their dance, to act out their mime, as "extra-being".'[43] The
physics of bodies, mixtures, reactions and mechanisms, requires the *meta*-
physics of incorporeal materiality such as phantasms and simulacra. The
result is not a shameful metaphysics but a joyful one, Foucault notes: 'A
dead God and sodomy are the thresholds of the new metaphysical
ellipse'.[44]

Let me now turn to analysing how this concern with the incorporeal
articulates itself in the later Deleuze. The mode of individuation which
differs from that of a person, subject or substance is given the name of
'haecceity' by Deleuze. Haecceities are composed of, on the one hand,
relations of movement between particles, and, on the other hand, capacities to affect and be affected.[45] This is visible in many examples of modern
literature, such as works by Hardy, Lawrence and Charlotte Bronte, in
which characters are 'presented' in terms of winds, temperatures, cli-
mates, durations, intensities of colour, etc. These haecceities can be
approached in terms of a demonology that 'expounds upon the diabolical
art of local movements and transports of affect', and which discloses 'the
importance of rain, hail, wind, pestilential air, or air polluted by noxious
particles, favourable conditions for these transports'.[46] They are concrete
individuations, not simply backdrops to the real action, which have an

autonomous status and which direct the metamorphosis of things and subjects.

It is not simply or only a question for a life-philosophy of roots: 'Thought always lags behind nature'.[47] In nature roots are taproots with a multiple, lateral and circular system of ramification. The rhizome is the open system par excellence. If an organism is partly a function of the frame in which biology encodes it, it becomes necessary to appreciate that such a frame captures only a small part of the information that machinic or symbiotic assemblages are able to express. In contrast to conventional phylogenetic lineages, which invariably assume the form of a genealogy, rhizomatics demonstrates the extent to which exclusively filiative models are unable to account for the creative aspects of 'evolution' (becomings and a-regressive involutions). A consequence of rhizomatics is the necessity to reconfigure evolutionary schemas, no longer adopting models of arborescent descent moving from the least to the more differentiated. A rhizome is constituted by an originary heterogeneity and involves transversal communication across phyletic lineages that serves to complicate genealogical trees. Arborescent schemas, whether in biology or computer science, posit hierarchical systems with centres of subjectification and central automata functioning in terms of an organized memory. Channels of transmission are pre-established, the system pre-exists the individual, and any deviation from the norms of the system is to be regarded as an aberration (one might note that the Freudian schema of memory conforms to this type of system).

Deleuze explores the existence of animal becomings that are said to both traverse human beings and affect both animals and humans alike. Animal becomings, it must be insisted upon, do not entail representation or imitation, simply because the becoming is situated on the molecular level of affect between particles of heterogeneous bodies, and not on the molar level of species and genus with its concentration on organs and their functions. It is for this reason that a becoming is said to produce only itself: 'What is real is … the block of becoming, not the supposedly fixed terms through which that which becomes passes.'[48] These becomings cannot be said to be evolutions *if* evolution is taken to be synonymous with descent and filiation. Becomings involve the coming into play of an order different than filiation, such as novel alliances found in symbiotic complexes: 'If evolution includes any veritable becomings, it is in the domain of *symbioses* that bring into play beings of totally different scales and kingdoms, with no possible filiation.'[49] Deleuze and Guattari adopt a model of 'creative involution' by disassociating involution from regression (the move towards less differentiation) and equating it with the establishment of non-linear blocks of becoming. This is what they call 'neoevolutionism' in which animal becomings involve the movement of populations: 'the animal is defined not by characteristics (specific, generic, etc.) but by populations that vary from milieu to milieu or within the same milieu; movement occurs not only or not primarily by filiative productions but also by transversal communications between heterogeneous populations'.[50]

If the universe does not evolve in accordance with the law of filiation, but involves heterogeneous components and combinations that are neither genetic nor structural, then nature can be shown to operate against itself in terms of 'unnatural participations' which involve neither filiative production nor hereditary reproduction of the same. Creative evolution is epidemic and contagious precisely because it involves transversal communication. The 'politics' of animal becomings are ambiguous simply because forms of society and state are able to appropriate animal becomings and subject them to filiative overcoding, such as reducing them to relations of totemic or symbolic correspondence.

Every animal becoming partakes of the anomalous (Moby-Dick, Josephine the Mouse Singer, the Wolf-Man). The anomalous is a 'phenomenon of bordering',[51] and it is within its terms of reference (a multiplicity, a population) that we can think in a novel manner the nature of demons and monsters.[52] The anomalous resists schemas of classification; it has something of the 'unnameable' and the 'monstrous' about it – one could call it 'the Outsider', the 'nameless horror' or 'viroid life'.[53] Conceived in its most important sense, biophilosophically, the anomalous cannot be said to be either an individual or a species. It has to do with the movement of a multiplicity and of populations, definable neither by their elements nor by their centres of unification, but solely and strictly in terms of the number of dimensions and variations they enjoy. The desire to be a demon is a desire not to be One but more than one, even less than one. No more One.[54] Sorcerers occupy an anomalous position within their social sphere, dwelling at the edge of fields or woods, at the borderline between villages, and operating 'between' life and death. Their relation to the anomalous is not one of filiation but of alliance, establishing a pact with evil spirits: 'The sorcerer has a relation of alliance with the demon as the power of the anomalous'.[55] The politics of this sorcery involve assemblages (couplings and copulations) that assume the form neither of the family nor of the state and religion: 'Instead they express minoritarian groups, or groups that are oppressed, prohibited, in revolt, or always on the fringe of recognized institutions'.[56] If the animal becomings take the form of a great 'temptation', of monsters that are aroused in the imagination as a demonic influence, this is because they are 'accompanied ... by a rupture with the central institutions that have established themselves or seek to become established'.[57] Evil spirits ensure that nature overcomes itself by evolving contra itself through modes of involution, breaking out of the ossification and rigidification of organismic life, and heralding the germinal life of the non-organic: 'it is not the mechanical which is opposed to the organic: it is the vital as potent pre-organic germinality (*puissante germinalité pré-organique*), common to the animate and the inanimate, to a matter which raises itself to the point of life, and to a life which spreads itself through all matter'.[58] Non-organic life invokes a *non-psychological* life of the spirit, a life that does not simply 'belong' either to nature or to organic individuality since it is the ungrounding of both, the flowers of evil which adorn the crowned an-archy.

Demons are demonic precisely because they exist without determinate function or fixed form. Where gods have fixed attributes, properties, functions, territories and codes, concerned to oversee and regulate boundaries, demons jump across intervals of space and time and betray existing codes and territories. This is why Deleuze argues that it is a poor recipe for producing monsters merely to 'accumulate heteroclite determinations or to over-determine the animal'. Rather, the more successful and subversive task lies in raising up the ground and dissolving the form.[59] Of course, this involves betrayal, most notably betraying the 'fixed powers which try to hold us back, the established powers of the earth'.[60]

Deleuze and Guattari will go so far as to claim that the becomings of philosophy and science are unthinkable without recourse to an appreciation of the role played by demons in all thought-experimentation. The demon is not to be construed as a God-like figure, a trickster, who assumes the role of the total observer able to calculate the past and the future from a given state of affairs (in the manner of the demon invented by Laplace). The demon invoked here denotes not simply something that exceeds our reasoning capacities but rather a common kind of 'necessary intercessor' playing the role of inventive subject of enunciation, such as the philosophical friend and rival, the idiot, the overman, etc. The demons of science – of Maxwell, of Heisenberg, and so on – function as 'partial observers' and play the role of a molecular perception and affection, in which knowledge becomes a perspectivism. This is not the perspectivism of a banal scientific relativism in which truth is said to be always relative to a subject. There is not a relativity of truth (the anthropocentric *naïveté* par excellence), but only 'a truth of the relative'. It is worth quoting Deleuze and Guattari at some length on this point:

> the role of a partial observer is to perceive and to experience, although these perceptions and affections are not those of a man, in the currently accepted sense, but belong to the things studied. Man feels the effect of them nonetheless (what mathematician does not feel the experience, the effect of a section, an ablation, or an addition), but he obtains this effect only from the

ideal observer that he himself has installed like a golem in the system of reference. These partial observers belong to the neighborhood of the singularities of a curve, of a physical system, of a living organism. Even animism, when it multiplies little immanent souls in organs and functions, is not so far removed from biological science as it is said to be, on condition that these immanent souls are withdrawn from any active or efficient role so as to become solely sources of molecular perception and affection. In this way, bodies are populated by an infinity of little monads.[61]

In contrast to science, art and philosophy can, in their relation to demonic powers, be assigned a political task. The revolutionary artist (whether painter, novelist, cinema author or creative thinker) always writes, says Deleuze, for a people (a population) to come, for non-denumerable multiplicities (that which escapes statistical capture). Where statistics concern individual phenomena, 'antistatistical individuality operates only in relation to molecular populations'.[62] To be a poet or an assassin? The poet is one who 'lets loose molecular populations in the hope that this will sow the seeds of, or even engender, the people to come, that these populations will pass into a people to come, open a cosmos'.[63]

Deleuze and Guattari criticize oedipalized readings of literature for preventing us from seizing the connection between a literary or writing machine and a field of social desiring-production that interrupts the order of the signifier. Literature is always a writing of the near future that concerns a revolution to come. The language of literature, therefore, is not to be defined solely in terms of what it says or what it signifies but by what causes it to move, to flow and to explode: 'The only literature is that which places an explosive device in its package'.[64] Oedipalized readings, by contrast, fail in that they reduce literature to an object of consumption that conforms to the established order. The result is to enslave the work (think of the number of times that even the most perspicacious of critics condemn Kafka, and we his readers, to failure!). Of course, the 'great voices' of literature, the ones capable of performing breakthroughs in grammar and syntax, always speak from the depths of psychosis.[65] In a revolutionary-becoming it is always a question of bringing into transversal communication the writing-machine, the painting-machine, the analytical engine, the social machine and the technical machines, removing them from their reified existence in the system of social and psychic repression, so that they become partial objects connected to one another 'in the flow that feeds one and the same desiring-machine, so many local fires patiently kindled for a generalized explosion'.[66]

If, as Simon Critchley has recently contested, philosophy 'begins' with disappointment, whether this disappointment be religious or political, this is only a small beginning, a beginning that perhaps had the wrong kind of investment (in the One, in identity, in control).[67] We might care to ask: does philosophy ever begin or does it only ever repeat? If it repeats, if philosophy is already more than philosophy, then what is repeated is never the beginning as such but rather the moment of excess (difference), the moment of overlife or germinal life. Nietzsche described himself as a perfect nihilist, that is, as a nihilist who has lived through the whole of nihilism but who has come to leave it behind him, finding himself in the 'labyrinth of the future'.[68] If nihilism has its causes in our 'categories of reason', falsely projected into the essence of things, then this must mean that any thinking 'beyond' nihilism requires a different thinking, a thinking of the monstrous that is monstrous. Nihilism was only a beginning caught up in a pathology of man, although it may be that this beginning arrives, like an uncanny guest, at a certain moment of time, such as the time of the end of man. The death of God is to be greeted, wrote Nietzsche, not by any sense of involvement or investment, but first by relief, quickly followed by exhilaration and expectation.[69] Nihilism is for the living who refuse death (no matter how much they prattle on about wanting to know the truth about dying); perfected nihilism remains, at the end of the day perhaps, for the living dead. One becomes a traitor to the human, all too human: 'Is it possible, without setting off loud protests on the part of militants of an edifying or dogmatic humanism, to think and to live the gentle rigour of friendship, the law of friendship *qua* the experience of a certain ahumanity ... beyond or below commerce of gods and men? And what politics would still be founded on this friendship which exceeds the measure of man ... Would it still be a politics?'[70] For, as Derrida notes, the concept of politics very rarely announces itself without an attachment of the state to the family (of man, always, perhaps), without, that is, a schema of filiation.[71]

Thinking beyond the law of number – against great numbers, where the greatest numbers include the strongest and weakest at same time[72] – is a thinking that also involves going beyond the law of genus and species/race (the politics of filiation) and calls for an altogether different language[73] (not simply 'more than one', as Derrida proposes, as the anomalous may also be less than one, completely other than one; after all, more than one is two which is another one). We should not be surprised that Derrida returns in recent work to the question of Nietzsche's overman since it is the overhuman which utters and stammers this other (esoteric) language. Such a return is entirely improper, strictly ahuman: 'To the charge "You shall be a monster, a shapeless mass", Nietzsche responds: "We have realized this prophecy".'[74]

Critchley's recent book inevitably given the pedagogic task it undertakes to perform gives due consideration to commonly accepted, if ultimately platitudinous, propositions regarding nihilism and modernity: 'To accept the diagnosis of modernity in terms of nihilism is to accept the ubiquity of the finite. That is, if God is bracketed out as the possible source of a response to the question of the meaning of life, then the response to that question must be sought within life, conceived as a finite temporal stretch between birth and death. So, under nihilistic conditions of modernity, the question of the meaning of life becomes a matter of finding meaning to human finitude'.[75] But, we must ask: are life and death able to live and die when stratified within the confines of the 'ubiquity of the finite'? Certainly, the banal placement of life in terms of a 'temporal stretch between birth and death' reveals little insight into the phenomenon of repetition, in which life gets caught up in a spectropoiesis, whether this poiesis be the event of the overlife that lives beyond bodies and organisms, but also through them, as in Deleuze, or the spectres of life in Derrida such as automata, machines, ghosts, beasts, the nameless Thing. In both cases one is dealing with a germinal life that haunts finite organisms and bodies, and overturns dramatically the meaning of finitude, speaking of a machinic surplus value (which is how both Deleuze and Derrida read Marx on capital). Spirits do not simply leave nature; rather, they animate non-organic and germinal life, inventing and reinventing themselves as evil spirits who burn nature in flames of metamorphosis, rediscovering the infinite in the spirit of evil.

Even though he invokes spectres and speaks of the 'event of death' (in this anlaysis the event is too casually conflated with a 'state of affairs') – which means for him 'the event of our death' – Critchley is thus left with very little, almost nothing, mourning the impossibility of a 'phenomenology of death' because, we are told, death is a 'state of affairs' about which we can find neither 'adequate intention' nor 'intuitive fulfilment', meaning that death is 'radically resistant to the order of representation'.[76] Hence the conclusion is reached that '*the ultimate meaning of human finitude is that we cannot find meaningful fulfilment for the finite*. In this specific sense, death is meaningless and the work of mourning is infinite'.[77]

The achievement of *Very Little … Almost Nothing* raises the stakes of a post-Nietzschean encounter with death, showing the need to cultivate atheism and scepticism in terms of a philosophical ethos. However, although Critchley desires to effect a movement beyond the phenomenology of death – the 'ungraspable facticity of dying' is said, with the aid of Blanchot and Levinas, to establish 'an opening onto a meta-phenomenological alterity' that cannot be made reducible to the power of the will or Dasein (there can be no subject of death) – for me this staging of the question of death remains caught within the confines of organismic life, the life of the 'I' and the self. For Critchley the 'recognition of meaninglessness' as something one can achieve leads to a 'deeper recognition of the profound limitedness of the human condition'.[78] He goes on to critique the illusions of suicide, locating in its alleged fantasy the 'virile leap into the void', and aiming to show the ridiculous character of a wanting to die; but one may want to ask about the phallic virility concealed in the idea of achieving and working towards one's very own recognition of meaninglessness.[79] The real difference between us, however, is over the question of affirmation. For Critchley death cannot be laid hold of and be made to work as the basis for an affirmation of life since it belongs to an ungraspable finitude. But if death is ungraspable it is not because of human finitude and the limitedness of *la condition humaine*, but because it belongs to the event. In other words, it does not belong to me (*Je* or *Moi*), *not even 'my' death*. It is precisely because death does not belong (to the subject) and cannot be owned (by the One) that it offers *the basis for an affirmation*. And it is precisely the event 'of' death which is not being thought in this instructive but inexcessive attempt to move beyond phenomenology.

Atheistic nihilism cannot afford to lose sight, and the site, of the participation, in the monstrous becoming of life, of the power of the demonic and the spectral.[80] As we see in Critchley's account, a fully realized or actualized atheistic nihilism too easily establishes for itself the power and the boundary of the Absolute, making the same mistake as the ascetic ideal of transforming a partial perspective into a total view of the world, and turning the reactive moment of a limited history into the – non-virtual, I would insist – 'truth' of all history. In short, on a spectral reckoning this nihilism is nothing other than the continuation and prolongation of the human, all too human ascetic ideal (which might perhaps partly explain why Nietzsche never in his writings associated atheism with an overcoming of this ideal). Nihilism, therefore, must be allowed to enjoy the character of an event, an event that is both 'decisive' and which lives on virtually and monstrously. When Nietzsche writes of this event as announcing the time of the future we are to take this future in its absolute futurity. Nihilism speaks of the future as the 'monstrous event that is on its way and wanders'.

We are to be modern, then, not simply in terms of being perpetually post, of continually outstripping ourselves – to be modern not at any cost, says Deleuze, but in terms of the power of the simulacrum by extracting from it the 'untimely' as that which exceeds our powers and puts us to the test, namely, as that which turns against modernity '"in favour, I hope, of a time to come"'.[81] This is to live – and die – at the edge of a 'critical modernity' and 'in relation to the future' that is attained 'by the phantasm of the eternal return as belief in the future'.[82] At this dis-juncture Deleuze raises the matter of two nihilisms (always more than one), which speak of a 'vast difference' between modes of destruction: one which destroys in order to conserve and perpetuate the established order of representations, models and copies, and an-other which destroys the models and copies in order to institute the chaos (an-archy) of the anomalous and enjoy the power that affirms divergence and the decentred circle, making of this power an object of affirmation: 'The opening must preserve this heterogeneity as the only chance of an affirmed or rather reaffirmed future. It is the future itself, it comes from there … The future can only be for ghosts. And the past.'[83] This is to free time from its thermodynamic arrow, which can only end in finite death (the death of the organism, of the body). The event lives on (death living on as the incorporeal event, as the time of ghosts, demons and spirits). There is neither absolute life nor absolute death. If we think monstrously enough this thinking may make a difference – *out of the repetition of difference and for a difference to come.* At the end of the remains of the day we shall be mourning not the limitedness of the human condition but the life and death that are to come. What if one day or night in the hour of your loneliest loneliness …[84]

Notes

1 D. H. Lawrence, *Complete Poems* (Harmondsworth: Penguin, 1993) p. 167.
2 Gilles Deleuze and Félix Guattari (1980), *A Thousand Plateaus*, trans. Brian Massumi (London: Athlone, 1988) p. 242.
3 Michel Serres, 'Language and Space: From Oedipus to Zola', *Hermes. Literature, Science, Philosophy*, ed. J. V. Harari and D. F. Bell (Baltimore: Johns Hopkins University Press, 1983) p. 43.
4 Sigmund Freud (1913), 'Totem and Taboo', *The Origins of Religion* (London: Pelican Freud Library vol. 13, 1990) p. 78.
5 'For we erre … by introducing the Daemonology of the Heathen Poets, that is to say, their fabulous Doctrine concerning Daemons, which are but Idols, or Phantasms of the braine, without any reall nature of their own, distinct from humane fancy.' In Thomas Hobbes (1651), *Leviathan* (Harmondsworth: Penguin, 1968) pp. 628–9.
6 Freud, *Totem*, p. 204.
7 Ibid., p. 128.
8 Deleuze and Guattari, *Plateaus*, p. 293.
9 Gilles Deleuze (1969), *The Logic of Sense*, trans. M. Lester and C. Stivale (London: Athlone Press, 1990) p. 154ff.
10 Deleuze and Guattari, *Plateaus*, p. 34.
11 In his essay 'The Uncanny' (1919) Freud will employ the same procedure, reading Hoffmann's tale of the 'Sand-Man' about the blinding of the eyes in terms of the dread of being castrated. Moreover, Freud will read the anxiety about eyes in terms of their intimate connection with the death of the father (the self-blinding of Oedipus is also invoked at this point). The Sand-Man is no 'one' other than the dreaded father. Freud will then go on to implicate ego disturbances, such as are undergone in the experience of the uncanny, in regression, to the time 'when the ego had not yet marked itself off sharply from the external world and from other people', especially in 'The Uncanny', *Art and Literature* (London: Pelican Freud Library Vol. 14, 1990)

p. 358. Again we witness the compulsion to repeat 'beyond' the pleasure principle, exposing the mind in thrall to a daemonic power, so that 'whatever reminds us of this inner "compulsion to repeat" is perceived as uncanny' (ibid., p. 361). What is uncanny in certain experiences is finding oneself unintendedly in the recurrence of the same situation, a recurrence which amounts to the return of the repressed. Freud contends that if this is the 'secret nature' of the uncanny then it is quite easy to understand why linguistic usage has extended the 'homely' (*das Heimliche*) into its exact opposite (*das Unheimliche*), 'for this uncanny is in reality nothing new or alien, but something which is familiar and old-established in the mind and which has become alienated from it only through the process of repression' (ibid., pp. 363–4). Freud then gives further examples to corroborate his thesis, such as the figuration of death in biology and the return of the dead, spirits and ghosts. See also Derrida's remarks on Freud on the uncanny in Jaques Derrida, *Spectres of Marx*, trans. Peggy Kamuf (London: Routledge, 1994) pp. 133, 173–5, where the automatism of repetition is related to the impersonal '*es spukt*'; that is, it is not clear, Derrida is suggesting, where the uncanniness comes from – its alien status needs to be reinscribed if one is to be true to the other (to the demonic powers). For Derrida the consequences of this move in Freud – which he also locates in Marx and Heidegger – are of tremendous importance for our understanding of the haunting which comes 'before life *as such*, before death *as such*'.

12 Ibid., p. 36.

13 Jacques Derrida (1972), *Disseminations*, trans. Barbara Johnson (London: Athlone Press, 1981) p. 52.

14 Ibid., p. 25.

15 C. Johnson, *System and Writing in the Philosophy of Jacques Derrida* (Cambridge: Cambridge University Press, 1993) p. 194.

16 Ibid.

17 Derrida, *Spectres*, p. 175.

18 Ibid., p. xx.

19 Gilles Deleuze (1968), *Difference and Repetition*, trans. Paul Patton (London: Athlone Press, 1994) p. 19.

20 Sigmund Freud (1920), 'Beyond the Pleasure Principle', *On Metapsychology* (London: Pelican Freud Library Vol. 11, 1991) p. 292.

21 Deleuze, *Logic*, p. 176.

22 D. H. Lawrence, *Women in Love* (Harmondsworth: Penguin, 1995) p. 185.

23 S. Zizek, *The Plague of Fantasies* (London: Verso, 1997) p. 89.

24 Lawrence, *Women*, p. 144.

25 Ibid., p. 128.

26 Ibid,. pp. 116–117.

27 Freud, *Totem*, p. 115.

28 E. Zola, *La Bête humaine*, trans. R. Pearson (Oxford: Oxford University Press, 1996) p. 44.

29 Deleuze, *Logic*, p. 325.

30 Ibid., p. 332.

31 Freud's own reworking of Weissmann in 'Beyond the Pleasure Principle', as well as Deleuze's critique of Freud on the death-drive and on Weissmann, is explored in detail in my *Germinal Life: The Difference and Repetition of Deleuze* (London: Routledge, 1999).

32 Deleuze and Guattari, *Plateaus*, p. 165.

33 Derrida, *Spectres*, p. 190.

34 Ibid., p. 184, n. 9.
35 Deleuze, *Logic*, p. 107.
36 Ibid., p. 105.
37 Gilles Deleuze and Felix Guattari (1991), *What is Philosophy?*, trans. G. Burchell and H. Tomlinson (London: Verso, 1994) p. 46.
38 Deleuze and Guattari *Difference*, p. 143.
39 Ibid., p. 139.
40 Deleuze, *Logic*, p. 281.
41 Deleuze, *Difference*, p. 145.
42 M. Foucault, 'Theatrum Philosophicum', *Language, Counter-Memory, and Practice*, trans. D. F. Bouchard and S.Simon (Oxford: Basil Blackwell, 1977) p. 170.
43 Ibid.
44 Ibid., p. 171.
45 Deleuze and Guattari, *Plateaus*, p. 261.
46 Ibid.
47 Ibid., p. 5.
48 Ibid., p. 238.
49 Ibid.
50 Ibid., p. 239.
51 Ibid., p. 245.
52 Deleuze seeks to think and map anomalous animal becomings from *Différence et répétition* to *A Thousand Plateaus* in terms of a conception of *univocal being*, in which Duns Scotus is dangerously supplemented by the 'atheists', and excessive rationalists, Spinoza and Nietzsche. This conception of being is best approached in terms of the question of a *distribution* that is without property, enclosure or measure. Stated in positive terms this distribution of being is 'nomadic' and ab-errant. It is also 'demonic' rather than 'divine' since only demons enjoy the delirious freedom of leaping over barriers and operating in the intervals between the fields of action set up by the gods. It is out of these reflections on the 'immeasurable state of things', and an attempt to come up with a new notion of hier-archy (where limits are to be thought in terms of excessive powers rather than in terms of normative laws), that Deleuze arrives at the proposition and thought-experiment: 'It is the monster which combines all the demons' (this monster is nothing other than univocal being thought deliriously and drunkenly).
53 For further insight into these notions, see H. P. Lovecraft, *At the Mountains of Madness and Other Novels* (London: HarperCollins, 1993) and *The Haunter of the Dark and Other Tales* (London: HarperCollins, 1994).
54 See Jacques Derrida on an-other democracy beyond the One, in *Politics of Friendship*, trans. G. Collins (London: Verso, 1997); compare Lawrence on Whitman and democracy, in *The Selected Letters of D. H. Lawrence*, ed. J. T. Boulton (Cambridge: Cambridge University Press, 1997) p. 171: 'God save me, I feel like creeping down a rabbit-hole, to get away from all these automobiles rushing down the ONE IDENTITY track to the goal of ALLNESS'.
55 Deleuze and Guattari, *Plateaus*, p. 246.
56 Ibid., p. 247.
57 Ibid.
58 Gilles Deleuze (1983), *Cinema 1. The Movement-Image*, trans. H. Tomlinson and B. Habberjam (London: Athlone Press, 1986) p. 51.
59 Gilles Deleuze (1968), *Expressionism in Philosophy: Spinoza*, trans. M. Joughin (New York: Zone Books, 1994), pp. 28–9.

60 Gilles Deleuze (1977), *Dialogues*, trans. H. Tomlinson and B. Habberjam (London: Athlone Press, 1987) p. 40.
61 Deleuze and Guattari, *Philosophy*, p. 130.
62 Deleuze and Guattari, *Plateaus*, p. 335.
63 Ibid.
64 Deleuze and Guattari (1972), *AntiOedipus*, trans. R. Hurley, M. Seem and H. R. Lane (London: Athlone Press, 1984) p. 134.
65 See Gilles Deleuze, *Critique et clinique* (Paris: Les Editions de Minuit, 1993) pp. 13–14, for further insight into links between psychosis, illness, the life-process and the peculiar 'health' of writing.
66 Deleuze and Guattari, *AntiOedipus*, p. 137.
67 Simon Critchley, *Very Little … Almost Nothing. Death, Philosophy and Literature* (London: Routledge, 1997) p. 2.
68 F. Nietzsche, Preface to section 3 of *On the Genealogy of Morals*, trans. R. J. Hollingdale and W. Kauffmann (New York: Random House, 1967).
69 F. Nietzsche, *The Gay Science*, trans. W. Kauffmann (New York: Random House, 1974) §343.
70 Derrida, *Politics*, p. 294.
71 Ibid., p. viii.
72 Ibid., p. 71.
73 Ibid., p. 299.
74 Deleuze, *Logic*, p. 107.
75 Critchley, *Very Little …*, pp. 24–5.
76 Ibid.
77 Ibid.
78 Ibid,. p. 27.
79 On the rational *and* courageous character of suicide see Hume's essay on the subject, in D. Hume, 'On Suicide', *Of the Standard of Taste and Other Essays*, ed. J. W. Lenz (Indianapolis: Bobbs-Merrill, 1965) pp. 151–61.
80 In this sentence the word 'participation' is used casually enough, but there is nothing casual about the philosophical notion we have of it. For insight into the stakes of 'participation' in Plato and post-Platonic thought, see Deleuze, *Expressionism*, 169ff.
81 Deleuze, *Logic*, p. 265.
82 Ibid.
83 Derrida, *Spectres*, p. 37.
84 Many of the ideas advanced in this chapter are worked through and over in greater detail in my *Germinal Life* (1999). This chapter reworks material first presented in this book coupled wih new material.

antony easthope

FREUD'S SPECTRES

It is known that Freud did everything possible to not neglect the experience of haunting, spectrality, phantoms, ghosts. He tried to account for them. Courageously, in as scientific, critical, and positive a fashion as possible. But by doing that, he also tried to conjure them. Like Marx. His scientific positivism was put to the service of his declared hauntedness and of his unavowed fear.[1]

Gods within and without

Reason and the irrational define each other's limits. In order to give at least some substance to that assertion I shall begin by sketching out an abbreviated history, which, since my topic is to be Freud, will contrast the three stages of religion as these are understood by psychoanalysis: animism, monotheism, modernity.

In the history of the West the opposition between reason and what was beyond it mapped onto the idea of a supernatural domain which was as external and objective as physical reality – and expressed in words such as these:

This is the word the Achaians have spoken often against me
and found fault with me in it, yet I am not responsible
but Zeus is, and Destiny, and Erinys the mist-walking
who in assembly caught my heart in the savage delusion
on that day I myself stripped from him the prize of Achilleus. Yet what could
I do? It is the god who accomplishes all things.
Delusion is the elder daughter of Zeus, the accursed
who deludes all.[2]

Homer's epic concerns the anger of Achilles. This is provoked because Agamemnon is forced to return a young woman, Chryseis, to her father in order to avert a plague, and so takes in her place Briseis, a slave girl belonging to Achilles. After Achilles's friend Patroclus has been killed Agamemnon apologizes to Achilles for what he has done: 'It is the god who accomplishes these things'.

Referring to this and similar passages E. R. Dodds, in his book *The Greeks and the Irrational*, argues that the presentation of psychic intervention is typical of Homeric and early Greek thought. Casual readers would be quite wrong to think that Agamemnon is simply excusing himself by blaming the supernatural powers of Destiny, Erinys, Delusion and Zeus – the assembled Greeks accept his explanation. A double structure is at work, as Dodds argues. On the one hand, 'all departures from normal human behaviour whose causes are not immediately perceived, whether by the subjects' own consciousness or by the observation of others, are ascribed to a supernatural agency, just as is any departure from the normal behaviour of the weather or the normal behaviour of a bowstring'.[3] But on the other, this idea of supernatural intervention safeguards and promotes the possibility of rational thought and rational action. When someone acts in a manner contrary to conventionally established and known expectations, then the action is not properly their own but has been dictated to them: 'unsystematised, nonrational impulses, and the acts resulting from them, tend to be excluded from the self and ascribed to an alien origin'.[4]

With the advent of Christianity the plurality of Greek gods is replaced by a monotheism (though a wide variety of principalities, spirits and powers, both orthodox and heretical, still frolic in the margins). But a similar strategy for demarcating an inside and outside is continued within the Christian opposition between God and his angels and the devil and his demons. Normal awareness is preserved because a clear border is set between itself and the possible intervention of external supernatural powers, for good and evil.

The implied ethic had always borne asymmetrically on men and women: since women were considered to be much less rational beings than men they were hardly responsible for their actions. These contradictions reveal themselves in the story Panurge tells Pantagruel:

> You know very well how at Brignoles, when the religious nun, sister Fatbum, was made big with child by the young Stiffly-stand-to't, her pregnancy became known, and she cited by the abbess, and in a full convention of the convent, accused of incest. Her excuse was, – That she did not consent thereto, but that it was done by the violence and impetuous force of the Friar Stiffly-stand-to't. Hereto the abbess very astutely replying, thou naughty wicked girl, why did'st thou not cry – A rape, a rape? then should all of us have run to thy succour. Her answer was, that the rape was committed in the

dortor, where she durst not cry, because it was a place of sempiternal silence. But, quoth, the abbess, thou roguish wench, why didst thou not then make some sign to those that were in the next chamber beside thee? To this she answered, that with her buttocks she made a sign unto them as vigorously as she could, yet never one of them did so much as offer to come to her help and assistance.[5]

Though the presumption is that sister Fatbum is limited in the possession of reason her replies evince the opposite.

With the first stirrings of modernity – exemplifying it in fact – the conception of an external force which might literally and physically act upon an individual's subjectivity, actually able to occupy and possess, begins to weaken, though it is still expressed within the confines of monotheism. That moment of transition is signalled in Hamlet. The hero is ordered to his revenge by the Ghost of his father, an actual presence on the stage. But a whole series of things suggests that this supernatural intervention acts upon Hamlet in ways very close to his own natural, subjective promptings. The literal objectivity of the Ghost is attenuated by the fact that, though seen by others, he speaks only to Hamlet. Before the Ghost addresses him Hamlet is already far from happy with the situation in Denmark – in fact, he greets the Ghost's announcement that Claudius murdered him with the words, 'Oh my prophetic soul!' Hamlet represents the new humanism which doubts the reality of ghosts, one reason why he delays, wonders if the Ghost may be the devil in 'a pleasing shape' and decides to put on a play as means to convict Claudius more conclusively.

Deities in the human breast

With romanticism the relocation of spiritual powers (and demons) from an external region into forms of subjectivity becomes effectively complete when the traditional line between rational and irrational becomes redrawn. Blake's well-known account is exemplary, from 'The Marriage of Heaven and Hell' (1790-93):

The ancient Poets animated all sensible objects with Gods, or genuiuses, calling them by the names and adorning them with the properties of woods, rivers, mountains, lakes, cities, nations, and whatever their enlarged & numerous senses could percieve [sic]

And particularly they studied the genius of each city & country, placing it under its mental deity;

Till a system was formed, which some took advantage of, & enslav'd the vulgar by attempting to realise or abstract the mental deities from their objects: thus began Priesthood;

Choosing forms of worship from poetic tales.

And at length they pronounc'd that the Gods had order'd such things.
Thus men forgot that All deities reside in the human breast.[6]

Blake's affirmation that all angels and demons, spirits and spectres, have only a subjective existence is radical. He makes no attempt to revive the animist world of antiquity with its objectively realized gods and goddesses; these were in any case created by perception and so by the projection of the deities which in fact reside within. He does contrast his avowed position with the rationalism of a power/knowledge system, though he cannot really explain the process of forgetting by which this form of abstract explanation could come to impose itself.

Romanticism does not simply relocate the deities. From Hegel to Wordsworth, Victor Hugo to Emily Bronte, it partakes of a wider historical change in which older expressions of subjectivity are re-evaluated while new forms of subjectivity come into existence. New feelings are reflected in a new idiom or rhetoric which in turn constructs those feelings. In an unprecedented articulation of inner psychology the word 'unconscious' begins to be used. There is no going back on the subjectivization of the deities.

Inheriting this fresh domain of subjectivity, Freud remains utterly uncompromising in his assessment of the supernatural. For example, in 'A Seventeenth-Century Demonological Neurosis' he discusses the records of a man who sold his soul to the devil but, through the good offices of the Virgin Mary, got it back again:

> The states of possession correspond to our neuroses, for the explanation of which we once more have recourse to psychical powers. In our eyes, the demons are bad and reprehensible wishes, derivatives of instinctual impulses that have been repudiated and repressed. We merely eliminate the projection of these mental entities into the external world which the Middle Ages carried out; instead, we regard them as having arisen in the patient's internal life, where they have their abode.[7]

Freud always sounds uneasy and defensive whenever he adopts a modest phrasing to say that all he has done is this. So it is here, when he says, 'We merely eliminate the projection of these mental entities'.

Freud's complete disbelief in the supernatural did not arrive as a *fait accompli*. It is consequence of a long historical progression from animism to monotheism to the death of God, as Lacan suggests. In the world of animism (exemplified by the apology of Achilles) 'the numen rises up at every step, at the corner of every road, in grottoes, at crossroads'[8] very much as Blake imagines, 'all sensible objects' becoming animated 'with Gods, or genuiuses'. Animism is a power, Lacan says, which 'cannot be overcome'[9] because (rather like power in Foucault) it comes from everywhere. Only when it is gathered into a single figure as monotheism can it be, as it were, confronted and dispersed. Not dispersed exactly but reinscribed, for it does not go away but (Lacan again) remains as the power of law bequeathed to us by 'the death of God'.[10] God, dead 'out there', lives on, with even more insidious effectivity, 'in here'. This reworking of knowledge and subjectivity forms the basis on which Freud works.

Freud's scientific rationalism

Freud's project is secular, rationalist and scientific, following the enlightenment strategy of establishing its own truth by denigrating an adversarial discourse, religion. Scientific thinking, he asserts, does 'not differ in nature from the normal activity of thought' which all of us employ in everyday life.[11] Science differs in being interested in things without immediate use for them; in examining sense perceptions sceptically, it aims to avoid merely individual influences. Overall, 'its endeavour is to arrive at a correspondence with reality', with what exists independent of our wishes.[12]

At the beginning of 'Instincts and their Vicissitudes' (1915) Freud sets out an account of how scientific understanding can only begin with a certain degree of abstraction (not simple observation) before moving between abstract and concrete, each being progressively modified in 'the advance of knowledge'.[13] Freud's epistemology is similar to that put forward by Marx in the 'Introduction' to the Grundrisse, the section on 'The Method of Political Economy'.[14] This is not surprising since both are taken from the common shelf of nineteenth-century scientific thought. Psychoanalysis, according to Freud, cannot construct a *Weltanschauung* of its own and must 'accept the scientific one'.[15] Within this larger project, psychoanalysis, a branch of psychology, is defined by its specific object as 'the science of unconscious mental processes'.[16]

In validating psychoanalysis as a science Freud never ceases to prefer it positively over its threatening but dubious forebear, religion. Science takes account of 'our dependence on the real external world' religion 'is an illusion'.[17] Of the three powers which may dispute the pre-eminence of science – art, philosophy and religion – only religion 'is to be taken seriously as an enemy'.[18] Freud's confidence that he can see off religion arises from the transition of modernity from an 'out there' to an 'in here', because he feels sure he can explain the first as the second.

God, whose existence imagines 'the forces of nature' in the form of a person,[19] this god-creator 'undisguisedly called "father"', is of course the father as 'he once appeared to the small child'.[20] The system in which God and the devil are accorded external and antagonistic existence can be explained otherwise: the idea of the devil is 'the best way out as an excuse for God' when things go wrong and plays the same part 'as the Jew does in the world of the Aryan ideal',[21] while the projection of the duality itself lets people evade responsibility for the fact that both good and evil reside in the human breast. The doctrine of reward in the afterlife 'is nothing other than a mythical projection' of the renunciation of pleasure enforced by the reality principle.[22] In sum, just as children experience neurosis on a personal level, so religion in its organized forms represents 'the universal obsessional neurosis of humanity'.[23]

Religion is not true but it is not good either, and certainly not needed to provide an ethic. When Kant pronounced a conjunction between 'the starry heavens and the moral law within us'[24] he touched on a great psychological truth, says Freud, for the supernatural is indelibly inscribed deep within subjectivity as the voice of conscience, the superego, whose energies, torn away from drive, turn against drive to produce human culture (as is argued in *Civilisation and its Discontents*). Culture is thus defined as a historical process of displacement and renunciation. For this a 'progressive strengthening of the scientific spirit seems to form an essential part'[25] since science comes nearest to succeeding in conquering the pleasure principle, both offering intellectual pleasure and promising practical gain in the end. (It is, Freud suggests, a secular version of the afterlife.) If the illusory comforts of religion let you down sooner or later, Freud has at his disposal deep resources of pessimism. 'Experience teaches us', he remarks, 'that the world is no nursery.'[26]

Freud's assurance is historically based, relying on the nineteenth-century development of the scientific method as well as its demystification of religion by referring it to the transition from external to internal. Freud is sure he can exorcise demons, ward off spectres, and has no need of angels. Yet we can't avoid bringing the force of his own writing to bear upon itself and ask whether his aggressive conjuring away of the supernatural does not contain elements of disavowal and defensiveness. I shall pursue this by looking at two responses.

Demonic thought

In a somewhat off-beat but fascinating article Terry Castle picks up the story of the numinous, external and internal, before Freud, in its romantic development. Although he mentions the better-known poets his concern is with forms of popular culture and in particular with documenting the massive contemporary interest in phantasmagoria – that is, visual effects produced especially by magic lanterns and stage magic. Castle recognizes that the early nineteenth century is an inheritor of the enlightenment but wants to demonstrate the 'latent irrationalism, haunting, so to speak, this rationalist conception of mind',[27] ambivalence as to whether ghosts were (1) objective and supernatural phenomena or (2) products of the mind.

Castle's argument is that proving ghosts do not exist externally – since they can be so vividly simulated – made ghosts seem 'more real than ever before – in that they occupied (indeed preoccupied) the intimate space of the mind itself'.[28] Subjective experience of the spiritual (and demonic) was not only equivalent to the old supernatural haunting but more sensational, more closely and inwardly unsettling since it took place inside your own head:

> If ghosts were thoughts, then thoughts themselves took on – at least notion-ally – the haunting reality of ghosts. The mind became subject to spectral presences. The epistemologically unstable, potentially fantastic metaphor of the phantasmagoria simply condensed the historical paradox by relocating the world of ghosts in the closed space of the imagination: one ended up supernaturalising the mind itself.[29]

I want to register a preliminary reservation here. The haunting reality of ghosts is not equal, identical and the same if one arises as supernatural event and the other as an effect of the imagination, however powerful. Castle knows this because he qualifies his assertion with the words 'at least notionally'. And when he talks about 'supernaturalising the mind' his verb is of course a metaphor.

This is the context for Castle's reading of Freud:

> By the time of Freud, the rhetorical pattern had resolved, as it were, into a cultural pathology: everyone felt 'haunted'. That is to say, the mind itself now seemed a kind of supernatural space, filled with intrusive spectral pres-ences ... Freud struggled with the paradoxes of spectralisation, largely by attempting to define a cognitive practice – psychoanalysis – which would exorcise these 'ghostly presences' ... Even as he attempted to demystify the uncanny forces of the psyche, he could not help reinventing the very theory of the unconscious itself as an essentially daemonic conception of thought.[30]

There is a certain sleight of hand here, as when Castle hedges his bets by saying 'a kind of supernatural space' and 'an essentially daemonic concep-tion of thought'. Freud's thought may concern the unconscious; it may in this respect take the demonic as its theme and object of investigation. But it does not follow that the form and method of his conception, his scientific metalanguage, is in any sense itself demonic. To enter this denial, though, relies on an opposition between an understanding of reality in terms of supernatural events and the procedures of scientific rationalism which refuse that understanding. Castle has already done his best to eradicate that distinction by saying there is no difference between actual ghosts and ghosts in the mind.

I want to agree with Castle's general view that Freud's writing does not eliminate a sense of the numinous and uncanny. However, I think Castle introduces an ahistorical simplification in his claim that it is a process simply of 'relocating' ghosts in the imagination. The space of the mind has changed with romanticism so that its haunting becomes part of a new conception of subjectivity. And the whole discursive reorganization which takes place at the time – leading to a much more abrasive opposition between objective and rational science on one side, and subjective and irrational feeling on the other – has changed the terrain radically. For all these reasons it is neither the same content nor the same location.

In the eye of the wolf

Castle's view is that Freud's thought is demonic: Deleuze and Guattari think it is not demonic at all, far from it. Since they seem to be obsessed with Freud, coming back to kick him again and again, and since they don't often say very much new along the way, and since I want to call up Wolfman and his famous dream for my own purposes later, I shall concentrate on what they say about that and take it to exemplify their position. And I shall defer for the moment citing the story of how Wolfman saw his wolves (and they him).

Freud reads the dream of the wolves in terms of the primal scene, a child's observation of or inference of the existence of intercourse between his or her parents. Seeing his mother's genitals as well as his father's penis (the act was *coitus a tergo*) the child feels threatened with castration by the father.

Deleuze and Guattari have three main objections to Freud's dealing with the wolves. Their overriding complaint is that his explanation is reductive and samey:

> Freud himself recognises the multiplicity of libidinal 'currents' that coexist in the Wolf-Man. That makes it all the more surprising that he treats the multiplicities of the unconscious the way he does. For him, there will always be a reduction to the One: the little scars, the little holes, become subdivisions of the great scar or supreme hole named castration; the wolves become substitutes for a single Father who turns up everywhere, or wherever they put him.[31]

Freud transforms complexity into simplicity, the multiplicities of the unconscious into a single father: 'Oedipus, nothing but Oedipus ... it flattens everything'.[32] Second, they protest that Freud's rationalism replaces experience with analysis: 'The trap was set from the start: never will the Wolf-Man speak. Talk as he might about wolves, howl as he might like a wolf, Freud does not even listen; he glances at his dog and answers, "It's daddy"'.[33] 'Kipling', they say, in the 'Mowgli' stories, 'understood the call of the wolves, their libidinal meaning, better than Freud'.[34] In consequence, the sharp edges of lived experience are blunted: 'Wolves watch, intently watch, the dreaming child; it is so much more reassuring to tell oneself that the dream produced a reversal and that it is really the child who sees dogs or parents in the act of making love.'[35] Otherness diminished becomes familiarity, the viscous flow of libido regulated and safely reterritorialized into a designated zone, the lava of desire frozen into immobility (and so on).

One reply would be to assert that what Freud says is true, it is scientific fact, and that Deleuze and Guattari make it easy for themselves by bracketing any possibility of truth (except for that of their own analysis) and concentrating upon the discursive effects of the psychoanalytic account. For the centrality of the phallus Freud could refer to the universal existence of an incest taboo and to the evident fact that society is patriarchal. If, as Juliet Mitchell says, 'psychoanalysis is not a recommendation for a patriarchal society, but an analysis of one',[36] Freud cannot be blamed for what he describes any more than Darwin for the zoological struggle he portrays.

In the end Freud certainly does point to the father. But a whole series of overlapping motifs and detailed interpretations intervene between Wolfman's dream and explanation in the paternal metaphor. There is a subtle and extended process in which representation in the dream is effected by reversal and suppression. (The violence of the parents' intercourse is converted into the uncanny stillness of the wolves in the tree.) Nor is the link between primal scene, subject and dream at all single or direct. Freud proposes: that the child feels coitus in terms of the father's aggression; that it excites him sexually as well as instigating fear of castration; that he wishes he were himself the object of the father's desire; that as a child he thinks of what is going on in terms of infantile sexual theory as anal intercourse. It is Daddy all right, but from this point of origin desire is deferred and deflected into all kinds of strange and inconsistent bypaths not simply at one with themselves.

Deleuze and Guattari recognize how much their own awareness of multiplicity and flow is indebted to Freud's conception of the unconscious – but they accuse the old man of misrecognizing his own insights, selling them out to analytic reason, making them comfortable to us. That accusation can certainly be made against the content of Freud's text but in its turn it ignores and misrecognizes the force of Freud's own text, his writing. Castle says Freud's thought is demonic, Deleuze and Guattari say it is not. My argument is that his thinking takes the form of scientific rationality but that the actual writing is spectral, full of angels and demons whose appearance is unsettling precisely because they emerge in the context in which they do. Freud's writing is uncanny.

The uncanny

Freud's discussion of the uncanny takes off from the observation that the meaning of certain words may sometimes be identical with its opposite – in German, for instance, *heimlich* and *unheimlich*. Considering examples from fiction (a story of a figure poised uncertainly between human and automaton, representation of a double) and from life (the experience of involuntary repetition), Freud asserts his own view that 'the uncanny (*unheimlich*) is something which is secretly familiar (*heimlich-heimisch*), which has undergone repression and then returned from it'.[37] There are, then, two conditions for the operation of the uncanny: the return of the repressed; the return of the repressed as something which used to be 'familiar and old-established in the mind and which has become alienated from it'.[38] Freud goes on to historicize this analysis, interpreting the familiar as supernatural ideas our ancestors believed in but which have become alien because a rationalist understanding has rendered them superannuated: 'As soon as something actually happens in our lives which seems to confirm the old, discarded beliefs we get a feeling of the uncanny; it is as though we were making a judgment something like this, "So, after all, it is true that one can kill a person by the mere wish!" or, "So the dead do live on and appear on the scene of their former activities!".[39] In the uncanny, ideas we think we have surmounted become once again plausible. Freud's explicit theoretical stance persistently advances scientific rationality against and in the place of its religious rival; but his recognition of the effect of the uncanny accepts that in practice and in experience – when 'something actually happens' in our lives – the old ideas are resurrected and show they have not been eradicated by an act of secular will.

When Freud turns to the relation between textuality and the effect of the uncanny he notes that a great deal that is not uncanny in fiction would be so if it happened in real life. In writing it is crucially a matter of context. Fairy stories are not at all uncanny because there we expect miracles all the time – and this holds also for the 'supernatural apparitions in Shakespeare's *Hamlet*'.[40] But the situation is altered 'as soon as the writer pretends to move in the world of common reality';[41] when the setting is 'one of material reality'[42] the effect of the uncanny arises in the juxtaposition of or interface between 'old, discarded beliefs' and modern reason – if the beliefs become plausible and seem confirmed by what happens.

Uncanny texts

At the beginning of George Romero's 1969 film, *Night of the Living Dead*, an average couple, brother and sister, drive through a bleakly deserted landscape in the American mid-West. They arrive at an equally deserted cemetery, shadowed by cypresses, but as they remark, still strangely light at 8.00 p. m. Their purpose is to place, at their mother's request, a memorial on their father's grave. The brother takes a secular position, complaining about the whole exercise: when his sister says, 'We still remember', he replies, 'I don't'; while she prays he lights a cigarette; she says, 'I haven't seen you in church lately' and he responds with, 'There's not much sense in my going to church'. He recalls how his grandfather used to tell him off as a child for doing things to frighten her: 'Boy, you'll be damned to hell'. He sees she is still easy to frighten and starts to menace her mockingly with the words 'They're coming to get you' in a Boris Karloff voice. He points out a distant figure who has appeared among the headstones, 'Here he comes now'. This member of the living dead approaches them, huge, with the ungainly steps of Karloff's monster, doubtfully positioned between constructed and human. He attacks the woman and kills the man while he is trying to save her. She runs off, pursued.

In this sequence the man's scepticism positively invokes modern rationality. But the fact that the 'old, discarded beliefs' are still alive is shown when he actively imitates the Karloff voice. At this point the animistic belief that words can make supernatural events happen is enacted. His cry of 'Here he comes now' conjures the arrival of a spectre in terrible reality. Through its lighting, movement and imagery the cinematic scene renders this sequence both unanticipated and convincing.

Freud's narrative of the Wolfman's dream occurs at the beginning of Chapter 4 of the case history, under the heading 'The Dream and the Primal Scene':

> I have already published this dream elsewhere, on account of the quantity of material in it which is derived from fairy tales; and I will begin by repeating what I wrote on that occasion:
> 'I dreamt that it was night and that I was lying in my bed. (My bed stood with its foot towards the window; in front of the window there was a row of old walnut trees. I know it was winter when I had the dream, and night-time.) Suddenly the window opened of its own accord, and I was terrified to see that some white wolves were sitting on the big walnut tree in front of the window. There were six or seven of them. The wolves were quite white, and looked more like foxes or sheep-dogs, for they had big tails like foxes and they had their ears pricked like dogs when they pay attention to something. In great terror, evidently of being eaten up by the wolves, I screamed and

woke up. My nurse hurried to my bed, to see what had happened to me. It took quite a long while before I was convinced that it had only been a dream; I had had such a clear and life-like picture of the window opening and the wolves sitting on the tree. At last I grew quieter, felt as though I had escaped from some danger, and went to sleep again.

'The only piece of action in the dream was the opening of the window; for the wolves sat quite still and without making any movement on the branches of the trees, to the right and left of the trunk, and looked at me. It seems as though they had riveted their whole attention on me.'[43]

For Wolfman, who experienced the dream, the wolves were just as he says, so terrifying he woke up. For us as readers of the narrative, set off and framed as it is by 'the world of common reality' – the detached rationalism of Freud's analysis – they become uncanny.

The effect is pervasive. Here, for example, almost at random, is the report of a casual conversation between Little Hans and his father recorded by the father and included in Freud's case history:

April 9th. This morning Hans came in to me while I was washing and bare to the waist.

HANS: 'Daddy, you are lovely! You're so white.'
I: 'Yes. Like a white horse.'
HANS: 'The only black thing's your moustache.' (Continuing) 'Or perhaps it's a black muzzle?'[44]

In a moment rather like that at the end of Hitchcock's film *Psycho* when the skull-face of Mrs Bates appears in superimposition behind her son's smile, the father here at first benignly transformed into a horse suddenly becomes changed into some beast with a predatory 'muzzle'.

Anna O. (a hysteric treated by Breuer) was nursing her father when she fell into 'a waking dream' in which she 'saw a black snake coming towards the sick man from the wall to bite him'; she tried to fend it off but her hand was paralysed; when she looked at it 'the fingers turned into little snakes with death's head (the nails)'.[45] Dreams as Freud amasses them in *The Interpretation of Dreams* come in many forms – banal, beautiful, grotesque, comic – but a lot of them are uncanny, as is this, selected for its brevity: 'He arrived at a railway station just as a train was coming in. What then happened was that the platform moved towards the train, while the train stopped still.'[46]

Freud's 1914 essay on 'The Moses of Michelangelo' is argued through in extraordinary detail which tries to account for the fact that this sublime law-giver and authority-figure, 'a concrete expression of the highest mental achievement',[47] far from looking serene and calmly authoritative, displays certain tiny signs of anxiety (the tablets under his right arm, for example, are upside down). Freud's analysis is that the statue shows a moment in a process, that Moses was distracted, started to get up, and forgot about the Tables, which 'began to slip', and were only retained because he squeezed them against his side with his arm: 'Another instant and the Tables would have pivoted ..., hit the ground with the upper edge foremost, and been shattered to pieces.'[48] Isn't the moment in which Moses nearly drops the Tables an effect of the uncanny in sculpture? Or rather the moment in Freud's exposition which reveals what we hadn't noticed before?

Another essay begins innocently enough with Shakespeare, *The Merchant of Venice*, and the scene at the end in which the suitors have to choose between three caskets. From there Freud enlarges his theme via a medieval collection of stories, the *Gesta Romanorum*, then back to Shakespeare for *King Lear* (three sisters, one of them silent), on to other myths and fairy stories, to the preliminary conclusion that the three caskets or boxes represent women and that there is something strange about the third of them. From a story in Grimm, Freud moves to his hypothesis – that in such cases the third of the sisters is dead and that in choosing her, the third, we choose 'Death itself'.[49] Another substantiating excursion through mythology and fiction leads round to the same conclusion with a similar uncanny effect, in the last sentence of the essay: 'But it is in vain that an old man yearns for the love of a woman as he had it first from his mother; the third of the Fates alone, the silent Goddess of Death, will take him into her arms'.[50]

The effect of the uncanny is endemic in Freud's writing, necessarily so. Although his project specifies itself as the displacement of religion by rationality he knows that the unconscious is itself peopled with 'old discarded beliefs' which still stagger around blinking in the light of reason. The *New Introductory Lectures* contain, surprisingly, a long discussion of Marxism; Freud does not believe that changing the economic base will change the ideological superstructure since 'the past, the tradition of the race and of the people, lives on in the ideologies of the superego, and yields only slowly to the influences of the present'.[51] Having described in vivid detail how prophylactic rituals around defloration, menstruation and childbirth in primitive society can be explained in terms of fear of woman, Freud comments that 'in all this there is nothing obsolete, nothing which is not still alive among us'.[52] When Freud remarks that 'a man who will kiss a pretty girl's lips passionately, may perhaps be disgusted at the idea of using her toothbrush'[53] surely this juxtaposition of modernity (procedures for dental hygiene) with a much older anxiety evinces in us a slight, uncanny quiver?

Displaced synecdoche: traces of the uncanny

The nearest fictional example I can think of to Freud's Wolfman's wolves comes from Edgar Allen Poe. In the short story, 'The Black Cat', the anonymous narrator is troubled by a (one-eyed) black cat which has made its home with him. Trying to kill the cat he kills his wife and walls up her body in the cellar ('as monks of the Middle Ages are recorded to have walled up their victims' – an old, discarded belief). Visited by the police he takes them round the house, and as they pass the tomb in the cellar they hear an 'inhuman shriek':

> For one instant the party upon the stairs remained motionless, through extremity of terror and awe. In the next, a dozen stout arms were toiling at the wall. It fell bodily. The corpse, already greatly decayed and clotted with gore, stood erect before the eyes of the spectators. Upon its head, with red extended mouth and solitary eye of fire, sat the hideous beast … I had walled the monster up within the tomb.[54]

Despite its similarities with the wolf dream – the animal unexpectedly staring at the speaker – I submit that this is nothing like as forcefully uncanny as Freud's text. Poe is working up a narrative designed to thrill, excite and lead to a *coup de théâtre*, 'I had walled the monster up within the tomb'. It becomes too like the fairy story and thus unlike psychoanalytic writing with its 'world of common reality'.

Freud believes the uncanny is more effectively rendered by suggestion than actual embodiment. Such a manoeuvre dodges modern scepticism and helps to bring the old into close association with the new. In the opening of *Night of the Living Dead* it is not, I think, the climax with the arrival of the creature itself which is seriously uncanny but rather the incidental remark at the beginning – that the light is strange (the filmed image shows this very well). A similar displacement occurs with Wolfman's dream.

How many wolves were there? 'There were six or seven' of them, Wolfman says, when he is looking intently at them to try to work out whether they are wolves, foxes or sheep-dogs (their ears are pricked up 'like dogs when they pay attention to something'[55]). No mention of their looking at him – this comes later, in the past tense, after he has screamed, woken up and gone to sleep again, when he mentions retrospectively that 'it seemed as though they had riveted their whole attention on me'. Strictly, then, the gaze of the wolves is recorded only in the form of a secondary revision, an effect repeated when Wolfman in the present, for Freud, draws a picture of the tree with the wolves. This is reproduced on the next page of the text and in it the wolves are indeed looking straight out.[56] There are five of them.

Today the uncanny seems to have two particularly effective features –

reversal between subject and object, and the power of the symptom (the omen or proleptic trace). Both figure in Wolfman's dream; both are constantly offered as the pleasures of the uncanny by mainstream cinema.

The subject intently caught up in their own active subjectivity (counting wolves) suddenly becomes an object for the strange subjectivity of the other (riveting their attention). This reversal seems especially to be played out in terms of the logic of the look and the gaze. Lacan explains this with the story of the little boy who says of the floating sardine tin, 'You see that can? Do you see it? Well, it doesn't see you.'[57] (No, it doesn't, but someone there might, since whatever I see instances a point from which I could be seen.) Janet Leigh in *Psycho* drives into the growing darkness until great black drops of rain (like blood?) fall on her windscreen and instead of the camera looking with her down the road, she is looked at by the camera, by us, as she pulls off the highway towards the uncertain sign, 'Bates Motel'. At the beginning of *Jaws* the naked woman who has run up the beach and swum out to sea is suddenly viewed (by what?) from below, outlined against the surface by the moonlight.

The second feature follows from recognition that the really affective moment is not when the spectre, demon, monster becomes visible but when it is presaged ('It's quiet ... too quiet'; 'What was that noise?'; 'Why is it still light this late?'). I think we might refer to this as displaced synecdoche, synecdoche because a part represents a whole, displaced because the part is set at a distance from what it stands for. In *Alien* the scalpel cuts into the carapace which had been on John Hurt's face; a drop of yellow blood falls on the floor – and burns its way through. In *Jurassic Park* the carload of visitors who have come to look at the dinosaurs notice the coffee in their plastic cups is vibrating from unseen mighty steps.

My contention is that Freud's writing is much more like this than is the work of contemporaries such as Yeats. Yeats's avowed purpose was to open his poetry to a world of spirits, yet he constantly recuperates any potentially mysterious alterity (the wild swans at Coole) until they become more of the same, merely vehicles for personal expression. Freud's writing becomes uncanny because it dramatizes a juxtaposition between the common sense of its analysis and the 'old, discarded beliefs' which come alive in it.

Freud's project seen otherwise

I tried to let Freud have his own say on the nature of his scientific, antireligious project. It is tempting, however, to wonder what this endeavour might look like seen from the other side, as it were. It might run like this.

Freud was notoriously conservative in what political views he did avow, sceptical whether any 'golden age ... can be realised'.[58] Yet *The Interpretation of Dreams*, which records Freud's foundation of psychoanalysis through the process of his own self-analysis, gives evidence for another story. A long passage[59] recalls a series of dreams in which Freud longed to go to Rome and was disappointed, in one dream, because he could only see it shrouded in mist, 'the promised land seen from afar', as he says, imagining himself as Moses. In another dream a different identification appears. Freud guesses that his longing for the eternal city derived from a childhood identification with Hannibal and also with the Carthaginians against the Romans in the Punic wars: 'I began to understand for the first time what it meant to belong to an alien race, and anti-semitic feelings among the other boys warned me that I must take up a definite position. To my youthful mind Hannibal and Rome symbolised the conflict between the tenacity of Jewry and the organisation of the Catholic church.'[60] Freud wishes to possess Rome, the Rome responsible for his oppression.

But reference to the Punic wars and the Carthaginians also points to the *Aeneid*, the story of Aeneas, his struggle to free himself from Dido, the Carthaginian queen, and his subsequent success in founding Rome, supported by Jupiter and opposed by Juno. Freud's fantasy seems to wish the project to succeed but with contrary identifications, thus: Hannibal for Aeneas, Carthaginian for Roman, Juno for Jupiter. In the *Aeneid* there are two journeys to the underworld: the famous one in Book VI when Aeneas descends to get the support he needs to win Rome; another, less well-known, in Book VII when Juno herself goes down to call up Hades against Aeneas, proclaiming 'If I cannot change the gods above, I shall move the world beneath'. These are the words Freud places as the epigraph to *The Interpretation of Dreams*, '*Flectere si nequeo superos, Acheronta movebo*'.[61] Could it be that this Freud/Moses/Hannibal wants to destroy the official gods of Rome/Jupiter/Aeneas but knows he cannot do so with a direct political attack, on the surface, in daylight, so he calls on the gods of the underworld and makes his approach from below? By mobilizing to his purposes the powers of Hell even in the heart of scientific reason?

So, the uncanny, which I've pointed out in the high-cultural scientific writing of Freud and in the fictional incitements of popular cinema, is the most of the spectral we can expect. Is that it or is there perhaps something more? My preference is to end not with a conclusion but rather by indicating other questions. There may remain for us other possibilities, even if I have only space to suggest them here in the form of displaced synecdoche.

In the *Duino Elegies* (1922) Rilke undertakes two moves. One is to treat the numinous as so radically subjective it becomes other than human:

Everywhere appearance and vision came, as it were, together in the object, in every one of them a whole inner world was exhibited, as though an angel in whom space was included, were blind and looking into himself. This world, regarded no longer from the human point of view, but as it is within the angel, is perhaps my real task, one, at any rate, in which all my previous attempts would converge.[62]

The other is to establish the 'angel' in the space once occupied by the Greek spirit or demon, δαμων, having the attributes of good and evil at once (as the 'First Elegy' says in its seventh line, 'Every angel is terrible', *schrecklich*).

Rilke's sense of the angelic has been picked up by Thomas Pynchon, whose novel *Gravity's Rainbow* echoes with allusions to the *Elegies*. One section refers to 'these star-blotting Moslem angels ... *O, wie spurlos zerträte Engel den Trostmarkt*', a phrase translated and transformed later on the same page as 'German dreams of the Tenth-Elegy angel coming, wing-beats already at the edges of waking, coming to trample spoorless the white marketplace of his own exile'. The reference is to line 20 of the 'Tenth Elegy', translated by Leishman and Spender as, 'How an Angel would tread beyond trace their market of comfort').[63] Rilke – and Pynchon in his wake – regard this idea of angels as profoundly significant, as something like a post-transcendental centre of value in their texts. But there is not much more you can say about these angels than that: their content and operation is defined by the specific contexts in which they appear; they don't seem to have a fixed identity as entities but, rather, an uncertain status (the reason, no doubt, they are the way they are). Are Rilke's angels any better than those of Yeats, which I accused earlier of being insufficiently numinous? Why do Rilke and Pynchon revisit them so intently? Do they know something Freud doesn't?

Notes

1 Jacques Derrida, *Archive Fever: a Freudian Impression*, trans. E. Penowitz (Chicago: Chicago University Press, 1995), p. 85.

2 Homer, *The Iliad*, trans. R. Lattimore (Chicago: Chicago University Press, 1961), XVIII, ll. 85–93.

3 E. R. Dodds, *The Greeks and the Irrational* (Berkeley and Los Angeles: University of California Press, 1963), p. 13.

4 Ibid., p. 17.

5 Rabelais, *Gargantua and Pantagruel*, trans. T. Urquart (London: Dent [1693], 1929), p. 324.

6 W. Blake, *The Complete Writings*, ed. G. Keynes (London: Oxford University Press, 1966), p. 153.

7 All references to Freud are to the Pelican Freud Library 1973–86, volume number followed by page reference. Freud, 14: 383–4.

8 J. Lacan, *The Ethics of Psychoanalysis 1959–60*, trans. D. Porter (London: Routledge, 1992), p. 172.
9 Ibid.
10 Ibid., p. 177.
11 Freud, 2: 206.
12 Ibid.
13 Freud, 11: 113.
14 K. Marx, *Grundrisse*, trans. M. Nicholaus (Harmondsworth: Penguin, 1973), p. 100–2.
15 Freud, 2: 193.
16 Freud, 15: 255.
17 Freud, 2: 211.
18 Freud, 2: 195.
19 Freud, 12: 197.
20 Freud, 2: 198.
21 Freud, 12: 311.
22 Freud, 11: 41.
23 Freud, 12: 226.
24 Cited in Freud, 2: 199.
25 Freud, 2: 216.
26 Freud, 2: 204.
27 T. Castle, 'Phantasmagoria: Spectral Technology and the Metaphysics of Modern Reverie, *Critical Inquiry*', 15:1 (1988), 29.
28 Ibid., p. 58.
29 Ibid., p. 52.
30 Ibid., p. 59.
31 G. Deleuze and F. Guattari, *A Thousand Plateaus, Capitalism and Schizophrenia*, trans. Brian Massumi (London: Athlone, 1988), p. 31.
32 Ibid., p. 34.
33 Ibid., p. 38.
34 Ibid., p. 31.
35 Ibid., p. 28.
36 Juliet Mitchell, *Psychoanalysis and Feminism* (Harmondsworth: Penguin, 1974), p. xv.
37 Freud, 14: 368.
38 Freud, 14: 363–4.
39 Freud, 14: 371.
40 Freud, 14: 373.
41 Freud, 14: 374.
42 Freud, 14: 375.
43 Freud, 9: 259.
44 Freud, 8: 215.
45 Freud, 3: 93.
46 Freud, 4: 534.
47 Freud, 14: 277.
48 Freud, 14: 271.
49 Freud, 14: 241.
50 Freud, 14: 247.
51 Freud, 2: 99.
52 Freud, 7: 271.

53 Freud, 7: 64.
54 E. A. Poe, 'The Black Cat', *The Complete Tales and Poems of Edgar Allen Poe* (Harmondsworth: Pemguin, 1982), p. 230.
55 Freud, 9: 259.
56 Ibid.
57 J. Lacan, *Four Fundamental Concepts of Psychoanalysis*, trans. A. Sheridan (London: Hogarth, 1977), p. 95.
58 Freud, 12: 185.
59 Freud, 5: 282–7.
60 Ibid.
61 Virgil, *Aeneid*, trans. W. F. Jackson Knight (London: Guild Publishing, 1989), VII, l. 312.
62 Cited by J. B. Leishman and S. Spender, trans., *Duino Elegies* by R. M. Rilke (London: Chatto & Windus, 1975), p. 10.
63 T. Pynchon, *Gravity's Rainbow* (New York: Viking, 1973), p. 341.

daniel conway

UNFAMILIAR HAUNTS: THE PRIMITIVE ONTOLOGY OF HEIDEGGER'S *DER SPIEGEL* INTERVIEW

Thinking does not overcome metaphysics by climbing still higher, surmounting it, transcending it somehow or other; thinking overcomes metaphysics by climbing back down into the nearness of the nearest. The descent, particularly where man has strayed into subjectivity, is more arduous and more dangerous than the ascent.[1]

In 1966 Martin Heidegger agreed to be interviewed by representatives of *Der Spiegel* magazine. On condition that the interview would be published only after his death, Heidegger made himself available for questions concerning his nazi entanglements, the practical consequences of his thinking, and his speculations on the future of humankind. The interview appeared in *Der Spiegel* in May of 1976, just days after his death, under the title 'Nur noch ein Gott kann uns retten' ('Only a God Can Save Us').[2]

My particular focus in this chapter is a consequence of Heidegger's *Der Spiegel* interview that was almost certainly unintended – namely, the emergence of the primitive ontology that silently shapes (and limits) the articulation of his post-metaphysical thinking. Responding to the unusual constraints of the interview format, as well as to the overtly political agenda of his interlocutors,[3] Heidegger manifests the atavistic metaphysical prejudices that haunt his philosophizing. The *Der Spiegel* interview thus affords us a rare glimpse of Heidegger when he is not in full command of the direction and theme of his philosophizing, when he is palpably exercised by his deepest anxieties concerning the future of humankind.

Sympathetic readers typically treat the emergence of this primitive ontology as a harmless aberration.[4] While there is certainly some merit to this interpretation, it strikes me as too simple, especially with respect to a complex thinker of the rank and stature of Heidegger. I consequently treat the emergence of this primitive ontology as revealing a hidden source of the energy that animates his post-metaphysical exertions. Borrowing from the work of Jacques Derrida, I maintain that Heidegger's *Der Spiegel* interview brings to light the 'hauntology' that both inhabits and possesses his more familiar philosophical investigations. As we shall later see in more detail, the *Der Spiegel* interview intimates the extent to which his thinking is haunted by the ghosts of humanism.

Especially to Heidegger's more reverent champions, the emergence of this hauntology might warrant disappointment or embarrassment on his behalf. Indeed, perhaps this warrant partly explains the relative lack of interest paid to the *Der Spiegel* interview by his readers. It seems to me, however, that the emergence of this primitive ontology places his later philosophy in a potentially more flattering light. Rather than attempt to dismiss or domesticate this primitive ontology, I wish instead to summon it as the basis for an alternative interpretation of Heidegger's practical philosophy. Towards that end, I wish to identify and put to work the evil spirits that haunt his later philosophizing.

If we are willing to acknowledge the primitive ontology that haunts Heidegger's thinking, then we need not endorse the standard interpretation of his later philosophy as apolitical, fatalistic and/or nihilistic. The Heidegger who lends voice to the primitive ontology of the *Der Spiegel* interview actually secures a minimal domain of praxis for certain human beings, thereby reserving for humankind a role in its own redemption. Indeed, only by virtue of this primitive ontology may we treat the poet-philosophers to whom he defers as lawgivers. It is their unique labour to illuminate the *Gestell* of planetary technics and to glean a saving insight into its essential, enframing nature. Harnessing the fructifying power of the poetic imagination, they will gradually return humankind to a more appropriate orientation to thinking. In so doing they will legislate the worldly preparations that may entice the absent divinity finally to appear.

Unheimlich manoeuvres

Why Heidegger agreed to be bound by the ontic constraints of a magazine interview is not entirely clear. To be sure, he gained thereby a unique opportunity to correct the historical record of his activities in the mid-1930s, especially during his tenure as Rector of the University of Freiburg.[5] But he certainly did not make very much of this opportunity, even insisting at one point that 'National socialism did indeed go in this direction' of 'help[ing] man as such achieve a satisfactory relationship to the essence of technicity' (61). In addition to squandering this opportunity to apologize for his entanglements with national socialism, he also subjected himself to the vagaries of a public forum and discourse that are profoundly unsympathetic to his (and perhaps any) approach to philosophy. As one might have expected him to have foreseen, in fact, his interviewers attempted to mould his philosophical insights into pithy, apothegmatic nuggets suitable for public consumption. Any gains he might have achieved in rehabilitating his reputation were very likely negated by his voluntary participation in the vulgar popularization of his philosophy. Even those critics who dismiss this interview as self-serving are willing to admit that it has not served him well at all.[6]

I begin my investigation of the *Der Spiegel* interview at approximately its midpoint. Here the interviewers raise the question of the status of praxis in late modernity, a question they are apparently unable to consider outside the context of techne. Their queries to Heidegger are consequently as pointed as they are narrow.

> **Spiegel**: Fine. Now the question naturally arises: Can the individual man in any way still influence this web of fateful circumstance? Or, indeed, can philosophy influence it? Or can both together influence it, insofar as philosophy guides the individual or several individuals, to a determined action?
>
> **Heidegger**: If I may answer briefly, if not clumsily, but after long reflection: philosophy will be unable to effect any immediate change in the current state of the world. This is true not only of philosophy but of all purely human reflection and endeavor. Only a god can save us. [*Nur noch ein Gott kann uns retten.*] The only possibility available to us is that by thinking and poetizing we prepare a readiness for the appearance of a god, or for the absence of a god in [our] decline, insofar as in view of the absent god we are in a state of decline. (57)

From the relentlessly technical standpoint of Heidegger's interviewers, the question of praxis comes down to this: does thinking either promise or possess the capacity to lead to the realization of a practical activity that might contribute to our salvation? That is, might thinking somehow cause, invite, enjoin, precipitate, occasion or effect the saving appearance of the absent divinity? We know from Heidegger's other writings that his 'official' answer to this question tends more cautiously to the negative: the thinking that might precede the appearance of the god is not a technical articulation of human mentation; nor is it properly suited to the realization of practical ends in even the broadest sense of political activity.[7]

In his response to his interviewers, however, Heidegger deviates somewhat from this 'official' position. Here, it seems, he faces a nettlesome dilemma: if he divorces thinking altogether from the appearance of the saving divinity, then he risks abandoning the project of renewing the dimension of human praxis; in that event, human beings would altogether lack the resources needed to remediate the benighted condition of the world in late modernity. If he reserves for human beings some measure of practical efficacy, whereby they might undertake to improve themselves or their orientation to the erratic career of Being, then he risks transforming the sprawl of global technicity into a technical problem requiring a technical solution. That is, he must somehow contribute to the articulation of a 'solution' to the 'problem' of global technics, but without ever presenting the sprawl of technicity as a technical problem to be solved by an application of technical rationality.

His apparent strategy in the *Der Spiegel* interview is to impale himself on the latter horn of this dilemma, but only after reducing this horn to the barest protruberance. He need attribute only a minimal, indirect agency to the poet-philosophers whom he beckons, for they are entrusted 'simply' with inaugurating the preparatory thinking that will ready the world for the advent of the absent deity. They are not expected to rule empires, found cities, cultivate civic virtues, enforce a social contract, formulate the moral law, frame a constitution, tame a leviathan, educate a prince, prosecute just wars or assume an original position. In fact, Heidegger suggests that the preparatory activity of these poet-philosophers might not constitute an agency at all: the god will appear (or not) only when humankind has finally overcome its preoccupation with its precious 'agency'. And this is very likely what he meant to convey.[8]

In the ontic parlance of the *Der Spiegel* interview, however, this is not exactly what he says. Indeed, sensing that Heidegger has not yet ruled out a technical solution to the crisis of global technics, his interviewers press him on the precise nature of the relationship he envisions between thinking and salvation:

> **Spiegel**: Is there a correlation between your thinking and the emergence of this god? Is there here in your view a causal connection? Do you feel that we can bring a god forth by our thinking?
>
> **Heidegger**: We can not bring him forth by our thinking. At best we can awaken a readiness to wait [for him]. (57)

From the narrowly technical perspective of his interviewers, Heidegger may appear to have sidestepped a straightforward question. Regardless of whether thinking brings forth the absent deity or awakens a readiness to wait (which in turn contributes to the appearance of the god), thinking is predicated of a practical capacity to contribute to our eventual salvation. Put somewhat differently: Heidegger has the opportunity here to deny categorically that thinking is practical in any way, shape or form, but he does not. As a consequence of his uncharacteristic latitude on this important point, his interviewers press forward:

> **Spiegel**: But can we help?

Heidegger: The first help might be the readying of this readiness. It is not
through man that the world can be what it is and how it is – but also not
without man. In my view, this goes together with the fact that what I call
'Being' … has need of man in order that its revelation, its appearance as
truth, and its [various] forms may come to pass. The essence of technicity I see in what I call 'pos-ure' [*Ge-Stell*], an often ridiculed and perhaps
awkward expression. To say that pos-ure holds sway means that man is
posed, enjoined, and challenged by a power that becomes manifest in
the essence of technicity – a power that man himself does not control.
Thought asks no more than this: that it help us achieve this insight.
(57–8)

Accepting his interviewers' parlance (as well as its indelibly technical
connotations), Heidegger attributes to thinking a limited, indirect, practical capacity – namely, the 'readying of the readiness' that might occasion
the appearance of the absent divinity. Rather than insist on a role for thinking that is absolutely untainted by practical considerations, he instead
identifies its practical benefits as preparatory and indirect. As a consequence, his interviewers are keen to identify the precise nature of the
practical efficacy that he wishes to attribute to thinking, and he is equally
resolved not to allow their premature capitulation to technicity to tincture
his responses. Here it becomes clear, in fact, that his participation in this
public forum virtually precludes the successful communication of his
philosophical insights. He can neither give his interlocutors the technical
answers they seek, nor revert to his customary mode of protracted philosophical explanation.

Convinced that Heidegger wishes to ascribe to thinking an indirect
practical capacity, his interviewers invite him to situate himself (or not) in
their rendition of the history of praxis in the tradition of western philosophy. They maintain that philosophy has long provided indirect help in
practical affairs, and they wonder if he has something similar in mind:

Spiegel: Yet, nonetheless, in former times (and not only in former times) philosophy was thought to accomplish a great deal indirectly – directly only
seldom – but was able indirectly to do much, to help new currents break
through … Do you mean now that this effectiveness of philosophy is at
an end? And if you say that the old philosophy is dead – that there is no
such thing any more, do you also include the thought that this effectiveness of philosophy, if it was ever there in the past, is in our day, at least,
no longer there?

Heidegger: A mediated effectiveness is possible through another [kind of]
thinking, but no direct one – in the sense that thought will change the
world in any causal way, so to speak. (58)

Heidegger neither refuses nor qualifies his interlocutors' understanding of philosophy as having 'accomplish[ed] a great deal indirectly'. He repeats his claim that thinking can be indirectly (or mediately) efficacious, but he now explicitly emphasizes the difference between practical efficacy and causality. An example of the relationship he has in mind is that which obtains between the absence of the god and our current state of decline.

> **Spiegel**: Excuse me, we do not wish to philosophize – we are not up to that – but we have here the point of contact between politics and philosophy. That is why you notice that we are drawn into a dialogue of this kind. You have just said that philosophy and the individual would be able to do nothing but ...
>
> **Heidegger**: ... but make ready for this readiness of holding oneself open for the arrival, or for the absence, of a god ... Making [ourselves] ready for the aforementioned readiness involves reflecting on what in our own day ... is. (58)

In this response, Heidegger introduces an important clarification: the 'making ready' that thinking can accomplish yields a readiness for either the appearance *or* the absence of the god who might save us. That is, the distinctly practical concerns that might lead one down the path of thinking, e.g., the need or desire to summon the absent god, must evaporate as one travels this path. Here Heidegger reveals that the practical efficacy he is willing to locate in thinking is neither technical nor anti-technical in its nature, but *extra*-technical. Thinking thus prepares the world for the advent of the absent divinity, but only by first granting us an insight into the essence of planetary technics.

The absent god will appear, that is, only when we are prepared to receive either its absence or its presence, only when we have cultivated an ontological indifference to the salvation of humankind *qua* favoured species. This is why Heidegger earlier qualified 'the only possibility available to us' as involving our preparations for a readiness either 'for the appearance of the god, or for the absence of a god in [our] decline'. The crisis of global technics will not be solved simply by the adventitious appearance of a god, for we may not yet be prepared to acknowledge the nearing of this god. We must also aspire to an adequate understanding of the historical conditions under which we have grown content to dwell in the absence of the divinity. Until we gain an insight into the *Gestell* of planetary technics, that is, we are not sufficiently prepared to receive the deity in its presence or absence. As Heidegger later elaborates, 'within its own limits [thinking] helps man as such achieve a satisfactory relationship to the essence of technicity' (61). This is why he believes that achieving an insight into the essence of the enframing power of technicity is of paramount importance. Because this saving insight will be gleaned only through thinking, he insists on a (non-causal) linkage between thinking and salvation.[9]

Following a brief exchange concerning the success of Heidegger's own thinking thus far,[10] he concludes his contribution to the interview with the following statement, which has been widely received as uninspiring in both tone and content:[11]

> **Heidegger**: ... But the greatest need of thought consists in this, that today, so far as I can see, there is still no thinker speaking who is 'great' enough to bring thought immediately and in clearly defined form before the heart of the matter and thereby [set it] on its way. For us today, the greatness of what is to be thought is [all] too great. Perhaps the best we can do is strive to break a passage through it – along narrow paths that do not stretch too far. (64–5)

As this extract demonstrates, Heidegger presents his practical philosophy in somewhat paradoxical terms. Although, as he readily admits, he 'knows nothing' about the possible practical effects of the thinking he describes,[12] and although he consistently disavows any first-hand authority on the progress of his own efforts at thinking, he nevertheless recommends thinking as the sole alternative available to humankind in late modernity. Although he claims to be of virtually no help in understanding how thinking might bear practical fruit, speculating that '300 years' may pass before anyone adequately understands these matters, he is sufficiently familiar with thinking to assert that it might someday yield a saving insight into the essence of planetary technics. While his simultaneous embrace of these alternative claims need not involve him in contradiction, it does render his precise relationship to thinking difficult to specify. For example: if he really knows so little about thinking, about its future and its promise, then why does he so categorically discourage those who would invest in thinking their ontic hopes for melioration and redemption?[13]

It would seem, in fact, that Heidegger is not able to remain silent for long about thinking – despite his admitted ignorance of its nature and effects. He is not content not to say what he cannot say, and he cannot abjure his need to articulate the unsayable. Indeed, the unsayable haunts him, demanding that he lend it voice – which means, of course, that whatever he *does* say is necessarily inadequate and probably misleading. While Heidegger is ordinarily willing to bear these risks within the hermetic confines of his later philosophizing, his *unheimlich* manoeuvres in the *Der Spiegel* interview escalate these risks to the very threshold of tolerance. Indeed, while not quite saying what he wishes to say about the extra-technical, para-practical efficacy of thinking, Heidegger succeeds – unwittingly, perhaps – in voicing the metaphysical bogeys that continue to haunt him.

Heidegger's primitive ontology

Heidegger's failure in the *Der Spiegel* interview to say what he means is attributable to a number of factors, including the inherent deformations of the interview format, the superficiality of a public discourse on philosophy, and the limits of the infra-poetic language by means of which he struggles to express his untimely insights. These privative constraints collectively illuminate what is missing from his contributions to the *Der Spiegel* interview, i.e., what he cannot articulate within the limited format of a magazine interview.

In addition to these privative defects, however, Heidegger also labours under the positive burden of his own metaphysical inheritance. The gulf that separates the said from the unsaid engenders a space in which a primitive ontology comes to light. Here he displays his ongoing (if involuntary) allegiance to the metaphysical prejudices that silently shadow his post-metaphysical experiments. While attempting to negotiate the constraints required by the magazine, he reveals the extent to which he remains haunted by ontological atavisms that have thwarted thus far the preparatory influence of his experiments in extra-technical thinking.

Only a god can save us: What an uncharacteristic remark from a thinker who wished to advance philosophy beyond the anthropocentric legacies of humanistic religion and morality! This pithy statement rings of a benedictory pronouncement, and it is treated precisely as such by the *Der Spiegel* editors who extracted it as the title for the interview article. This benediction furthermore resembles the kind of summary 'teaching' with which philosophers are typically associated in popular anthologies and quiz shows, for it dispenses a moral message of the consummatory sort that Heidegger ordinarily eschewed. As such, this benediction announces the stirring of something altogether *unheimlich* in the economy of his thought.

In fact, this benediction lends voice to an emergent ontology that stands in marked contrast to the ontological experiments with which Heidegger's readers are more familiar. The ontology that comes to light in his benedictory pronouncement is not the pathbreaking 'fundamental ontology' outlined in *Sein und Zeit*. Nor is it the abstractly poeticized, post-metaphysical ontology previewed in the *Beiträge zur Philosophie*. Nor, for that matter, is it the disclosive, Hölderlinian ontology that he invokes in some passages of the *Der Spiegel* interview itself. In fact, the ontology announced in Heidegger's benedictory pronouncement is surprisingly ontic in its scope and sweep, surprisingly confluent with the mainstream currents of onto-theology in the western metaphysical tradition.

In the primitive ontology illuminated by his benedictory pronouncement, Heidegger identifies three basic terms, all of which figure prominently, in varying aspects, in the dominant metaphysical systems of western philosophy and religion.

1 *The god*

The divinity is known to Heidegger not only in its absence, which is related to the state of decline that currently besets humanity, but also in the promise of its advent, which leads him to speculate on the possibility of our salvation at some unspecified point in the future.

His reference to the possible appearance of the absent divinity is somewhat surprising in light of his own concern, recorded elsewhere, that 'man at the present stage of world history' is not yet prepared to 'ask at all seriously and rigorously whether the god nears or withdraws'.[14] Since Heidegger here belays his own admonition, not merely asking but answering the question concerning the nearing or withdrawal of the god, we should certainly take notice. Either he feels adequately prepared to locate the god in withdrawal (perhaps because 'we' have progressed to a 'new' stage of history?), or he has relaxed the caution that ordinarily informs his thinking on such matters. Indeed, what is most surprising about his benedictory pronouncement is not, as his critics allege, its pessimistic/fatalistic/nihilistic appraisal of the plight of humankind. What is most surprising is his confident appeal to the existence of a divinity that might save us. Although he is not sanguine about our prospects for persuading this divinity to appear, he does not openly despair that no such divinity exists. Rather than conclude from the absence of the saving divinity that no such divinity exists, or that no such divinity is likely to appear, he confidently alludes to the possible nearing of the absent divinity. Especially in light of the proliferation in late modernity of philosophical and theological challenges to the existence of a deity attuned to the human condition, this is an extraordinary assumption on his part.

Despite his sympathy for the thesis of the 'death of God', Heidegger thus refuses to treat the divinity's current absence as a permanent, irremediable condition. Following Nietzsche and Hölderlin, that is, he interprets the 'death of God' as the historically specific disintegration of a formerly viable web of beliefs and values. Although indisputably catastrophic, this disintegration may nevertheless occasion, or so Heidegger believes, the advent of new gods and a new, ontologically enhanced theology. (This is why he portrays the *Gestell* of planetary technics as posing a 'challenge' as well as an obstacle to us.) He consequently refuses to treat the world in late modernity as throughly disenchanted. He thereby responds (albeit implicitly) to those critics who paint him as a godless philosopher,[15] as well as to those critics who associate the death of God with Auschwitz.[16] Without denying the benighted state into which humankind has fallen in the twentieth century, he maintains a surprisingly robust faith in the providential ministrations of a redemptive divinity.

Heidegger does not name this divinity, but his characterization of its absence and possible advent furnishes some clues to its likely identity. The deity in question is neither Dionysus nor Apollo, nor any of the pantheonic gods of Greek antiquity. Nor does Heidegger mean to appeal to the saving power of Yahweh, Christ, Allah or any of the gods worshipped in the major religions of influence in western civilization. Nor does he have in mind Siva, Krishna, Buddha, Brahman-Atman or any of the gods worshipped in eastern religions. (He pointedly opines in the *Der Spiegel* interview that 'a [conversion of the modern, technical world] cannot happen by taking over Zen-Buddhism or other Eastern experiences of the world' (62).) Nor does he appeal explicitly to any known chthonian numina or woodland spirits, despite his overt fascination with pagan deities. And he certainly does not mean to invoke the belated return of the retired watchmaker whom deists tepidly revere.

In fact, Heidegger is careful to speak throughout the *Der Spiegel* interview only of the *advent* or *appearance* of the god who might save us, and not of the *return* of this deity. This suggests that he does not have in mind any of the gods heretofore known to humankind. He apparently wishes to invoke the messianic properties of a new, as yet unknown divinity, one whose existence and nature will presumably be ontologically consonant with the insight to be gleaned by us into the essence of planetary technics.[17] For this reason, perhaps, he is careful not to speak of the god in positive terms, with the exception of its potentially redemptive properties.

Jürgen Habermas interprets this novel theological attunement as indicative of Heidegger's campaign to introduce a pagan, mythological element into the religious consciousness of late modernity. Endorsing the thesis advanced by Otto Pöggeler, Habermas observes,

> Pöggeler is surely correct to emphasize the biographical turning point of 1929 ... [At that time,] Friedrich Hölderlin and Nietzsche came into view as the authors who were to dominate the following decades. This paved the way for the *neo-pagan turn* that pushed Christian themes into the background in favor of a mythologizing recourse to the archaic; even at the end of his life, Heidegger placed his hopes in 'a' god who can save us.[18]

The 'neo-pagan turn' described by Habermas thus opposes the afterworldly onto-theology of western metaphysics with a this-worldly theology of immanence, which is intended to complement the post-anthropocentric ontology towards which Heidegger's later writings gesture.[19]

Echoing Habermas, John D. Caputo avers that Heidegger's *Kehre* actually enables multiple this-worldly religious attunements. According to Caputo, what Habermas calls the 'neo-pagan turn' also involves a literal orientation of Heidegger's thinking:

> The god that emerges in Heidegger's late writing is a profoundly poetic god, a woodland god arising from a poetic experience of the earth as something sacred and deserving of reverence. This is a cosmo-poetic god, not the ethico-religious God of the Hebrew and Christian scriptures, not a God of the suffering, of mercy and justice and flesh laid low. It has nothing to do with the God whom Jesus called *abba* or with bibilical works of healing and mercy, with the widow, the orphan, or the stranger. Indeed, Heidegger's later writings are more suggestive of a certain Buddhism, a certain meditative, silent world reverencing, than of Judaism or Christianity and the emancipatory power of biblical justice.[20]

As Caputo suggests, the 'neo-pagan' turn eventually sanctions a more general openness to non-western, non-transcendent deities. From sylvan reverie to Buddhist reverence: in search of a deity around whom a post-metaphysical, post-anthropocentric theology might coalesce, Heidegger casts a fairly wide net. As we shall see, however, the grand sweep of his 'neo-pagan turn' attests not only to his wish to dissociate himself from the old gods of onto-theology, but also to his failure to discover any genuinely new gods.

2 The 'us'

Humankind is known to Heidegger in its present state of decline and in its irrecuperable incapacity to bring about its own redemption. In order to survive the crisis of planetary technics, humankind requires the providential intervention of the absent divinity. Rather than surrender entirely to the fatalism with which he flirts, however, Heidegger reserves for humankind a proto-redemptive capacity for 'thinking and poetizing'. So although humankind cannot save itself, some of its representative exemplars can play an indirect, mediated role in preparing for its salvation.

3 That from which only a god can save us

The unnamed threat to the future of humankind is primarily known to Heidegger in privative terms. He links the absence of the deity to the 'state of decline' that presently imperils humankind. He thereby suggests that the advent of the deity is the necessary condition of our redemption. Like Nietzsche, who described the 'death of God' as an event as yet unknown to most human beings, Heidegger believes that precious few people yet experience the abject disenchantment of the world in late modernity. The absence of the deity is largely alien to our experience because the empire of planetary technics has imperceptibly colonized the space that might otherwise have been occupied by a reverence for this deity. Indeed, we are chronically distracted from this impending peril by the wonders wrought by technology. It is therefore a mistake to treat planetary technics itself as an evil – as *the* evil – to be combated; the unchallenged hegemony of planetary technics is not the cause of our decline.

Where, then, lies the 'cause' of our current, godless plight? This is precisely the question that Heidegger's poet-philosophers must ponder if they are to help us to prepare ourselves for the planetary readiness that may entice the messianic god to appear. As Heidegger cautions, however, the taking up of these questions comprises an enormous task, for we do not as yet have even a rudimentary understanding of the meanings of 'causality' and 'agency'.[21]

Heidegger fleshes out this skeletal ontology by identifying the four basic relations that obtain between these three relata: (1) humankind stands in need of salvation; (2) the god who might save humanity is absent; (3) the god's absence is related somehow (although not causally) to the 'state of decline' in which humankind presently finds itself (for 'in view of the absent god we are in a state of decline'[22]); and (4) humankind lacks the resources needed to realize its own salvation, even if it may possess the resources needed to contribute to the preparations for the advent of the divinity. These relations define the ambit of the primitive ontology that comes to light in the *Der Spiegel* interview.

Heidegger's emergent ontology is not only primitive in the sense that it occupies a primal place in the economy of his thought. It is also primitive in the sense that it perpetuates many of the standard metaphysical prejudices of western onto-theology. For example: although Heidegger's later philosophy is predicated on a resistance to the anthropomorphisms of western onto-theology, the 'us' that only a god can save is a distinctly human 'us'. Even if we are willing to concede that other (and perhaps all) planetary beings stand to be saved if the absent god were to appear, we must nevertheless acknowledge that the fate of *human* beings lies at the centre of his concerns in this interview. Like his onto-theological predecessors, in fact, Heidegger assigns a lexical priority to the relations between the divinity and humankind. He anticipates the advent of the absent god not for the salvation of the world, the animal kingdom, the rain forest, or the thesaurus of beings, but for *us*. Philosophy itself is presented as an enterprise preoccupied with the welfare of humankind in general, and his anxiety about the future of humankind fits squarely within the mainstream tradition of this enterprise. The *Der Spiegel* interview thus reveals the residual humanism that tinctures Heidegger's later philosophizing.

This residual humanism in turn lends voice to the moral idealism that informs his benedictory pronouncement. By 'idealism' I have in mind any sustained distinction between the world as it *is* and the world as it *ought* to be, such that the former receives a denigratory evaluation or rank. Indeed, the uncharacteristically moralizing tone of Heidegger's remarks in the *Der Spiegel* interview is partially attributable to the periodic eruptions of an unwanted idealism. Divine providence is needed, after all, only because human beings have allowed/invited the sprawl of planetary technics, apparently in ignorance of its essential enframing nature. As a consequence, humankind has not yet progressed sufficiently towards the retrieval of its long-abandoned practice of extra-technical thinking. Human beings are not yet what they can/ought to be, and their deficiencies are measured by the absence of the saviour god and the unchallenged hegemony of planetary technics.

Here Heidegger is no longer content merely to report the uprooting of all beings, which is characteristic of the protracted oblivion of Being in late modernity. Rather than simply receive and appreciate this particular moment in the destinal sending of Being, he also delivers his moral judgment of it – especially insofar as it threatens the extinction of humankind itself. His lapse into moral idealism thus prevents him from regarding Being in the unique aspect under which it grants itself to late modernity. At this point, at least, he is not prepared simply to behold the *Ereignis* and adopt a posture of respectful releasement. Nor is he inclined simply to let beings be, especially if doing so would exacerbate the peril of human extinction. Despite his ingenious attempts to move beyond the anthropocentric prejudices of western philosophy, here he clearly pledges allegiance to them.[23]

For all his enthusiasm concerning the advent of new gods, moreover, Heidegger in fact reverts to a very old story of human decline and divine redemption: only a god can save us. The god is not merely absent, but also *needed by humans*, who cannot secure the conditions of their own salvation by dint of their own efforts. In uttering his benedictory pronouncement, Heidegger employs a verb – *retten* – that strongly connotes the eschatological inflections of Protestant theology. Whereas he elsewhere meditates at length on the meaning of *retten* (while somehow managing to misplace its multiple biblical resonances behind its idiosyncratic appropriation by Hölderlin in *Patmos*[24]), here he deploys the verb, without qualification or apology, in its more familiar context of meaning. Indeed, to stand in need of salvation is to require the intervention of a particular kind of deity, a deity all-too-familiar to the history of western onto-theology.

Heidegger's recourse to the verb *retten* thus suggests that his shadow ontology treats the absence of the god not simply as a negation, but as a defect. After all, any number of entities are missing from the world. Unlike these other missing entities, however, the absent god is needed to preside over the salvation of humankind. By treating the absence of the divinity as a defect, Heidegger thus delivers an unmistakably moral judgment: humankind stands in *need* of salvation, which presupposes an antecedent condition of deficiency, fallenness, incompleteness or sinfulness. Human beings will be joined by the divinity in an ontological relationship marked not by equality, complementarity, mutuality, reciprocity, harmony or unification, but by the imbalance and inequality predicated of salvation. Indeed, so long as the saving divinity is absent, the world is neither harmonious nor complete, for it must continue to stage the pandemic uprooting of all beings. While unchaperoned by compatible deities, the planetary infestation known as 'humankind' plunges the world into chaos and disharmony, disastrously investing in global technics the faith that it should render unto the absent deity. Just as 'we' require salvation, that is, so does the world need to be saved from us.

The misanthropic message is therefore clear: on its own, humankind is deficient and will continue to manifest this deficiency in a systematic, technological denaturing of the world. So long as Heidegger treats the absence of the saving divinity as a defect, he unwittingly distorts his call for the advent of new gods into an entreaty for the return of the old god. The god who might appear is treated as an absent saviour god, as a messiah in withdrawal, whose timely advent would redeem humanity's lamentable 'state of decline'. Put quite simply, a world that only a god can save is not a particularly pagan or neo-pagan world. Such a world recalls more resonantly the familiar, doomsday eschatology of Protestant theology, which juxtaposes an incommunicative deity with an irremediably self-destructive humanity. Despite his fascination with pagan poly- and pantheisms, moreover, Heidegger consistently refers throughout the *Der Spiegel* interview to one (male) god, thus suggesting the continued influence on his thought of the Judeo-Christian lineage of messianic, patriarchal monotheism.

Although Heidegger expressly insists that he does not model our current 'state of decline' on a fall from grace (61), he occasionally portrays the path of thinking as one from which humankind has disastrously strayed. He thus explains, for example, that 'The danger into which Europe as it has hitherto existed is ever more clearly forced consists presumably in the fact above all that thinking – *once its glory* – is falling behind in the essential course of a dawning world destiny which nevertheless in the basic traits of its essential provenance remains European by definition.'[25] The influence of this primitive ontology thus imparts a familiar trajectory to Heidegger's speculations on our prospects for salvation. What he advertises as the advent of an as yet unknown messianic divinity bears a suspicious resemblance to the return of a *deus absconditus*. What he calls humanity's 'state of decline' invokes a fall from grace, and the preparatory ministrations of the poet-philosophers recall the good works that may someday warrant the dispensation of divine grace.

To be sure, Heidegger does not reprise the strict fatalism of Luther and Calvin,[26] and he does not predicate human salvation solely on the unearned gift of divine grace.[27] In the *Der Spiegel* interview, at least, he reserves for some human beings the practical task of readying humankind to prepare for the advent of the absent god. So although we have indisputably fallen into decline, we are not altogether powerless to contribute to our own redemption – hence Heidegger's attribution to thinking of an undefined measure of practical efficacy. That is, our salvation is not entirely dependent upon an adventitious turning-towards-us on the part of Being; we may play a role in influencing its change of course.

Charting Heidegger's hauntology

Granted, the evidence surveyed thus far could hardly be considered conclusive. Even if one concedes that Heidegger's *Der Spiegel* interview lends voice to a primitive ontology, why should its emergence interest us? Is it not simply a harmless departure from his more rigorous ontological investigations?

Richard Bernstein insists that Heidegger's benedictory pronouncement need not cast a shadow over his later philosophy. According to Bernstein, we can rely on some of Heidegger's later writings, including 'The Question Concerning Technology', to 'gain a new perspective' on the *Der Spiegel* interview.[28] Although I do not dispute Bernstein's claim that he 'can give a more subtle reading of the striking claim that "only a god can save us"',[29] his interest in exacting 'greater subtlety' seems somewhat misplaced, especially in light of Heidegger's unpredecented decision to subject himself to the unusual discursive conditions of a magazine interview. In comparing Heidegger's unguarded remarks in the *Der Spiegel* interview with similar passages from his later published writings, we might gain a more consistent and polished interpretation of his philosophy, but we also lose the opportunity to ponder the immediate philosophical and political implications of the (relatively) raw sentiments he conveys to his interviewers.

Bernstein's interpretive strategy thus places us at risk of forfeiting a unique angle of vision into the complex economy of Heidegger's thought. On what other occasion do we enjoy such relatively unmediated access to his deepest existential anxieties? In what other text is he obliged to answer pointed questions and to express his philosophical insights on terms other than his own? In what other context does he allow his readers to encounter him when he is not in full command of the tempo, direction and subject matter of his thinking? His benedictory pronouncement in the *Der Spiegel* interview is important, that is, precisely because it *lacks* the 'greater subtlety' that Bernstein wishes to import on its behalf. We are well acquainted with the Heidegger who crafts subtle philosophical arguments; perhaps we would do well to make the acquaintance of the Heidegger for whom 'greater subtlety' is an unaffordable luxury.

To be sure, some notice must be taken of the unusual setting in which Heidegger adverts to this primitive ontology. He is speaking to journalists, not philosophers, and he is limited by their preferred format to short, pithy answers that readily lend themselves to distortion, oversimplification, misunderstanding and caricature. The very fact that the *Der Spiegel* editors extracted his benedictory pronouncement as the title for the interview article displays a certain level of hostility to the philosophical sophistication he recommends. Still, Heidegger agreed to sit for the interview, and he was no stranger to *Der Spiegel*. Nor were his interviewers strangers to his thought. He was also promised a posthumous publication of the interview, which, one conjectures, should have allayed any fears of a negative public response and encouraged in him a greater degree of candor. Finally, although he apologizes for answering the question about the future of humankind 'briefly, and perhaps clumsily', he also introduces his benedictory pronouncement as the product of 'long reflection' (57). It thus conveys in some sense his considered judgment on the question.

But the most compelling reason for taking seriously the emergence of this primitive ontology is the possibility that it plays a central (if largely invisible) role in the development of his larger philosophical project. To paraphrase Nietzsche: only those who are haunted by metaphysics have good reason and sufficient creative energy to entertain the possibility of a post-metaphysical future. As Habermas suggests in the extract cited above, Heidegger's 'neo-pagan turn' did not eliminate the 'Christian themes' that had dominated his thought, but only 'pushed [them] into the background'. This imagery thus attests to the crowded economy of Heidegger's later thought, which attempts to foreground an inchoate neo-paganism while restricting vestiges of an undigested Christianity to the background. If Habermas is correct, then the emergence of Heidegger's primitive ontology is neither an aberration nor a mistake, but the inevitable return of the repressed. On this (admittedly speculative) interpretion, his flickering faith in the advent of a saviour god should be treated as integral to his philosophizing; it cannot be ignored without penalty to an understanding of his thought as a whole. If Habermas's interpretation is accurate, then we should not be surprised if the endogenous tensions that strain this economy eventually exhibit outward signs of fissure and stress – as, for example, when the backgrounded 'Christian themes' of his philosophy obtrude into the foreground of his thinking.

Borrowing the terminology of Jacques Derrida, we might say that Heidegger's primitive ontology *haunts* his more familiar post-metaphysical investigations. His shadow ontology silently spooks him onward, invisibly shaping the directions and determinations of his thought. This primitive ontology thus comprises what Derrida calls a *hauntology*,[30] for its ghostly revenance possesses his various attempts to overcome the tradition of western metaphysics. Heidegger's hauntology thus emerges as the unacknowledged other of his ontology, as an undisclosed energy source that motivates his post-metaphysical adventures and sets them on their particular course. As Derrida explains, 'To haunt does not mean to be present, and it is necessary to introduce haunting into the very construction of a concept. Of every concept, beginning with the concepts of being and time. This is what we would be calling here a hauntology. Ontology opposes it only in a movement of exorcism. Ontology is a conjuration.'[31]

According to Derrida, the category of hauntology is meant to include any unclassified term that 'does not belong to ontology, to the discourse on the Being of beings, or to the essence of life or death'.[32] The category thus collects any ontological dangler that 'itself is neither living nor dead, present nor absent', but which 'spectralizes'.[33] Despite its revenant provenance, in fact, Derrida assigns to the category of hauntology a distinct priority: 'We will take this category [of hauntology] to be irreducible, and first of all to everything it makes possible: ontology, theology, positive or negative theology.'[34] As this passage suggests, we would be doubly mistaken to dismiss Heidegger's benedictory pronouncement as a harmless epiphenomenon. His hauntological allegiances are not only integral to his thinking, but also originary to his more familiar ontological exertions.

By dint of his recourse to the category of hauntology, Derrida indicates that what is most vital within an ontology is often that which has been left for dead. This stipulated 'death' frees the ontologian to conduct his investigations afresh, ostensibly innocent of the mistakes and prejudices of his predecessors. But ontology does not grant its practitioners a clean slate, onto which they might expectorate *ex nihilo*. That which is left for dead must, and will, lend its infernal energies to the articulation – and deformation – of any 'new beginning' or 'second innocence'. No philosophical structure or method, regardless of its rigour, can permanently bury its dead. A hauntology thus comprises those ontological relics that are presumed or figured to be 'dead' (i.e., in the sense of having been relinquished, abandoned, overcome, sublated or transcended), but which continue to haunt the ontologian's enterprise as its unacknowledged pre-conditions. This means that the enterprise of ontology always already operates under the sponsorship of a silent partner whose seminal invest-ments are not accurately reckoned.

Under certain conditions of endogenous strain and disruption, a hauntology may eventually come to light – not merely as an apparition, but as the revenant vitality that shapes and directs the ontological investiga-tion in question. Hauntology lives when ontology dies, and *vice versa*. Derrida thus explains that

> This logic of haunting would not be merely larger and more powerful than an ontology or a thinking of Being (of the 'to be,' assuming that it is a matter of Being in the 'to be or not to be,' but nothing is less certain.) It would har-bor within itself, but like circumscribed places or particular effects, escha-tology and teleology themselves. It would *comprehend* them, but incomprehensibly. How to *comprehend* in fact the discourse of the end or the discourse about the end? Can the extremity of the extreme ever be com-prehended? And the opposition between 'to be' and 'not to be'?[35]

Heidegger's hauntology comes to light as he attempts to adapt his philo-sophical enterprise to the artificial constraints imposed on it by *Der Spiegel* magazine. Removed from the comfort and familiarity of his pre-ferred approach to philosophy, he unwittingly voices the archaic meta-physical prejudices that haunt his philosophical labours.[36] In Derrida's words, the *Der Spiegel* interview authorizes a kind of 'exorcism,' which allows Heidegger's ghosts to announce themselves as such:

> To exorcise not in order to chase away the ghosts, but this time to grant them the right, if it means making them come back alive, as *revenants* who would no longer be *revenants*, but as other *arrivants* to whom a hospitable memory or promise must offer welcome – without certainty, ever, that they present themselves as such. Not in order to grant them the right in this sense but out of a concern for justice.[37]

As this passage suggests, the 'exorcism' Derrida has in mind is not intended to banish the revenants and bring an end to their haunting. Instead, the aim of this exorcism is to extend the concerns of justice into the infernal realm, in order that the hauntological familiars of ontology might receive their due. Rather than rouse evil spirits and command them to desist their inhabitations, Derridean exorcism endeavours to relax (if only temporarily) the conditions of spectralization – the conditions, that is, under which the 'evil' spirits were originally separated out from the 'good' spirits and left for dead. As we shall see, this brand of exorcism is especially apposite to the case of Heidegger, for it is only by loosing the 'evil' spirits of his hauntology that we can construct on his behalf a practical response to the enframing crisis of global technics. That Heidegger continues to be haunted may redound to his credit with readers who are similarly spooked, for these familiar haunts suggest the possibility of a distinctly human response to the crisis of late modernity.

Nur noch ein Dichter kann uns retten?

Heidegger's *Der Spiegel* interview is widely received as stubbornly evasive and disappointingly apolitical.[38] Even his interviewers grow exasperated with his chronic postponement of the question of a political response to the crisis of modern technicity. Yet Heidegger does not completely foreclose the domain of human praxis.[39] The contemporary world has indisputably declined into a benighted state, but it has not yet been plunged into total darkness. Disenchantment and secularization may thrive in late modernity, but they do not yet rule unchecked.[40] There are heroes amongst us who might yet bridge the gulf that separates an anxious humanity from the god that might save it. Heidegger thus voices a faint hope for the future of humankind, which is amplified dramatically against the backdrop of his shadow ontology. The guarded, anthropocentric optimism that has no place in his later published writings finds an unlikely home in his primitive ontology.[41]

The warrant for Heidegger's scintillant hope derives from his reckoning of the residual poetic capacities available to 'us' in late modernity. Rather than conclude that all possibilities for praxis have been permanently eclipsed, he alludes to the one option remaining for meaningful practical engagement: 'The only possibility available to us is that by thinking and poetizing we prepare a readiness for the appearance of a god' (57). Heidegger's characterization of the only alternative remaining to humankind has not inspired widespread enthusiasm. It is widely supposed, in fact, that his ostensibly practical appeal to 'thinking and poetizing' merely applies a quasi-mystical gloss to the resignationism of his benedictory pronouncement. To invoke the saving power of poetry is simply another – perhaps more palatable – way of declaring the dimension of human praxis to be effectively closed. The validity of these concerns is perhaps confirmed by the arresting modesty of the aspirations that Heidegger owns in his concluding statement: 'For us today, the greatness of what is to be thought is [all] too great. Perhaps the best we can do is strive to break a passage through it – along narrow paths that do not stretch too far' (65).

Especially to those readers who remain committed to the possibility of an intelligible practical response to the threat of global technics, Heidegger's practical agenda appears deflationary, fatalistic, and dangerously

naive.[42] It is a noteworthy irony, however, that the (faint) optimism of Heidegger's later philosophy emanates not from his more celebrated ontological exertions, but from his revenant hauntology. Within the context of a
post-anthropocentric ontology, after all, Heidegger's poet-philosophers
could not be portrayed as concerned primarily with the fate of humanity.[43]
Only his residual entanglements in humanism and its prevailing metaphysics of morals allow him to attribute to these poet-philosophers the
minimal agency needed to ready us to prepare humankind for the advent
of the absent divinity. For those readers who are similarly entangled, the
emergence of his shadow ontology may indeed be welcome, for it alone
sanctions something resembling a practical response to the pandemic
uprooting of all beings. Indeed, his confidence in the existence of a saving
divinity bespeaks a humanistic (i.e., anthropocentric) orientation that only
his shadow ontology could support.

In this light, Heidegger's readers might actually celebrate his failure to
complete the 'neo-pagan turn' he plotted for his thinking, for only in the
context of his revenant hauntology does he allow for the possibility that
human beings might contribute to their own redemption. The half-gods
and heroes whom his 'neo-pagan turn' would presumably have banished
are responsible for preparing humankind for the coming of the deity. The
shadow ontology thus infuses his 'neo-pagan' theology with a glimmer of
anthropocentrism. And only this glimmer can rescue his practical philosophy from the charge of nihilistic resignationism.

As we have seen, Heidegger refuses to describe the preparatory thinking of these poet-philosophers in the causal, technical terms favoured by
his interviewers. But he nevertheless assigns to it a distinct ontological priority. Although he is careful not to attribute to these poet-philosophers an
agency so robust that they could summon the absent god, he nevertheless
insists that some attenuated practical linkage obtains between their thinking and the realization of the state of preparedness whereupon the absent
deity might appear. He thus attributes to these poet-philosophers the minimal agency that is consistent with his slim hopes for meaningful practical
engagement. Although our salvation ultimately lies in the unseen hands of
an absent god, some human beings might nevertheless play a constructive
role in preparing the world for the advent of the reclusive deity.

Wary of portraying these poet-philosophers as gods in their own right,
he is neverthelesss concerned to reserve for them a practical role that is
conducive to the appearance of the saving divinity. That is, some human
beings in late modernity are distinguished by a capacity that could be
fairly described as quasi-divine, in the sense that they can indirectly precipitate the appearance of the god who might save us. Speaking of a poet
to whom he felt an unusually close kinship, Heidegger explains, 'For me,

Hölderlin is the poet who points into the future, who waits for a god, and who, consequently, should not remain merely an object of research according to the canons of literary history' (62).[44] This 'pointing into the future' need not refer to anything Hölderlin does *qua* agent, i.e., *qua* causally efficient, self-possessed originator of action, so much as it denotes an event or occurrence that his poeticizing catalyzes or unwittingly facilitates. It would therefore be a mistake to regard these poet-philosophers as self-conscious or self-appointed saviours of humankind.

We know from Heidegger's later writings that this gift for preparatory thinking is both rare and evanescent, residing only in those poets who lend voice to the reclusive career of Being. As his interviewers note (while sensing the influence of a latent elitism), Heidegger thus places his hopes for the future of humankind in a select group of exemplary human beings, whose gifts for poetized thinking outstrip those of ordinary mortals. Following their lead, we might eventually take the measure of the *Gestell* that enframes late modernity. In light of the distinctly political inflections of the *Der Spiegel* interview, in fact, we might fairly characterize these poet-philosophers (although Heidegger himself does not) as constituting a redemptive vanguard, whose preparatory labours could eventually lead others down/toward the path of thinking and thereby facilitate the advent of the absent deity.

Despite his persistent opposition to the humanism that informs so much of western political theory, Heidegger thus derives his faint hope for the future from a fairly traditional distinction between human types. The poet-philosophers amongst us are more intimately attuned to the sojourn of being, and they shall cultivate in us the thinking that might eventually yield a saving insight into the essence of modern technicity. At least within the ambit of his primitive hauntology, that is, Heidegger squarely situates himself within the dominant tradition of western political philosophy. Like so many of his predecessors, he identifies a superlative human type and assigns to it the task of leading humankind to its optimal political arrangement. Following the lead of Plato, Aristotle, Machiavelli, Rousseau, Hegel, Marx, Mill, Nietzsche and others, in fact, Heidegger identifies these exemplary human beings as constituting a new, improved breed of philosopher. This should not be understood as necessarily comprising a criticism of Heidegger, for had he not identified these poet-philosophers as an exemplary human type, his 'response' to the crisis of global technics would very likely have been deemed inadequate.

But these mysterious poet-philosophers are not (merely) thinkers in any traditional sense. Since it is their unique labour to restore a linkage between those human beings who require salvation and the god who might appear, these poet-philosophers might also be viewed as political leaders. Indeed, perhaps it is appropriate here to recall Nietzsche's sketch of those 'philosophers' to whom he similarly entrusts the future of humankind:

> *Genuine philosophers, however, are commanders and legislators:* they say, *'thus* it *shall* be!' They first determine the Whither and For What of man, and in so doing have at their disposal the preliminary labor of all philosophical laborers, all who have overcome the past. With a creative hand they reach for the future, and all that is and has been becomes a means for them, an instrument, a hammer. Their 'knowing' is *creating*, their creating is a legislation, their will to truth is – *will to power.*[45]

Ignoring for now the muscular imagery that Nietzsche favours, we might productively explore the similarities between these philosophers and the poet-philosophers whom Heidegger beckons.

The 'pointing toward the future' that Heidegger ascribes to Hölderlin may recall the 'reaching for the future' that Nietzsche's philosophers attempt 'with a creative hand'. Indeed, since Nietzsche's philosophers are 'lawgivers' in no conventional sense of this term, perhaps their nomothetic capacities are expressed, as Heidegger suggests of his poet-philosophers, in the unique 'making' that poetry comprises. Indeed, perhaps the 'Whither' and 'For What' of humankind are determined in the twilight of the idols by philosophers who undertake a new articulation of thinking – by philosophers, that is, who are also poets. It is their task to legislate the preparations that might ready humankind for the advent of the saving divinity. From Nietzsche we thus learn that Heidegger's poet-philosophers possess a legislative capacity, and from Heidegger we gain a clearer understanding of at least one sense in which Nietzsche might legitimately call philosophers 'commanders' and 'legislators'.

In order to complete our sketch of Heidegger's hauntology, we must attempt to explicate its fourth term: the lawgiver. This fourth term not only resolves the ontological vision suggested in Heidegger's benedictory pronouncement, but also accounts for the limited measure of hope he expresses therein. The salvation of humanity requires not simply the appearance of the absent god; it also requires the realization within certain exemplary human beings of their legislative mission and destiny. This realization in turn suggests a (minimal) dimension of praxis that may be consistent with the unique historical conditions and exigencies of late modernity. The 'preparatory thinking' that is so often ridiculed by Heidegger's readers may thus shelter the legislative praxis that will prepare the world for the advent of the saving divinity. Indeed, Heidegger seems to imply that the emergence of these poet-philosophers as lawgivers is a necessary condition of the advent of the deity. Their emergence constitutes the sole recognizable sign to the absent deity that humankind warrants redemption. If not for the legislative office of these poet-philosophers, in fact, we would dwell beyond redemption and bereft of hope. The only hope for humankind thus lies in the preparatory thinking practised by the poet-philosophers whom Heidegger reveres as legislators of the redemption of humankind.[46]

What would it mean for us to regard these poet-philosophers as 'commanders' and 'legislators'? Nietzsche's peculiar use of these designations is not meant to refer to those political figures who preside over the enactment and enforcement of positive law. To legislate in his sense means to envision a new, unknown future for humankind and to convey this vision in defiance of conventional appropriation by prevailing social orders. By offering a poetic articulation of this vision, the lawgiver thus contributes indirectly to its eventual realization. If this Nietzschean interpretation is correct, then we need not imagine Heidegger's poet-philosophers as fantastic, otherworldly, alien or angelic beings. They are fully natural, mortal creatures, beset by the same weakness of will and darkened horizon that characterize all human beings in late modernity. Yet they also participate in an agency (or patiency) that Heidegger describes as maintaining some intimate, unspecified relation to the divine.

These poet-philosophers 'command' and 'legislate' by leading humankind to an insight into the enframing influence of planetary technics. By simultaneously revealing and illuminating the *Gestell* of late modernity, the poets solve the riddle of the 'challenge' posed to us by the pandemic uprooting of all beings. As Heidegger explains,

> The essence of technicity I see in what I call 'pos-ure' (*Ge-stell*), an often ridiculed and perhaps awkward expression. To say that pos-ure holds sway means that man is posed, enjoined, and challenged by a power that becomes manifest in the essence of technicity – a power that man himself does not control. Thought asks no more than this: that it help us achieve this insight. (58)

When we finally apprehend the *Gestell* for what it is, it appears not simply as a prison or curse. It also comprises a challenge to discover an exit from the labyrinth it constitutes. That is, the frame imposed on late modernity by the sprawl of global technicity 'poses' us in a way that could also lead to its own self-overcoming. Only when we understand the enframing of global technics for what it is can we 'do' anything about it – if, at that point, there is anything that needs to be done. The challenge of 'pos-ure' is accepted on our behalf by the poets, who attempt to discover and convey its essence.

Heidegger locates the legislative capacity of these poet-philosophers in their command of language.[47] The poets point into the future by virtue of their apophantic attunement to language, whereby they invite beings to manifest themselves in their essential presencing. They name and identify that which envelops us so completely as to preclude detection; they thus attempt to say what cannot yet be said about the totality of technicity in late modernity. By dint of their unconventional linguistic fabrications, these poet-philosophers thus deflect the enframing vectors of global technics and thereby secure the differential clearing wherein humankind might someday discover a trailhead to the path of thinking. Their poetic gifts thus enable them to suspend (occasionally and temporarily) the familiar limitations that typically characterize humankind in late modernity. Although the activity of the poets requires the contribution of novelty and creativity on their part, is is also a result of the poets having been 'posed' in this way by the frame of late modernity. We should therefore understand the poets to be simultaneously participating in and reacting against the *Gestell* that both frames and positions them. Indeed, it is their task to legislate the transformation of the *Gestell* of late modernity from a prison-house into a shelter.

For an illumination of the nomothetic labours performed by these philosopher-poets, we might turn productively to a consideration of Heidegger's favourite poet. In his *Rheinhymne*, Hölderlin not only attributes to the poets a similar intermediary function (e.g., propagating divine lightning to humankind), but also includes them among the 'half-gods' whose superlative capacity for mourning hallows the world. Building upon this characterization of the poets in his commentary on Hölderlin's *Rheinhymne*, Heidegger describes these half-gods as 'overmen and undergods' [*Übermenschen und Untergötter*] who populate (and safeguard) the liminal realm between gods and men.[48]

As Heidegger's commentary perhaps suggests, his poet-philosophers are expected to patrol the gulf that separates a declining humanity from the saving divinity that might appear. It is their unique labour to legislate a healing of this rupture and to ready a world in which gods and men no longer occupy ontologically separate realms.[49] Insofar as they preside over the communication between the sundered domains of the human and the divine, these poet-philosophers can be seen as messengers who intercede on behalf of humanity with the reclusive divinity. By dint of their preparatory thinking, they mediate between the human and the divine, partaking of both domains while dwelling restfully in neither. Their homelessness might fairly be viewed as a condition of our homecoming.[50]

By tracking the emergence of Heidegger's hauntology in the *Der Spiegel* interview, we thus position ourselves to recover the practical dimension of his later philosophy. Owing to the formative influence of the shadow ontology, his influential confrontation with late modernity need not culminate in the paralyzing jeremiad for which he is so widely criticized. The poet-philosophers whom he summons in his *Der Spiegel* interview might play a productive role in mounting a distinctly human response to the crisis of global technics. To arrive at this interpretation, however, it has been necessary to read Heidegger against Heidegger, thereby steering his hauntology into collision with his more familiar ontological teachings. As a result of this collision, the visage we see reflected in the *Der Spiegel* interview bears only a passing resemblance to the magisterial Heidegger with whom we are more familiar. We thereby make the acquaintance of a decidedly unfamiliar Heidegger, a haunted Heidegger, but one whom we might recognize as more fully human in the complexity of his philosophizing.

Notes

1 Martin Heidegger, 'Letter on Humanism', trans. Frank J. Capuzzi and J. Gray in *Martin Heidegger: Basic Writings*, ed. David Farrell Krell (New York: Harper & Row, 1977) pp. 15–191.

2 See 'Only a God Can Save Us' (1966 interview with Martin Heidegger), trans. William J. Richardson, in *Heidegger: the Man and the Thinker*, ed. Thomas Sheehan (Chicago: Precedent Publishing, 1981) pp. 45–67. My practice throughout this chapter is to reference citations to the *Der Spiegel* interview by placing the relevant page numbers from the Richardson translation in parentheses following the citation.

3 Claiming to have reached 'the point of contact between politics and philosophy' (58), his interviewers imply that Heidegger's anaemic response to the crisis of modernity may countenance the emergence of a political leader, who, in lieu of the absent god, would provide the external stimulus that will galvanize the practical capacity of thinking. The 'god or someone else' who must provide the 'well-known stimulus from outside' (58) recalls not only the popular enthusiasm for a charismatic *Führer*, but also the ill-chosen rhetoric of Heidegger's own *Rektoratsrede*.

4 See, for example, Richard J. Bernstein, 'Heidegger's Silence: Ethos and Technology', in *The New Constellations: the Ethico-political Horizons of Modernity/Postmodernity*, ed. Richard J. Bernstein (Cambridge: Polity Press, 1991) pp. 119–20.

5 Even in the *Der Spiegel* interview, under the assurance of a posthumous publication, Heidegger maintains his silence with respect to the atrocities of the nazi regime. The *Der Spiegel* interview thus compounds his obtrusive post-war silence on the subject of nazi politics and the holocaust, a silence that Bernstein deems 'resounding, deafening, and damning' ('Heidegger's Silence', p. 136). Lang helpfully focuses on Heidegger's silence on the Jewish question in particular: Berel Lang, *Heidegger's Silence* (Ithaca, NY: Cornell University Press, 1996) ch. 6. For a sympathetic account of the place of Heidegger's silence within the context of his larger philosophical project, see Miguel de Beistegui, *Heidegger and the Political: Dystopias* (London: Routledge), ch. 6.

6 As an example of the kind of claim that is widely viewed as self-serving, Heidegger avers that he too was victimized by the nazis. In response to his interviewers' question, he apparently agrees that 'the Party kept a watchful eye on [him]' (54). He

recounts a number of professional and academic slights that he endured following his resignation as Rector, and he also reminds his interviewers that 'In the last year of the war, 500 of the most important scientists and artists were released from any kind of war service. I was not among them. On the contrary, in the summer of 1944, I was ordered up the Rhine to build fortifications' (54).

7 For example, he explains, 'But the deed of thinking is neither theoretical nor practical, nor is it the conjunction of these two forms of behavior' ('Letter on Humanism,' p. 240).

8 See Bernstein, 'Heidegger's Silence', pp. 119–22.

9 Thiele locates a primary practical benefit of thinking in its capacity to engender the space of radical questioning: 'Only a nonwillful doing grounded in reflective thinking will avail. Thought, however, is not in the business of overcoming. It only summons. Although the technological world is full of quandaries and challenges, thought can provide no answers. But it does keep questioning alive. And once the nature of modern technology is brought into question, its hold is loosened.' Leslie Paul Thiele, *Timely Meditations: Heidegger and Postmodern Politics* (Princeton, NJ: Princeton University Press, 1995) p. 212.

10 When asked by his interviewers about the success thus far of his own experiments in thinking, Heidegger demurs: 'How far I come with my own effort at thought and in what way it will be received in the future and fruitfully transformed – this is not for me to decide' (61). Heidegger was not always so modest, however, and his humility on this occasion sounds suspiciously strategic. According to Zimmerman, 'The self-deluding and self-mythifying Heidegger believed that he had been destined to proclaim the saving vision of his hero, Hölderlin, and that he himself was thus the world-historical figure who would transform the fate of the West.' Michael E. Zimmerman, *Heidegger's Confrontation with Modernity: Technology, Politics, Art* (Bloomington and Indianapolis: Indiana University Press, 1990) p. 54.

11 Several critics have wondered if 'preparatory thinking' constitutes an adequate response to the crisis of modernity. For example, Bernstein endorses Hans-Georg Gadamer's claim that Heidegger's anti-practical emphasis on preparatory thinking betrays a 'terrible intellectual hubris'. Bernstein himself calls for a renewed attention to the rejuvenation of praxis through a cultivation of phronesis ('Heidegger's Silence', pp. 126–36). Alan Milchman and Alan Rosenberg insist that 'for thinking and questioning to even arise, there must already be a limit to the process by which human beings are turned into standing reserve'. Such a limit would 'manifest itself in a Refusal; a refusal to become standing reserve and to perish and to die.' Alan Milchman and Alan Rosenberg, eds., *Heidegger and the Holocaust* (Atlantic Highlands, NJ: Humanities Press) p. 228.

12 Heidegger thus explains, 'I know nothing about how this thought has an "effect." It may be, too, that the way of thought today may lead one to remain silent in order to protect this thought from becoming cheapened within a year. It may also be that it needs 300 years in order to have an "effect"' (60).

13 For a similar line of criticism, see Richard Wolin, 'French Heidegger Wars', in *The Heidegger Controversy: A Critical Reader*, ed. R. Woiln (Cambridge, MA: MIT Press, 1993), pp. 272–96. Wolin remarks that 'It comes as little surprise that, when pressed by his interlocutors during the course of the *Der Spiegel* interview for a tidbit of philosophical wisdom concerning a possible solution to the dilemmas of the modern age, Heidegger can only answer emphatically in the negative: whatever the solution may be, "it is not democracy"; instead, "only a god can save us." His devaluation of the modern project of human autonomy is so extreme, that he will only

admit to a deus ex machina solution – in the most literal sense of the term. The powers of human intelligence and volition are so thoroughly downplayed, the modern ideal of self-fashioning subjectivity is so far devalued, that all we are left with is an appeal to myth that is abstract, irrational, and sadly impotent' (p. 296).

14 'Letter on Humanism', p. 230.

15 This criticism is forcefully pressed by Levinas. 'But on the issue of Heidegger's participation in "Hitlerian thinking",' Levinas explains, 'I do not believe that any kind of historical research, arhival data, or eyewitness accounts … can equal the certainty that comes to us in the famous Testament in *Der Spiegel*, from his silence concerning the Final Solution, the Holocaust, the Shoah … [D]oesn't this silence, in time of peace, on the gas chambers and death camps lie beyond the realm of feeble excuses and reveal a soul completely cut off from any sensitivity, in which can be perceived a kind of consent to the horror?' Emmanuel Levinas, 'As if consenting to horror', trans. Paula Wissing, *Critical Inquiry* 5, winter 1989, p. 487.

16 This claim is made, for example, by Philippe Lacou-Labarthe, *Heidegger, Art, Politics: The Fiction of the Political*, trans. Chris Turner (Oxford: Basil Blackwell, 1990) p. 15.

17 On the 'new god' anticipated and revered by Heidegger, see John D. Caputo, *Demythologizing Heidegger* (Bloomington and Indianapolis: Indiana University Press, 1993) pp. 169–85.

18 Jurgen Habermas, 'Work and *Weltanschaung*', in *The Heidegger Controversy from a German Perspective*, trans. John McCumber, *Critical Inquiry* 15, winter 1989.

19 According to Dallmayr, 'In Heidegger's work the turning involved first of all a move away from anthropocentrism and a man-centered will to power, as it is reflected in a global power politics and planetary technology. At a more concrete level the turning involved a stand against the domestication of the earth, particularly under the auspices of a native or national culture.' Fred Dallmayr, *The Other Heidegger* (Ithaca, Ny: Cornell University Press, 1993) p. 48.

20 Caputo, *Demythologizing Heidegger*, p. 184.

21 In his 'Letter on Humanism', for example, Heidegger explains that we still fail to understand the essence of causality: 'We are still far from pondering the essence of action decisively enough. We view action only as causing an effect. The actuality of the effect is valued according to its utility. But the essence of action is accomplishment. To accomplish means to unfold something into the fullness of its essence, to lead it forth into this fullness – *producere*. Therefore only what already is can really be accomplished. But what "is" above all is Being. Thinking accomplishes the relation of Being to the essence of man. It does not make or cause the relation. Thinking brings this relation to Being solely as something handed over to it from Being. Such offering consists in the fact that in thinking Being comes to language. Language is the house of Being. In its home man dwells' (p. 193).

22 The nature of this relationship is more fully clarified in the rendering suggested by Maria P. Alter and John D. Caputo, trans., in '*Der Spiegel*'s interview with Martin Heidegger', in *The Heidegger Controversy*, ed. Wolin. Their translation reads: 'The sole possibility that is left for us is to prepare a sort of readiness, through thinking and poetizing, for the appearance of the god or for the absence of the god in the time of foundering [*Untergang*]; for in the face of the god who is absent, we founder' (p. 107).

23 My attention to the residence of a residual humanism in Heidegger's later philosophizing is indebted to a similar attempt at immanent critique by Charles E. Scott, *The Question of Ethics: Nietzsche, Foucault, Heidegger* (Bloomington: Indiana Uni-

versity Press, 1990), esp. ch. 4. Scott persuasively demonstrates the extent of the influence of the ascetic ideal on the development of Heidegger's thought and ingeniously recuperates Heidegger's ascetic investments by reading them as occasions on which the question of ethics comes to light.

24 Martin Heidegger, 'The Question concerning Technology' in *Martin Heidegger: Basic Writings*, ed. David Farrell Krell (New York: Harper & Rowe, 1977) pp. 316–17.

25 'Letter on Humanism', pp. 220–1, emphasis added.

26 As Bernstein helpfully remarks, 'Destining is never a fate that compels. Indeed, the all-important distinction between fate and destining enables us to begin to comprehend what Heidegger means by freedom' ('Heidegger's Silence', p. 106).

27 In response to what he takes to be an overly deterministic formulation on the part of his interviewers, Heidegger retorts, 'It seems to me that you take technicity in much too absolute [a sense]. I see the situation of man in the world of planetary technicity not as an inextricable and inescapable destiny, but I see the task of thought in this, that within its own limits it helps man as such achieve a satisfactory relationship to the essence of technicity' (61). On the question of Heidegger's fatalism, see Habermas, 'Work and *Weltanaschaung*', pp. 448–53.

28 Bernstein, 'Heidegger's Silence', p. 119.

29 Ibid.

30 Jacques Derrida, *Spectres of Marx*, trans. Peggy Kamuf (New York: Routledge, 1994), pp. 10–16. Although Derrida refers here explicitly to the hauntology that inhabits Marx's philosophy, his subsequent segue to Heidegger's philosophy suggests the validity of my application of the term to the latter. Derrida would seem to confirm the validity of this application in his remarks on Heidegger on pp. 173–4. I also view this discussion as an elaboration of Derrida's treatment of Heidegger in *Of Spirit: Heidegger and the Question*, trans. Geoff Bennington and Rachel Bowlby (Chicago: Chicago University Press, 1989).

31 Derrida, *Spectres of Marx*, p. 161.

32 Ibid., p. 51.

33 Ibid.

34 Ibid.

35 Ibid., p. 10.

36 Ibid., pp. 173–4.

37 Ibid., p. 175.

38 For a similar line of criticism, see Wolin, 'French Heidegger Wars', pp. 272–96.

39 Refusing his interviewers' attribution to him of 'pessimism', Heidegger explains, 'I don't say that [we are] "overwhelmed" [by modern technicity]. I say that up to the present we have not yet found a way to respond to the essene of technicity' (56).

40 Dews helpfully demonstrates that the assumption by many prominent philosophers in late modernity of radical disenchantment has not yet been empirically confirmed: Peter Dews, *The Limits to Disenchantment: Essays on Contemporary European Philosophy* (London: Verso, 1995). Heidegger's own failure to investigate (rather than simply assert) the limits of the disenchantment of late modernity is evident both in his later writings and in his haunted responses to his *Der Spiegel* interviewers.

41 The similarly faint hope evinced by Heidegger in 'The Question Concerning Technology' also rests on nothing more than the logical possibility 'that the frenziedness of technology may entrench itself everywhere to such an extent that someday, throughout everything technological, the essence of technology may come to pres-

ence in the coming-to-pass of truth' (pp. 316–17). Two comments are in order: (1) Heidegger offers no evidence that, or how, the 'frenziedness of technology' might yield an insight into the essence of global technicity; (2) the faint hope that Heidegger stirs could be extremely dangerous if it were to encourage us either to abandon our meliorative, practical efforts or to accelerate intentionally the 'frenzy' of technology in order to glean a saving insight into its essence.

42 In a succint appraisal of the political implications of Heidegger's later philosophizing, Rosen explains that 'Very simply stated, openness to Being, or to that which regions Being, is compatible with doing nothing, or with doing anything at all. Anarchism is as compatible with Heidegger's ambiguous doctrine as is extreme conservatism and even despotism. There is no reason, foundation, ground, or principle intrinsic to the Event to give us any guidance or to restrict us in any way whatsoever on this delicate point. It therefore remains permanently unclear why Heidegger's resolution of the problem of nihilism is not itself nihilism on the grand scale.' Stanley Rosen, *The Question of Being: A Reversal of Heidegger* (New Haven, CT: Yale University Press, 1993). For an extension of a similar line of argumentation, see Richard Wolin, *The Politics of Being: The Political Thought of Martin Heidegger* (New York: Columbia University Press, 1990), pp. 137–47. According to Wolin, '[O]ne must seriously inquire whether Heidegger's own philosophical arrogance did not in fact motivate him to fall back on the specious notion of *Seinsgeschick* as a vehicle of historical explanation. For didn't this theory possess the distinct advantage of absolving both himself and Germany (the privileged "nation in the middle") of all direct historical responsibility for the misdeeds of National Socialism?' (p. 145).

43 Caputo thus maintains that Heidegger's later writings 'remythologized the forest and left human suffering to itself' (*Demythologizing Heidegger*, p. 170).

44 It is interesting to note that when asked if he would 'count [himself] among those who, if they would only be heard, could point out a way', Heidegger responds with an emphatic 'No!' (60).

45 Friedrich Nietzsche, *Beyond Good and Evil: Prelude to a Philosophy of the Future*, trans. Walter Kaufmann (New York: Random House Vintage Books, 1989) p. 136.

46 Any enthusiasm for Heidegger's characterization of the poets as lawgivers must be tempered by an acknowledgment of his selectivity in engaging with the poets of his choice. For an excellent account of Heidegger's engagement with the poets, see Véronique M. Fóti, *Heidegger and the Poetic: Poesis/Sophia/Techne* (Atlantic Highlands, NJ: Humanities Press, 1992). As Fóti persuasively argues, his silence concerning the poetry of Paul Celan constitutes a 'missed interlocution' (p. 78).

47 As Fóti observes, 'due to the primordially apophantic character of language, poetry or *Dichtung* has, for Heidegger, priority among the arts. The poets, then, are those who first of all breach the circle of the rule and leave it marked with the traces of rupture' (ibid., p. xvii).

48 My discussion in this paragraph draws liberally and extensively from Dallmayr's careful reckoning of Heidegger's debts to Hölderlin (*The Other Heidegger*, pp. 143–5).

49 Dallmayr's rich account of Heidegger's engagement with the Swabian poet Johann Peter Hebel suggests a similar intermediary role for the poet-philosophers who will ready us for the advent of the saving divinity. According to Dallmayr, Heidegger not only learned from Hebel the importance for late modernity of the emergence of 'housefriends', or teachers of fellowship, but also resolved to become such a teacher (ibid., p. 197). See also Fóti's discussion of Heidegger's engagement with Hölderlin (*Heidegger and the Poetic*, pp. 55–9).

50 I am indebted here to Dallmayr's interpretation of Heidegger as summoning the poets to preside over the remediation of the world. Addressing in particular Heidegger's engagement with Hebel, Dallmayr observes, 'In this situation, a global housefriend is desperately needed: someone who is able to mediate between Western modernity and native traditions, between scientific nature and calculating reason, on the one hand, and the naturalness of historically grown life-worlds, on the other' (*The Other Heidegger*, p. 198).

howard caygill

THE SPIRITUAL DAYLIGHT OF THE PRESENT: HEGEL, BLAKE AND THE ADVENT OF SPIRIT

But I arose, and sought for the mill & there I found my Angel, who surprised asked me how I escaped!
I answered. All that we saw was owing to your metaphysics: for when you ran away, I found myself on a bank by moonlight hearing a harper.[1]

The philosophy of spirit is an important part of legacy of the 'radical reformation' and cannot be separated from the conviction that the 'age of the son' was coming to an end and to be succeeded by an 'age of the spirit' – the 'spiritual daylight of the present'. The periodization of history according to the three epochs of the father, the son and the spirit originates in the writings of the twelfth-century Calabrian monk Joachim of Fiore (1135–1202). In a number of works, the most important being the *Book of Concord* and the *Book of Figures*, Joachim elaborated the characteristics of the three ages of father, son and spirit. The age of the father, spanning the period between Adam and Christ narrated in the Old Testament, was the age of law, sensible perception, slavery and fear with the cosmic figure of the fixed stars and the prevailing colour of green. The age of the son, for Joachim spanning the period from Christ to St Benedict, was the epoch of grace administered by the church, of partial wisdom, partial liberty and faith with the cosmic figure of dawn and the colour blue. The full, apocalyptic age of the spirit was characterised for Joachim by monastic liberty, full wisdom, freedom and love, with the cosmic figure of daylight and the colour red.

Joachim regarded the advent of spirit in terms of the perfection of monastic organization, for which he saw intimations in monastic reform. Following him, the new mendicant orders of the first decades of the thirteenth century, particularly the Franciscans, saw in their reforms of the

Christian life intimations of the age of the spirit, extending out of the monastery and into secular society. The tendency of the radical mendicants to universalize the age of spirit was intensified in the reformation when themes such as the priesthood of believers and the generalization of monastic disciplines to secular society were once again interpreted as premonitions of the age of spirit. Such readings of the advent of spirit worked into radical Protestant theology, philosophy and poetry and even beyond into the secular millenarian movements of the nineteenth century.

Joachim's texts engaged very sensitively with the question of how textually to present the intimations of the age of spirit. The *Book of Concord* did so by means of allegorical interpretations of the Old and New Testaments, while the *Book of Figures* combined words and images in multicoloured apocalyptic diagrams and their interpretation. One such diagram shows three coloured interlocking circles (green, blue, red), each corresponding to a particular age and their interrelation showing how the father, son and spirit remain separate but also united in the three ages of history.[2] This apocalyptic diagram is framed by the figures of alpha and omega, signifying the beginning and the end of time. The development of a figural representation of the ages is significant for understanding the post-reformation strategies for presenting intimations of the age of spirit. For Hegel, the prolepsis of the age of spirit – the spiritual daylight of the present – entailed the renunciation of colour and poetry in favour of the grey on grey of philosophy, while for Blake the prophecy of the advent of the age of spirit required its intensification. What is at stake in such choices of textual strategy is not just that 'Hegel is more ponderous in his expression than William Blake',[3] but the very character and possibilities of a philosophy of spirit.

Towards the beginning of the self-consciousness section of *The Phenomenology of Spirit* Hegel describes the 'turning point' (*Wendungspunkt*) of consciousness into self-consciousness as a step into 'the spiritual daylight of the present' [*in den geistigen Tag der Gegenwart*]. With it spirit steps away from the opposition of the 'colourful appearances of the sensuous here and now' (*aus dem farbigen Schein des sinnlichen Diesseits*) and the 'empty night of the super-sensuous beyond (*aus der leeren Nacht des ubersinnlichen Jenseits*)[4] and enters a spiritual present which is neither here and now nor beyond and a daylight without colour or darkness. The 'spiritual daylight of the present' seems to invite a metaphysics of spirit as white light and absolute presence, with its characterization as 'the I that is a we and the we that is an I', understood as the total community; however, as Hegel insisted in the Preface to *The Phenomenology of Spirit*, white light and presence are abstractions that point to the removal of spirit.

If the removal of spirit is manifest in the fixed abstract oppositions of metaphysics its recovery is to be found in the animation of concrete transitions. From the standpoint of spirit, the 'I that is a we and the we that is an I' is not the fused community totally present to itself but the Bacchanalian revel keeping its shape through constant movement. Similarly, the colours of the sensible here and now are not resolved in the white light of spirit, but animated by the juxtaposition and superimposition of colours: 'nowhere is there any harsh or sharp line, transition is everywhere, light and shadow are not effective as purely direct light and shadow, but they both shine into one another'.[5] Indeed, *Schein* is defined in the *Lectures on Aesthetics* not as appearance opposed to truth but as an internally animated appearance, 'a hither and thither of reflections of sheens of colour, this mutability and fluidity of transitions'. If spirit is to be sought in its movements, juxtapositions and transitions the question arises of whether philosophy – which famously paints grey on grey – is capable of recovering it. Hegel insists that the pure labour of the concept is enough, that pure philosophy is capable of a fuller recovery of spirit than art and poetry. Again in the Preface he rails against a poetic thinking that would 'bring to the market the arbitrary combinations of an imagination disorganised by thoughts – images that are neither fish nor fowl, neither poetry nor philosophy'.[6]

Kierkegaard's critique of Hegel charted the progression of the phenomenology of the shapes of spirit as precisely the arbitrary combinations of concepts and images that Hegel berates in the Preface. The recovery of spirit and a glimpse of the spiritual daylight of the present perhaps requires a heterogenous philosophy – neither fish nor fowl – one in which the limits of word and image, concept and imagination are disorganized. William Blake's *The Marriage of Heaven and Hell*, written between 1789 and 1790, is such a work, dedicated like *The Phenomenology of Spirit* to evoking spirit through the reanimation of philosophy but avoiding any dialogue between natural and philosophical consciousness and instead proceeding by means of a collision between textual, visual and chromatic orders.

The Marriage of Heaven and Hell comprises twenty-seven engraved plates (twenty-eight including the title page) combining text with marginal and interlinear imagery all coloured by a combination of printing and watercolour techniques. A page of 'text' seems almost to illustrate Hegel's reflections on colour, with the chromatic order organized according to a subtle register of superimposition and juxtaposition. The text is an explicit attempt to reanimate philosophy, recovering its spirit from the priests and from 'analytical' philosophy. The opening plate of the text – 'The Argument' (blue soul superimposed upon red spirit) – begins and ends with the revolutionary refrain (in red): 'Rintrah roars & shakes his fires in the burdened air; / Hungry clouds swag on the deep' (Plate 2). Between the refrains is a narration in blue against a light-blue wash of the inversions of truth and justice by the 'sneaking serpent' of the priestly philosopher. *The Marriage of Heaven and Hell* ends with a kaleidoscopic 'Song of Liberty' which heralds the morning of the American and French revolutions and the end of the night of the law and its servants. The revolutions are interpreted by Blake in terms of Joachimite theology of history, as heralds of the third age of the spirit following the night of the law of the father and the grace of the son dispensed through the churches. The Joachimite structure also informs the recurrent critique of Swedenborg through the pages of *The Marriage of Heaven and Hell*. Swedenborg seemed to promise the advent of an age of the spirit, but in founding a church remained immured in the age of the son: 'And Lo! Swedenborg is the angel sitting at the tomb; his writings are the linen clothes folded up' (Plate 2).

The contents of *The Marriage of Heaven and Hell* are organized under a number of headings beginning with the 'Voice of the Devil' and continuing with a series of five 'Memorable Fancies' or satirical narratives punctuated between the first and the second by seventy 'Proverbs of Hell'. It is important to remember the Joachimite structure of the text – the move from the ages of the father and the son to the age of spirit – in order not to mistake its antinomian character. The antinomian pulse of the text is carefully introduced in the second part of the introductory 'Argument' where, framed between an image of a naked figure basking in flames and one of a woman giving birth, Blake introduces what has been termed his 'doctrine of contraries': 'Without [red] Contraries [blue superimposed upon red] is no progression. Attraction and Repulsion, Reason and Energy, Love and Hate, are necessary to [red] Human existence [blue superimposed upon red]' (Plate 2). From this statement Blake goes on to qualify such contraries as the perspectives on spirit adopted by 'the religious' who can only interpret spirit in terms of oppositions, primarily those between good and evil and reason and energy: 'From these contraries spring what the religious call Good and Evil. Good is the passive that obeys Reason. Evil is the active springing from energy [blue]. Good is Heaven. Evil is Hell [red]' (Plate 2) The division into contraries is a product of 'the religious', as indeed is the antinomian inversion of the terms. Blake however seeks a philosophy of spirit which does stop at contraries and their inversion, which as Jeane Moskal claims[7] only repeats, albeit in inverse form, the view of 'the religious'.

The antinomian reading of *The Marriage of Heaven and Hell* seems to be endorsed by 'The Voice of the Devil' which with the aid of three ethereal trumpeters proclaims that 'All bibles or sacred codes have been the causes of the following Errors [blue]'. The reference to sacred codes situates the cause of error in the age of the father – the age of law – and presents the errors of law about itself, about the son, and about the spirit. '1. That Man has two real existing principles Viz: a Body and a Soul. 2. That energy, called Evil, is alone from the Body & that reason, called Good, is alone from the Soul 3. That God will torment Man in Eternity for following his energies [blue]' (Plate 3). The devil then inverts the decrees of the father and claims 'the following contraries': '1. Man has no body distinct from his Soul for that called Body is a portion of the Soul discerned by the five Senses, the chief inlets of Soul in this age. 2. Energy is the only life and is from the Body and Reason is the bound or outward circumference of Energy. 3. Energy is Eternal Delight [red]'. The contraries remain inversions of the sacred code of the father; the separation of body and soul is qualified by the body becoming the sensuous perception of soul, reason becoming the limit of energy, and eternal torment becoming eternal delight (eternity remaining safely in place). The ironic interlinear designs put in question the veracity of the devil's voice, as does the image in the lower third of the plate of a struggle – above the sea of space and time – between a devil bound in flames and an angel for possession of the child of spirit born in Plate 2.

On the third plate of 'The Voice of the Devil' the oppositions and their inversions are intensified to the degree that Jehovah becomes 'no other than he [deleted 'the devil'] who dwells in the flaming fire' (Plate 6). Yet immediately after achieving the antinomian limit of inverting God into Satan Blake qualifies the movement by hinting that the inversions all depend upon the absence of spirit: 'But in Milton; the Father is Destiny, the Son, a Ratio of the five senses & the Holy Ghost, Vacuum' (Plate 6). The subsequent 'Memorable Fancies' and 'Proverbs of Hell' represent attempts to fill the vacuum of spirit. Blake's intimations of spirit are given a number of names – energy, genius, infinity, excess and prodigiousness – each of which is presented in the memorable fancies.

The first memorable fancy is dedicated to spirit conceived as genius, and finds the narrator in Hell, 'delighted with the enjoyments of Genius: which to Angels look like torment and insanity' and collecting the 'proverbs of Hell'. The seventy proverbs develop a complex counterpoint of themes ranging from antinomian inversions to figural intimations of spirit bound together by colour contrasts and a gradual change in the complexion of the wash: the first sixty appear against a meridian blue and yellow while the last ten are set against a crespucular blue and magenta wash. At the antinomian end of the range is Proverb 21, which says 'Prisons are built with the stones of Law, Brothels with bricks of Religion', reversing the values of law and religion by showing that they create their own transgressions of opposites. In between the antinomian and the spiritual are proverbs such as the infamous 67: 'Sooner murder an Infant in its cradle than nurse unacted desires' (Plate 10). Depending on the spiritual insight of the reader, this proverb can be read as a monstruous transgression of the commandment against murder or its antinomian inversion. Each of the contraries assumes that the unacted desire belongs to the adult rather than to the child; if the unacted desires are those of the child then the proverb takes on a different meaning – to nurse the unacted desires of an infant in the cradle is to deny it full life and figuratively to commit murder. The proverbs include a number of figural intimations of spirit such as the third, 'The road of excess leads to the palace of wisdom', and the thirty-fifth, 'The cistern contains; the fountain overflows'. The proverbs end in the twilight with the phrase 'Enough! Or Too much' referring back to Proverb 46 on the limits of knowledge: 'You never know what is enough unless you know what is more than enough'.

After the 'Proverbs of Hell' the first memorable fancy ends with a reflection on the poetic genius which imbued the world of the senses with spirit. Blake then explains that the creations of spirit were exploited by priests and philosophers 'who took advantage of & enslaved the vulgar by attempting to realize or abstract the mental deities from their objects: thus began Priesthood' (Plate 11). Here spirit in the guise of genius creates its own deities – father and son – but is lost when 'men forgot that All deities reside in the human breast'. The text with red and yellow wash begins in a pink/magenta ink drawn from the colour of the dawn sky over the sea of the scene of the birth of the gods out of genius at the top of the page and ends in a grey/brown ink which anticipates the scene of God the father consigning his son to oblivion.

The first intimation of spirit as poetic genius, and its loss, prepares for the alliance in the second memorable fancy of the theme of poetic genius with that of the infinite. The narrator dines with the prophets Isaiah and Ezekiel and learns the former's definition of spirit in terms of the senses discovering 'the infinite in every thing'. Here Blake develops the theme of spirit expanding the senses through spirit first proposed in the prototypical illuminated texts 'All Religions are One' and 'There is no Natural Religion'. Ezekiel develops the theme further by claiming that God or 'Poetic Genius (as you now call it)' was 'the first principle' which introduced the infinite into perception, a view less monotheistic than monotheurgic and 'which was the cause of our despising the Priests and philosophers of other countries and prophecying that all Gods would at last be proved to originate in ours & to be the tributaries of the Poetic Genius' (Plates 12 and 13). Blake ends the memorable fancy by using imagery drawn from the practice of engraving to explain how the senses can be prepared to receive the infinity of spirit. The senses would be subjected to corrosive acids or spirits, 'melting apparent surfaces away and displaying the infinite which was hid'. The surfaces are those given by the senses or 'the gates of perception' through which, once cleansed, 'everything would appear to man as it is: Infinite / For man has closed himself up till he sees all things thro' narrow chinks of his cavern'.

After the corrosive work of spirit in the second memorable fancy the third looks at the intimation of spirit through the gift of energy. It begins in a printing house in Hell where the hoarders and the devourers of knowledge (snakes and dragons) are contrasted with the prolific creators such as the eagle 'who caused the inside of the cave to be infinite'. The prolific creators release and bestow energy, a grace of the spirit and not of God the father or son – 'Some will say, Is not God alone the Prolific? I answer, God only Acts and Is, in existing beings or Men' (Plate 16). The spirit works through the senses, but these are both vehicles of spirit and potential obstacles to its passage. Thus the generosity of spirit is allied to the corrosive work on the gates of perception commenced in the third memorable fancy, both dedicated to a maximization of energy. The text begins in red and then gradually changes hue towards blue with an image of spirit – the eagle ascending, clutching a serpent – contrasted with an image of the five somnolent senses crouching in a black cavern.

The fourth and fifth memorable fancies parody the attempts to restrain infinite spirit on behalf of the law of the father and the grace of the son. In the fourth the angel of philosophy uses Aristotle's analytics and metaphysics as a servant of ecclesiastical power by making the infinite a scene of horror and terror rather than of beauty and peace. The inspired narrator declares it but 'lost time' to converse of spirit with a systematic reasoner who in the end 'only holds a candle in sunshine', having closed the doors of perception to the infinite. The fifth and final memorable fancy returns to the antinomian voice of the devil who, conversing with an angel, shows Christ to have broken all of the ten commandments. The demonstration provokes the angel to change colour, becoming almost blue but 'mastering himself', returning through yellow to white pink. The chromatic transformation is echoed in the text, with the devil beginning to speak, as ever, in blue, the angel's change of colour described in angelic red, followed by the angel's pious reply appearing in satanic blue and the devil's proof of the transgressions of Christ in angelic red tinted towards the end of his discourse with blue. The inversion of the colour code is consummated by the angel reaching into and being consumed by the flames of Hell and emerging a devil.

After the evocations of spirit in the memorable fancies *The Marriage of Heaven and Hell* ends on the threshold of the age of spirit with a 'Song of Liberty'. The text, set against a bright-yellow wash and moving between degrees of ochre and blue, is sung by a narrator (the 'I') and a chorus (the 'we') and sings of the battle at the end of the ages of the father and the son and the advent of the age of spirit. It begins in the night with the earth shivering at the birth of the spirit of liberty in the American revolution and its movement across the Atlantic and then moves to a battle between the eternal 'starry king' of the law and the 'new born fire'. The 'new born wonder' is cast down into the void 'like the sinking sun in the western sea' and the father reassumes command over the ruins of the world – 'With thunder and fire: leading his starry hosts thro' the waste wilderness he promulgates his ten commands glancing his beamy eyelids over the deep in dark dismay', only to see the 'son of fire' rise in the east, 'spurning the clouds written with curses stamps the stony law to dust, loosing the eternal horses from the dens of night crying Empire is no more! And now the lion and the wolf shall cease.' With the advent of the age of the spirit the chorus ends *the Marriage of Heaven and Hell* with a curse on the cursers of life (the priests and philosophers who deny spirit) – 'Let the Priests of the Raven of dawn no longer in deadly black, with hoarse note curse the sons of joy' – and proclaims that in the age of spirit 'every thing that lives is Holy'.

The intimations of the age of spirit throughout *The Marriage of Heaven and Hell* in its text, imagery and colours anticipate *The Phenomenology of Spirit* and its intimations of the age of spirit or 'spiritual daylight of the present'. Both see spirit animating the senses through the discovery of infinity in the finite and both end on the threshold of the age of spirit – the new world proclaimed after the death of the son in the final paragraph of *The Phenomenology of Spirit* and the proclamation of the chorus in *The Marriage of Heaven and Hell*. Yet the Blake text, by returning to Joachim of Fiore's figural and chromatic intimation of the age of spirit, remains oriented to the future rather than to retrospection and the grey on grey of the metaphysical ghosts of the father and the son. It is precisely a text that is 'neither fish nor fowl' with its swirling colours, figures and words that open the way for an affirmative philosophy of spirit in which spirit exceeds the bounds of received metaphysical oppositions.

Notes

1   William Blake, *The Marriage of Heaven and Hell*, ed. Geoffrey Keynes (Oxford: Oxford University Press, 1975) Plate 15.
2   See plate xib in Bernard McGinn, *Apocalyptic Spirituality* (London: SPCK, 1979) p. 105.
3   Cyril O'Regan, *The Heterodox Hegel* (New York: State University of New York Press, 1994) p. 323.
4   G. W. F. Hegel, *Phänomenologie des Geistes* (Frankfurt: Ulstein Verlag, 1973) p. 113.

5 G. W. F Hegel, *Aesthetics*, trans. F. M. Knox (Oxford: Clarendon Press, 1975).
6 Hegel, *Phänomenologie*, p. 50.
7 Jeane Moskal, *Blake, Ethics and Forgiveness* (Tuscaloosa and London: University of Alabama Press, 1994).

graham ward

THE CONTEMPORARY
CITY OF ANGELS

The American sociologist, Robert Wuthnow, recently observed:

> the mysterious has become a growth industry. One manifestation of this growth is the enormous interest in angels. In only three years, Sophy Burnham's *A Book of Angels* sold 450,000 copies. So many readers wrote letters to the author reporting their encounters with angels that her edited anthology of these letters (*Angel Letters*) sold another 175,000 copies. Joan Wester Anderson's book, *Where Angels Walk*, proved even more successful, selling more than a million copies.
>
> As if to capitalize on the popular interest, in 1993 First Lady Hilary Rodham Clinton decorated the White House Christmas tree entirely in angels, declaring 'this is the year of the angels'. Overall, the number of books on angels (according to the Library of Congress) rose from 20 published between 1971 and 1975, to 31 between 1976 and 1980, 34 between 1981 and 1985, 57 between 1986 and 1990, and 110 between 1991 and 1995. During the last of these periods, total sales of angel books were estimated to exceed 5 million copies.[1]

In his masterpiece *The Production of Space*, Henri Lefebvre writes: 'Any "social existence" aspiring or claiming to be "real", but failing to produce its own space, would be a strange entity, a very peculiar kind of abstraction unable to escape from the ideological or even the "cultural" realm. It would fall to the level of folklore and sooner or later disappear altogether, thereby immediately losing its identity, its denomination and its feeble degree of reality.'[2] What I wish to do in this chapter is 'explain' (inverted commas here because I claim no epistemological validity, no objectivity for the rationality of my argument; I simply attempt to persuade) – to explain why it is that angels seemingly disappeared from the systems of belief which created the space termed modernity and why it is that they are making a dramatic comeback in the new cultural spaces (complex and heterogeneous) of postmodernity. Michel de Certeau would ask, what is it that makes a belief believable. And it is something of the same kind of enterprise that I am embarking on here. We did not, could not, believe in angels any longer because, returning to Lefebvre, angels produced no space; they did not give themselves as objects organizing a certain perspective within which they could be viewed or figure forth something meaningful. Put another way, they were no longer visible because of what determines, for us, those three foundational categories Lefebvre alludes to: 'social existence', being 'real' and spatiality. But this opens up alternative possibilities, because if we accept the production of social existence, what is considered 'real' and space, then there may be (may have been and may well yet be) forms of social existence, reality and spatiality in which angels can again appear (and be believed in). And maybe we are heralding again a time of advent. Maybe we are beginning again to believe in them. And so, in this chapter, I wish to 'explain' why this might be so and to understand what they are figuring for us today.

The release of hybrids

Angels are not the only 'creatures' experiencing a revival of interest. They are part of a cultural context which, in witnessing the implosion of modernity, are welcoming again the hybrid and making the claim 'We have never been modern' (not really). We can take a cue here from the historian of science Bruno Latour, who, in his book entitled *We Have Never Been Modern*, distinguished one of the fundamental trajectories of modernity to be the aspiration for purity.[3] The counter-effect of this trajectory was the suppression, or erasure, or fear of or redefinition of *the hybrid*. That which did not conform to the rules of conduct or the laws of science (which the ethics of natural law conflated) was criminal, pathological or perverted. Such phenomena were to be publicly, clinically, scientifically exposed and shown to be in need of reformation, healing or disciplining. The natural was the understandable, the rational, that which conformed.

What took place sociologically was the development of an underworld: a world of the prostitutes, the transvestites, the sodomites, the paedophiles, the criminal, the insane, the vagabonds, the gypsies. What took place, imaginatively, was the development of the dark side of the romantic: the gothic, creatures of supernatural, the demonic, the pornographic, the suicidal and the sublime. Here Wagner's *Nieberlungen* and Rhine Maidens stalked the same lands as Shelley's Frankenstein, Byron's Cain, Stoker's Dracula, Le Fanu's Uncle Silas, the Golem myths of Judaism and Goya's witches. Angels too had a place here: in the esoteric writings of

Lavater and Swendenborg, in the paintings of the Pre-Raphaelite Brotherhood and, following the revival of mediaevalism, the fashion for gilded cherubim in the homes and cold marble angels over graves. Unlike the romantic 'monsters' their faces were more publicly acceptable. For rather than exemplifying the hybrid – which they might well have done since Old Testament scholars in the nineteenth century recognized that angels were imported into ancient Judaism via Babylon, where *kerub* (from which we derive *cherubim*) were bulls with wings and the faces of the human beings – angels became figures for modernity's obsession with the pure.

Writing in Germany in 1827, Carl Hase (in a book entitled, mysteriously enough *Gnosis*) wrote: 'Those who have a heart for the beautiful and the ideal will gladly think of angels. It was the desire for a living creature better than ourselves yet benevolently participating in our human joys and sorrows which first heard the angel-song in the quiet night.'[4] The title of the book is significant, for gnosticism is associated with the exaltation of the spiritual above the material – in fact, with cosmic mythologies in which the binary principle of good and evil is mapped onto the binary division between spirit and flesh. The angels of romanticism were figures for the ethereal and sublime. Furthermore, they were gendered feminine. Since Winklemann and the development, in Germany, of the gymnasium, the male body had been undergoing a Hellenization of its own in which slender, hairless, feminised bodies were sought after. Romantic angels of the male gender were either children or feminised. A paradox is articulated by these gendered figures: as representations of the beautiful and the ideal body they are escapes from actuality of embodiment, rejections of corporeality. As Grace Jantzen and other feminist thinkers have emphasized, this production of the eternal feminine (by and in dialectical opposition to the masculine), this divinizing of woman as the perfect other with whom synthesis is sublime (witness the end of *The Flying Dutchman*) is a manifestation of the male fear of death. The body beautiful, particularly the idealization of feminine beauty, was implicated in a necrophilia: angels and afterlife, angels and the other shore. These figurations of the pure (the required disciplining of the body to imitate these figurations) are profoundly gnostic.

What has changed in today's interest in the hybrid and in the angel is twofold. First, the hybrid is no longer the monstrous other out there, the other that must be kept out there, kept at bay (like Stevenson's Mr Hyde). The hybrid is part of the social; we are all recognized to be hybrids now, for the natural order has buckled and warped. With our implants, pacemakers, false teeth, cosmetic surgeries, contact lenses; with our diet over years of genetically engineered food; with our notions of hygiene; with the pharmaceuticalization of our bodies and the electronic extension of those bodies (mentally with computers, physically with cars and planes and space shuttles) – we are already becoming cyborgs. The question of what now is human is a real question. The collapse of liberal humanism in the wake of twentieth-century atrocities, galloping social atomism fuelled by advanced market economics and the explorations of the dark, violent side of the psyche have launched that question into the black holes of deep space.

The Protestant theologian Karl Barth, writing about angels in his *Church Dogmatics* in the late 1940s, strikes a contemporary note. While attacking on the one hand, as a biblicist, the speculative nonsense of those great angelologists of the Christian tradition – Pseudo-Dionysus in his *De Hierarchia Coelesti* and Thomas Aquinas (nicknamed the 'angelic doctor') in both his *Summa Theologicae* and his *Summa Contra Gentiles* – Barth attacks, on the other, those liberal theologians seduced by positivisms and keen to demythologize the Bible's record of angelic hosts. He writes that

> when the Bible speaks of angels (and their demonic counterparts) it always introduces us to a sphere where historically verifiable history, i.e., the history which is comprehensible by the known analogies of world history, passes over into non verifiable saga or legend. That is to say, when it is a matter of angels in the Bible, we are in the sphere of the particular form of history which by content and nature does not proceed according to ordinary analogies.[5]

With angels the material orders scrutinized and tabulated by modernity – nature verifiable by number – are questioned; also questioned is what it is we 'know', the nature of the analogical knowledge (knowledge built upon seeing things *as* other things, and *in relation* to other things) and therefore the production of the 'comprehensible' itself. We no longer speak of knowledge, we speak of the production of knowledge, and we speak of belief. As Wittgenstein puts it in a book of devastating philosophical scepticism, ironically entitled *On Certainty*: 'The difficulty is to realise the groundlessness of our believing'; 'What I know, I believe'; 'Knowledge is in the end based on acknowledgements'; 'At the end of reason comes persuasion'.[6]

Michel Serres and the tongues of angels

Serres's *La Légende des anges* was published in 1993 and translated into English in 1995 as *Angels: A Modern Myth*. The translation 'myth' does not capture the connotations of the French *légende*. For Serres's book is concerned with languages, speaking, messages, communication, translation (in its various meanings), transmission and transmutation. These are all aspects of his angelology, his talk about angels. The Latin *legere* (to bind or collect together as well as to appoint, or send out on a commission, as well as to read aloud or cite) can be heard in the French *légende*. *Legens*, the Latin participle, can be used as a substantive meaning 'reader'. The French *légende* is also linked to citation, as well as meaning 'key' or 'caption' beneath a painting or map. Serres plays with the word 'key' and 'map' and, in a volume richly illustrated, draws attention to the captions beneath paintings and photographs. *Légende* is much richer in association than 'myth' allows. In a dialogue between two characters, female and male, named Pia and her brother Jacques, Serres writes: 'Jacques says derisively: "But angels are fictitious beings." Pia counters, learnedly, "Take them in a figurative sense. And remember that both your 'fictitious' and my 'figurative' come from the same Latin root."'⁷ Just as Michel de Certeau uses 'fable' with the associations not of fiction as opposed to fact, but *facere*, to make, to do, and Michel Foucault will speak of his genealogies as *récits*, so Serres emphasizes the construction and the production of what we know. For Serres we compose our world in and through our employment of figures. Not only do we compose, but we also discover we are immersed within a world that speaks in, to and through us. We dwell within the endless relays and interchanges of language in transit – language understood widely to include the exchange of signs, the making of gestures, the production of rhythms and complex patterns of chains of activity. Hence the series of dialogues which constitute the text is staged in an airport, a place of transition with the coming and going of several people speaking several languages. Angels, for Serres, are like the convex mirrors in the background of certain seventeenth-century Dutch paintings which reflect back upon the painter painting. They are figures of a self-reflexivity in which communication is conscious of itself. They are not mythic. Like the word Barth uses for the genre of discourse in which the action of angels is described, 'saga', which bears within it the German *Sagen*, *légende* is not simply being used generically by Serres; it is being used to suggest the whole history of the transmission and commission, the speaking about or citation of these figures. Serres's book stands within that transmission, mediating and passing it on into another future.

The book, then, is not only about angels; it is angelic. Taking up a traditional notion of angelic intelligence and mechanics in which they move as fast as they can think, the movement of the thought tracks the passage of angels. The direction of the thought is governed by the 'good news' that angels are commissioned to tell out. The twilight of the angels comes when the good news arrives, when the word becomes flesh. This insistence upon incarnationalism structures the book, which shifts liturgically through the day and through refigured scenes of the scriptural narrative of the birth of

Christ. The dawn opening sketches an annunciation scene between Pia (a doctor at the airport's medical centre) and her lover Pantope (who flies constantly all over the world as a travel inspector for Air France). Following the birth of Christ refigured as a midnight mass and the birth of a child to an Israeli woman in the airport, in the final section entitled 'Noel' the work of the angels is accomplished and they take their leave. 'Angels will still be able to continue expressing their language, writing and singing, transporting and coding messages ... but henceforth their role will be subaltern, their age will have come to an end, and both their role and their end will have been fulfilled, because the message is here ... Throughout the whole world, all the networks are crying out about hunger, are screaming a thirst for incarnation, in a situation where the body is horribly lacking. But at last, the Good News: the Messiah, the message, is flesh, immanent'.[8]

It is this incarnationalism which bears the ethical and political significance of Serres's appeal to angels. The *légende* bears us, on messianic wings, towards a utopic horizon in which there is a new respect for the corporeal. At the moment 'the body is horribly lacking', Serres comments. That is, a limited number of bodies are being pampered and cared for in what he calls Newtown (the city founded upon informational technology by those who know how to access, use and profit by it) by exploiting and then disregarding the violated, abused and disfigured bodies of those still in Oldtown. The death of a destitute man called Gabriel, at the beginning of the book, brings forth these tidings. He announces by his very presence and act (for there is no distinction between the messenger and the message if the angel is good) the systematic destruction of humanity. Newtown is ruled over and organized by the fallen angels (where, in the distinction between messenger and message, the messenger wants to be glorified above or in place of the message). These constitute powers, thrones and dominions; the realm of the false gods who work to create simulacra of paradise and angelic existence for its best citizens. Not that Serres embraces a gnosticism here: the volatility of angels means there is always the temptation for rising or falling and a difficulty in assessing the good from the fallen. What is required then is mercy and love. The operation of the former (countering the effects of social Darwinism) is associated with the angel of consolation (the archangel Michael with the small foot); the operation of the latter, which brings about rebirth, is associated with entering 'the triangle of the seraphim'.[9]

Not only new bodies will be formed (and therefore a new ethics and politics governed by a recognition of the interdependence of all bodies), but new knowledges and states of being. Serres's angelology announces these new knowledges, for they figure forth a new enchantment of the real. This re-enchantment has to arise from the sublation of what Serres has viewed as socially dangerous and violent from his early writings: the cultural dominance of the hard sciences. Max Weber first described the advance of technology as withdrawing mystery from the world and disenchanting it. Serres's angelology is one more strategy for calling forth new knowledges by bringing together the so-called natural sciences and the social sciences or humanities. Hence throughout the book a series of analogies are created, establishing new connections: information theory is related to Hermes as a forerunner of the angels; spectrograms of the human voice are paralleled with Jacob's ladder and the continual ascent and descent of the angels upon it; the greenhouse effect is likened to the myth of Prometheus, Los Angeles to the heavenly Jerusalem. In another work, *Parasites*, Serres draws together literature, parasitology and sociological analysis. An intermixing of discourses which seeks to constitute new relationalities in our thinking, establish a new holism, is fundamental to Serres's work. Only this creative activity of making connections, of communicating one thing to another, one discursive world to another, will, for Serres, stall the accelerated dis-enchantment of the world which exploits in its (death-)drive to control. Newtown is established here: it is these uncontrolled technologies that produce 'the aggressive hell of commercial advertising' and a new form of global city 'which allows us to place our hopes only in itself and in its achievements. Furthermore, people can only enter it if they know how to access it everywhere.'[10] Such blatant forms of power-to-exclude and segregate manifests for Serres, the problem of evil.

The new knowledges of angels bring a recognition of 'a state of interconnectedness'.[11] It is a recognition that must produce humility, because it understands that the pursuit (and achievement) of personal glory, power and excellence is at the expense of others. But Serres goes further than this, as indeed he must. For he needs to expound the basis upon which the holism he propounds (and the analogies he constructs) is possible. The re-enchantment of the world through angels suggests that ultimately what holds all things in place, for Serres, is a theological worldview. The book, which draws together (*legere*), encyclopedically, so many different fields of reference, which moves between popular science, literature, philosophy and sociology, is finally framed theologically. All the connections can only be made, all the relations only hold, if a third and transcendent party is honoured above and beyond the analogical communications themselves. The angels announce a pantheistic world of immanent fluxes, a world in which the word is to be made flesh. But beyond the angelic hosts is the most high or the all high God to whom all glory is due: 'if our will becomes sufficiently good for us to make an agreement between us to accord the glory only to a transcendent absent being, then we will be able to live in peace.'[12] The book concludes: 'This unique solution to the problem of evil thus leads not to a demonstration of the existence of God, but to the fact that it is necessary for him to exist, and to the refutation of polytheism, which is what dominates us today. Without a God who is one and unique, and without his exclusive glory – these being the sole foundations for peace – the war of all against everyone will continue to rage.'[13]

I pass no comment on the Hobbesianism evident here – the social contract guaranteed by a covenant with the almighty God. The utopianism is unabashed, but then Serres's work is to implement transformation by being angelic, performing the creative bridge-building that will incarnate our words by making us all messengers who live out absolutely our messages. The angelology arises as the repressed voice of enlightenment rationality, with its social Darwinianism and its scientific reductionism. The angels in Serres's work call for and create a new spatiality within which there can be optimism and *renaissance*. In an interview with his pupil and colleague, Bruno Latour, he said: 'Hiroshima remains the sole object of my philosophy.'[14] Doxology is recognized at the only way of redeeming Hiroshima.

Wim Wenders and the knowledge of angels

In one of Wim Wenders's most recent films, *The End of Violence* (1997), a detective (Doc) who is tracking down a film director (Mike Max) who has gone missing and is thought to be a murderer, tells the director's wife (Page): 'I think everything's connected. Did you know that in nuclear physics if you look at a so-called particle you change it? Imagine, just by looking at something you can actually change what it is … We're connected and we've never even met.' The film explores that interconnectedness, which is graphically portrayed by shots of a major road intersection outside Los Angeles and dramatized in the prominence in the narrative of video surveillancing of the city. The interconnectedness is both reassuring (the detective finds the woman he loves and the main character is cleared of a murder because the event is caught on camera) and disturbing (in the voyeuristic intrusion of surveillance and the sinister threat of a power controlling the narrative). Connectedness is also narrativized in terms of computer links, video conferencing, the use of e-mail and mobile phones. Wenders's world is Serres's global city. In fact, Serres himself uses Los Angeles as a metaphor for his infotech Newtown; his city of the fallen angels. In Wenders's world the intricate networks of communication and the continuous relays of information artificially relate human beings. For most of the characters are isolated atoms, immigrants, refugees, men (always) on the run. They make small gestures of belonging: on the run Mike Max finds refuge with the Mexican family who service his Beverley

Hills mansion; Ray, who supervises the observatory (which controls the city's surveillance cameras) begins an affair with a South American refugee who acts as a cleaner. But the belonging never lasts: the cleaner betrays her supervisor, who is shot; the film director's wife leaves him and then threatens him with a gun when he returns. The absence of connection is dramatized in terms of the four plots running concurrently, linked through what is caught on camera (and those who are controlling what is caught on camera, in the observatory). What connections are made can appear either planned (and therefore possibly sinister) or arbitrary. For the connections themselves are tangential (at no point do any of those involved in the four plots understand their complicity one with the others).

At the end of the film, Mike, by leaving his wealth and position as a film director behind, has escaped the networks of global connection which constantly threaten violence and intrusion. He stands facing the sea while another level of the plot unravels: the South American cleaner is about to be assassinated by those who control the surveillance cameras because she knows too much. Her daughter stands next to Mike and begins a conversation. They discuss Spanish words, how many he knows and how to pronounce them.

> **Mike**: Los Angeles.
> **Girl**: (correcting his pronunciation) Los Angeles.
> **Mike**: Sky?
> **Girl**: Cielo.
> **Mike**: I thought cielo means heaven.
> **Girl**: Cielo means both heaven and sky. (Pause) They're watching us.

The camera zooms out and sweeps the promenade. We see (without commentary) that the mother is allowed to return to her child and the threat of assassination dispelled. In what is almost a trademark of Wenders's films a voiceover (Mike's) accompanies the camera's movement as the shot pulls smoothly to a distant point in the sky and panoramically surveys the sunlit Californian coastline, serene and blue.

> Funny, just when you think you've got it all figured in a heartbeat it changes again. (Pause) Thing is, all those years while I was waiting for that sudden attack *I* became the enemy. And when the enemy I expected finally came, they set me free. Strange. (Pause) Now when I look over the ocean I don't expect nuclear submarines, alien attacks anymore. I see China now. And I hope they can see us. (Fade out)

The violence, threats and paranoia dissolve into an appeal for omniscience. Bathed in sunlight, desire finds its *jouissance*, its sabbath rest. Movement – at least Mike's movements in this film – serves to escalate violence. Angels, like the satellites which comb the world and record what they see, like cameras passively watching, offer hope for a utopian future. They act as guarantors that someone knows what is going on. Their knowledge protects all of us. The close intimacy of the voiceover reassures us but the panning long shot of the ocean comes from nowhere. Freed from the secular forms of tracking and surveillance, exiled from the social, Mike seems to place himself in the hands of transcendent all-seeing powers which are benevolent. He seems to place himself in the hands of angels, and an omniscience which is innocent (affirmed by the words and perspective of a child[15]). If Serres's concern with communication is with the word as flesh, the message, then his focus is upon the tongues of angels, whereas for Wenders, for whom communication is fundamentally visual, attention is given to the knowledge of angels.

What the knowledge of angels seems to give Wenders is a transcendental authority to direct films. For Mike Max, the filming-within-the-film, the intrusive, voyeuristic cameras controlled from the observation tower, all suggest power and its potential for abuse; its potential for generating violence rather than ending it. The director is guilty, not for the crime he is being hunted down for, but for the focus for power he has allowed himself to become. His seeing changes the world we see, on Doc's analysis of sub-atomic physics. A guilt attaches to Wenders seeing and making us see. He is not confident that his seeing facilitates a redemption of the real – to quote the subtitle of Siegfried Kracauer's important book from the early Frankfurt school on film-making. In accepting the exile from globalization and the film industry's implication in it – in handing his studios and production over to his estranged wife, Page – in surrendering his vision for the seeing of the angels, the director enacts a kenosis and receives the grace of absolution.

The End of Violence suggests a new development in Wenders's exploration of the knowledge of angels which explicitly began ten years earlier with *Wings of Desire* (1987) and its sequel *Far Away, So Close* (1993). These two films form a diptych. In the first the angel Damiel falls in love with a woman and, leaving his friend Cassiel, falls to earth to create a new kind of relationship. The film is shot in West Berlin, and the Berlin wall and Germany's nazi past are constantly alluded to and revisited in documentary clips. In the second film, Cassiel, who comes to earth to join Damiel in his family bliss, finds the human, technicolour world (the angel-scenes are shot in black and white) painful and violent. He eventually returns to the angelic realm. The film is shot in the former East Berlin, the wall has now been torn down, Germany is still affected by the fruits of past events, though Cassiel's interventions redeem the possible present violence of those fruits. For example, he manages to smuggle a hoard of nazi guns away from a group of arms dealers. A little girl held at gunpoint by the arms dealers is saved by Cassiel, who is killed in saving her; but then he returns home to Raphaela, his angelic friend.

In both films Wenders plays with the political rather than engages it and critiques it. The darkness, despair and guilt of post-war which divided Berlin in the first film is portrayed, self-consciously so, when Peter Falk, as himself, is brought into Berlin to star in a film being made about the nazi concentration camps. But the darkness is constantly juxtaposed to the main focus of the film, the romance between the circus woman and the angel. In his notes for the film, published as *The Logic of Images*, Wenders wrote: 'One day, in the middle of Berlin, I suddenly became aware of that gleaming figure, 'the Angel of Peace", metamorphosed from being a war-like victory angel into a pacifist … [T]here have always been childhood images of angels as invisible, omnipresent observers; there was, so to speak, the old hunger for transcendence.'[16] The political is tempered by the utopic – the end of violence and the ushering in of an age of peace: Berlin's Angel of Peace rules over all.

Far Away, So Close opens with one of Wenders's circling, flying shots this time of Cassiel on the top of the Angel of Peace. And, once more, in this film, after the kenosis of Cassiel to the hell of earthly living and his cru-cifixion on behalf of a child (whom he had already saved from a fatal fall over the balcony of her apartment earlier in the film – a salvation which brought him to earth), the film ends on shots of the barge carrying the nazi armaments towards their final resting place in the sea. It is dawn, the river is misty, the colours are blue and violet touched by an orange sunrise and the view is panoramic. A voiceover, a duet composed of Cassiel and Raphaela speaking together, exhorts:

> You. You whom we love. You do not see us. You do not hear us. You imagine us in the far distance, yet we are so near. We are the messengers who bring closeness to those in the distance. We are not the message. We are only the messengers. The message is love. We are nothing. You are everything to us. Let us dwell in your eyes. See your world through us. Recapture through us that loving look once again. Then we'll be close to you and you to Him.

This is very close to the utopic ending of Serres's work.

In his film notes, Wenders self-consciously constructs a myth for these angels:

> When God, endlessly disappointed, finally prepared to turn his back on the world for ever, it happened that some of his angels disagreed with him and took the side of man, saying he deserved another chance. Angry at being crossed, God banished them to what is then the most terrible place on earth: Berlin. And then he turned away. All this happened at the time that today we call; 'the end of the Second World War.'[17]

It is a cosmic myth which does not map onto the films themselves. Particularly in *Far Away, So Close* Cassiel falls to earth because of his love, not his will (as Damiel) and, as the final voiceover suggests, the intention is to return the world in love 'to Him'. Earlier in the film, in a dialogue between Raphaela and Cassiel we are informed that humankind has hardened its heart and is now unable to see and hear the angelic presence. It is the world, not the angels, that has fallen. The redemption of that world lies in recalling these angelic figures, giving their knowledge (the way of seeing) cultural space. Luce Irigaray would concur.

Luce Irigaray and the flesh of angels

As a philosopher of sexual difference, Irigaray has been concerned throughout most of her work with, on the one hand, a critical project (deconstructing a male-centred cultural symbolic) and, on the other, a constructive project (transfiguring the cultural symbolic in a way that takes account of women). It is with reference to the second of these projects that she develops her angelology. Her understanding of the constitution of culture as a field of symbols issues from her critical engagement with Freudian and Lacanian psychology. For Lacan, the development of subjectivity requires the entry into language and the exchange of signs. These signs give representation to the subject's imaginary (that realm in which a subject's experience of the world is internalized in terms of various images, rhythms and intuitions). But the order of the symbolic, according to Lacan, is governed by the phallus and phallic-driven desire: 'The phallus is the privileged signifier of that mark in which the role of the logos is joined with the advent of desire.'[18] The phallus is a metonym for stabilized identity, full self-present meaning, the word of God. This consummation of identity is never possible; the journeying towards it and the mourning for its absence go on until death.

Irigaray's writing on angels, like Serres's, arises from a concern for a new kind of incarnationalism: the word made flesh in a way that owns the sexuate nature of all flesh and the sexual difference necessary for fleshing at all.

> [Angels] are not unrelated to sex. There is of course Gabriel, the angel of the annunciation. But other angels announce the consummation of marriage, notably all the angels in the Apocalypse and many in the Old Testament. As if the angel were a representation of a sexuality that has never been incarnated ... The fate of all flesh which is, moreover, attributable to God ... They proclaim that such a journey can be made by the body of man, and above all the body of woman. They represent and tell of another incarnation, another parousia of the body.[19]

Where the lapsed Catholic Wim Wenders pays homage to St Thomas Aquinas, in both emphasizing the significance of the knowledge of angels and presenting them as not having bodies and therefore unable to sense and limited in the impact they might have upon the world, the lapsed Catholic Luce Irigaray employs them as figures for the Christian construal of the resurrected body.

There are two distinct stages of the 'journey that can be made by the body'. The first of these relates to Irigaray's feminist project: the becoming divine or the incarnation of the woman. In her seminal essays 'Belief Itself' and 'Divine Women', in order to disrupt and transform the male symbolics of the body she figures woman, she speaks woman [*parler-femme*] as associated with the elements – earth, water, fire and air – and as hybrids. Divine women are 'half-creatures of the sea, half creatures of the air'.[20] By means of this figuration, women's fecundity is rendered cosmic. But something more is needed: a god is necessary to facilitate the infinite, to operate as the ideal, the form to which divine woman aspires. Men have such a god, as Feuerbach had pointed out. In fact, men have a whole hom(m)osexual community of gods in the Trinity. 'We have no female trinity. But, as long as woman lacks a divine made in her image she cannot establish her subjectivity or achieve a goal of her own.'[21] The embodied subjectivity of woman, the transfiguration of woman's flesh from fish to bird, requires this transcendental ideal. This female god has not yet come, but it is being imagined (through Irigaray's deconstruction of the male-focused god) and it is being symbolized in terms of alternative models of subjectivity. And so, pointing to the lacuna in Freud's account of the development of sexual identity, Irigaray posits the morphology of an identity around the two vaginal lips of woman as different from the phallic morphology of men. And, having critically examined the Christian tradition, she asks: 'Does respect for God made flesh not imply that we should incarnate God within us and within our sex: daughter-woman-mother.'[22] Here are alternative genealogies, new possibilities, a good news for women.

But who is to deliver this good news to the church? For 'Theology and the ritual practices [of the mass] it demands would seem to correspond to one formulation of all that is hidden in the constitution of the monocratic patriarchal truth, the faith in its order, its word, its logic.'[23] Who is, then, to ensure both its proclamation and reception? It is answering this question, in writing what elsewhere Irigaray will term 'the epistle to the last Christians',[24] that the hybrid bodies of those half-fish and half-bird become associated with the transfigured flesh of angels. Three angelic sites are visited in Irigaray's exposition of this transfigured flesh: the Old Testament account in Exodus of the ark of the covenant between God and the tribe of Israel in which two sculptured angels are described as facing each other;

the annunciation scene with the Virgin Mary; and the apocalyptic bridal banquet. The annunciation, in particular, is concerned with the transmission of messages, but in all three scenes 'a mediating angel or angels come to give us news about the place where the divine presence may be found, speaking of the word made flesh, returning, awaited'.[25] Evil angels, like Serres's demonic horde, are those who block the mediating process by drawing attention to themselves. As figures for mediation, the angels, then, incarnate the condition of representation and presentation – that which makes the message possible, the speaking and writing as woman. The enfleshment of angels is found in the very practice of speaking and writing, representing and presenting. For the angels mediate 'by keeping a space open and marking the trail from the oldest days to the farthest future of the world'.[26]

The Virgin Mary represents the woman who receives the angelic message and brings it to birth within her own body. In this way, Mary represents becoming divine, she incarnates what Irigaray will term the 'sensible transcendental' without whom there is no Christ and only with whom can there be redemption.[27] In modernity's refusal and rejection of angels, the message they enflesh goes unheard or is distorted. That is why Irigaray calls for the rethinking and rebuilding of 'the whole scene of representation',[28] beginning with speaking as woman [parler-femme]. Only then can the second stage of the 'journey that can be made by the body' be entered upon. This second stage is the realization of sexual difference and the divinity it presences. Men too are now brought into this transfiguration and the utopic age of the spirit or the bride dawns.[29] This is what the apocalyptic angels figure, for Irigaray. This is also, for her, what the two angels that stand at the two ends of the mercy seat which covers the ark of the covenant figure. A new forgiveness, a reconciliation, is announced by the way in which their wings reach over but never touch each other; and it is in this way that they 'guard the presence of God'. The guarding has two directions: towards human beings and towards God. For the 'doubling of the angel ... would keep Yahweh from being closed up in the text of the law ... They guard and await the mystery of a divine presence that has yet to be made flesh. Alike and different, they face each other, near enough and far enough for the future still to be on hold.'[30]

Angels, and here Irigaray returns to a more orthodox angelology, represent the movement of thought itself; thought which is always embodied, impassioned and sexuate. They figure the speaking and writing of Irigaray herself who, in receiving them, in standing with the Virgin Mary in her annunciation, proclaims 'the production of a new age of thought, art, poetry, and language: the creation of a new *poetics*'[31] when the horizons of the world are constituted in terms of sexual difference.

Cultural metaphors

We cannot conflate these three contemporary angelologies. They are far from being identical, as my subheadings – 'The Speech of Angels', 'The Knowledge of Angels' and 'The Flesh of Angels' – suggest. Serres (whose father was a converted Catholic though he associates himself with the Cathars) and Irigaray think angels within a broadly Christian schema – although downplaying the historical particularity of Christ while insisting upon the incarnation of the more nebulous word made flesh. Wenders has his film *Far Away, So Close* open with the passage from Matthew's Gospel about true seeing: 'If therefore thine eye be single, thy whole body shall be full of light' (7:22). Nevertheless, he detaches himself from any biblical framework, though there are close correspondences between his depiction of angels and those of Thomas Aquinas. For Thomas will insist also that the bodies of angels are non-corporeal, that their substance is spiritual, and that they can only assume human bodies to communicate, not become them. Serres and Irigaray pass from human bodies to angelic ones easily, with Irigaray quite emphatically stating that the angelic body is the perfection of human corporeality. Angels announce, for both of them, the incarnation of the spiritual to which we must give birth although what would be significant for her was that despite Serres's account of relationality, participation and reciprocity – which she would embrace – he still hierarchizes the angelic realm. Wenders, like Aquinas on this matter, is more dualistic – as his employment of technicolour for the human world and black and white for the angelic world makes visible. None of them espouse an institutional commitment to religion, for all the emphasis upon communication (or, in Wenders' the lack of communication) there is only the eschatological hope of communion (although Wenders again presents loving communities at the end of both *Wings of Desire* and *Far Away, So Close*).

But the question remains how we account for this resurfacing of the Christian imaginary? Nostalgia for the middle ages and the hegemony of the church? Both Serres and Irigaray will recognize the appeal of the mediaeval: 'Is it not true that in this age of sophisticated technical apparatus we still frequently turn to the Middle Ages in search of our images and secrets?' Irigaray asks.[32] Serres informs Bruno Latour that 'we are living today (and even more so in the United States than in Europe) closer to the Middle Ages than to the salons of the Age of Enlightenment'.[33] If not nostalgia for the liturgical cosmos of the mediaeval Catholic church, then this angelology certainly does claim to speak for a culture which has come to the end of the age of enlightenment, a culture disillusioned with the wielding of technical power for its own sake, a culture that is post-industrial and post-liberal. How then do we read this cultural metaphor of the angels? As new-age spirituality, as a response to the rootlessness, the heady irreality, the crisis of legitimation, authority and validation which characterizes postmodernity, a culture caught between the virtualities of cyberspace and the TV soap? Does the hyperventilating experience of postmodern living lead to *fin-de-siècle* fantasies – fantasies which are comforting, drugging, utopian and dripping with the red and golds of millenarianism?

No doubt sociological, psychological, ideological and historical explanations can be produced. But the production, not simply the fact, of these contemporary angelologies exceeds explanation. For they are not retreats into illusion or fantasies and away from a hard and rational reality, a normalcy. There is no hard reality for any of our three thinkers – no benchmark of the brutal given to appeal to. Each announces a world of constantly exchanging signs, the real as the production of a shifting commerce of messages written, delivered, stalled, distorted, misunderstood. The ontology is soft – matter, time and space have liquefied – making belief possible, maybe even necessary. Belief itself is produced, as Irigaray points out.[34] But belief in what? What we are witnessing here is the manufacture of new urban mythologies, a longing for transcendence, a desire to become divine while being constantly reminded by Hiroshima (Serres), the German death camps (Wenders), continuing exploitation (Irigaray) of the results of our attempts to play God. In the era of the death of God, we replaced him. Nietzsche tells us it is we who killed him. Now new negotiations with the divine are opening. Or are they? Something stirs the contemporary passions, and who can say whether this is an hysterical hope for security or the spirit of God blowing on the cold embers of souls who are remembering something whispered from their past, and who had forgotten how to sing of anything but loss. Serres's difficulty in distinguishing the good from the bad angels leads him to desire the purity of mediation, and he writes a series of dialogues as if he is not there. But he is there. A warp in the mediation is evident. Wenders employs film stars like Natasha Kinski and William Defoe to play his angels, his films always reflecting back upon their own production and the guilt he feels about that production. Irony stipples his vision. Irigaray's *parler-femme* is self-consciously utopic and mimics the very stereotypes of the feminine (element-bound, ineffable, dreaming of other worlds, the mystic as hysteric) she is attempting to subvert. Paradox installs itself in the heralding of her new age of the bride. But ultimately all three of our contemporary thinkers enjoin us to celebrate the ambivalence itself. They are upbeat and doxological in their acts of persuasion. To return to Lefebvre, the ambivalent offers new spacing. It is again becoming sacral. The undefined is again taking on the gravitas of grace – as 69 per cent of Americans believe in angels, according to a poll conducted for *Time* magazine in 1994.[35]

Notes

1 Robert Wuthnow, *After Heaven: Spirituality in America Since the 1950s* (Berkeley and Los Angeles: University of California Press, 1998), pp. 120–1.

2 Henri Lefebvre, *The Production of Space*, trans. Donald Nicholson-Smith (Oxford: Blackwell, 1991), p. 53.

3 Bruno Latour, *We have never been Modern*, trans. Catherine Porter (Cambridge, Mass.: Harvard University Press, 1993).

4 Quoted in Karl Barth, *Church Dogmatics* III.3, trans. G. W. Bromily and R. J. Ehrlich (Edinburgh: T.&T. Clark, 1960), p. 377.

5 Ibid., p. 374.

6 Ludwig Wittgenstein, *On Certainty*, ed. G. E. Anscombe and G. H. Wright, trans. Denis Paul and G. E. Anscombe (Oxford: Blackwell), propositions pp. 166, 177, 378 and 612.

7 Michel Serres, *Angels: A Modern* Myth, trans. Francis Cowper (Paris: Flammarion, 1993), p. 121.

8 Ibid., p. 285.

9 Ibid., p. 274.

10 Ibid., p. 72.

11 Ibid., p. 55.

12 Ibid., p. 288.

13 Ibid., p. 290.

14 Bruno Latour and Michel Serres, *Conversations on Science, Culture and Time*, trans. Roxanne Lapidus (Michigan: University of Michigan Press, 1995), p. 16.

15 Children are often given a redemptive role in Wenders's films. Their innocence enables them to be closer to the angelic perception of things, as the children in both *Wings of Desire* and *Far Away, So Close* exemplify. '[T]he Wenders child represents the richness and immediacy of being, where connection rather than fragmentation prevails' (Robert Phillip Kolker and Peter Beicken, *The Films of Wim Wenders* (Cambridge: Cambridge University Press, 1992), p. 53). Furthermore, for this is a lesson about words and the objects they refer to, children possess a 'prelapsian ability to enjoy unmediated language and the simple relationship of word and thing, of language and being' (Ibid., p. 55). Los Angeles is not the name of a city, or just the name of a city; it is, for the child, immediately related to heaven and those who watch out for us. It is a significant feature of *Far Away, So Close* that the angel saves the child. This is the suggestion in *The End of Violence* – that the child alone cannot redeem the adult; a more transcendental innocence is required. The child only confirms the new position and perspective Mike Max has been forced to find for himself within the world. 'As I see children as models for seeing and thinking and feeling, perhaps I also see them as models for sustaining relationships' (Wenders in *The Act of Seeing: Essays and Conversations*, trans. Michael Hoffmann (London: Faber & Faber, 1997), p. 45).

16 Wim Wenders, *The Logic of Images: Essays and Conversations*, trans. Michael Hoffmann (London: Faber & Faber, 1991), p. 77.

17 Ibid., p. 78.

18 Jacques Lacan, *Ecrits*, trans. Alan Sheridan (London: Tavistock, 1977), p. 187.

19 Luce Irigarary, *An Ethics of Sexual Difference*, trans. Carolyn Burke and Gillian Gill (Ithaca, NY: Cornell University Press, 1993), pp. 15–16.

20 Luce Irigarary, *Sexes and Genealogies*, trans. Gillian Gill (New York: Columbia University Press, 1993), p. 60.

21 Ibid., p. 63.
22 Ibid., p. 71.
23 Ibid., p. 27.
24 See the last section of Luce Irigarary, *Marine Lover of Friedrich Nietzsche*, trans. Gillian Gill (New York: Columbia University Press, 1991).
25 Irigarary, *Sexes and Genealogies*, p. 36.
26 Ibid., p. 40. It is difficult not to hear in these words a reference to Walter Benjamin's angel of history.
27 See here 'Equal to Whom' for a discussion of the place of the Virgin Mary in Christian redemption. In Graham Ward (ed.), *The Postmodern God* (Oxford: Blackwell, 1997), pp. 198–213.
28 Irigarary, *Sexes and Genealogies*, p. 42.
29 Irigaray frequently draws upon the mediaeval idea of the three ages elaborated by Joachim of Fiore (1132–1202): the age of the father relating to the Old Testament, the age of the son relating to the New Testament and the final age being the age of the spirit of the bride. See *An Ethics of Sexual Difference*, pp. 147–9.
30 Ibid., pp. 44–5.
31 Ibid., p. 5.
32 Irigarary, *Sexes and Genealogies*, p. 58.
33 Latour and Serres, *Conversations on Science, Culture and Time*, p. 25.
34 See also Michel de Certeau, 'Believing and Making People Believe', in *The Practice of Everyday Life*, trans. Steven Rendall (Berkeley and Los Angeles: University of California Press, 1984), pp. 177–89.
35 Quoted in Wuthnow, *After Heaven*, p. 120.

INDEX

Book titles can be found listed under their author's names. Similarly, film and paintings are listed under director or artist.